Islamist Parties
and Political Normalization
in the Muslim World

ISLAMIST PARTIES

AND

POLITICAL NORMALIZATION

IN THE

MUSLIM WORLD

EDITED BY

QUINN MECHAM

AND

JULIE CHERNOV HWANG

UNIVERSITY OF PENNSYLVANIA PRESS

PHILADELPHIA

Published by
University of Pennsylvania Press
Philadelphia, Pennsylvania 19104-4112
www.upenn.edu/pennpress

Printed in the United States of America
on acid-free paper
1 3 5 7 9 10 8 6 4 2

Library of Congress Cataloging-in-Publication Data
ISBN 978-0-8122-4605-6

Contents

Introduction

The Emergence and Development
of Islamist Political Parties

QUINN MECHAM AND JULIE CHERNOV HWANG

In the wake of the Arab uprisings of 2011, Islamist political parties have emerged at the forefront of formal politics in a number of countries, including Egypt, Tunisia, and Morocco. In Egypt, for example, which held the country's freest ever electoral competition in 2011–2012, Islamist parties combined to win more than two-thirds of the parliamentary seats in an assembly elected to help design the new Egyptian constitution. The parties of the Egyptian Muslim Brotherhood and their Salafist competitors demonstrated remarkable political dominance in the wake of a political uprising that was not in itself an Islamist revolution. Despite regime changes that have propelled Islamists in some countries into the bright lights of high politics, Islamist parties have long played an important role in both formal and informal political life in a wide range of countries in the Middle East and beyond. They have historically been important political players in the Muslim-majority countries of Asia, although they have sometimes remained parties of a dedicated minority. Why have Islamist parties spread throughout so much of the Muslim world and been so successful in their political contexts? Why have they been more successful at the ballot box in some Muslim-majority countries than in others? How has the potential for capturing power and participating in governments changed these parties over time? Answering these questions will be critical to understanding the political trajectory of many countries that define themselves at least in part by their Islamic identity.

This volume is a collective effort by a number of notable scholars to examine the evolution and behavior of Islamist parties across two very different regions of the world with large Muslim populations: the Middle East and Asia. The challenge of examining one type of political party across a diverse set of countries with divergent political histories is both a difficult one and a deliberate one. Scholarship on Islamist parties as one, reasonably distinct type of political party has been increasing over the last decade, and we have seen a number of prominent contributions that examine Islamist parties in particular country contexts, both in the Middle East and in the Muslim-majority countries of Asia. In this volume we have expanded the comparison to include six countries across both regions presented back to back in order for students or specialists in either region to compare the experiences of these parties under diverse political conditions. These cases are presented in the context of a theoretical framework for Islamist party participation in electoral contests.

We orient the volume around a number of key questions and ideas that have emerged from contemporary studies of Islamist movements and parties, as well as studies of party behavior more generally. Examples of these questions include the following. What, if anything, makes Islamist parties distinct from other types of parties? How similar are their political platforms and their constituencies to one another? How do Islamist parties relate to non-Islamist parties as potential competitors or collaborators? How do ties to broader Islamist movements affect their behavior in elections? How does participation in an electoral system affect the behavior and ideology of an Islamist party over time? How do Islamist parties interact in compromised electoral systems, in which regime incumbents have substantive competitive advantages? These are the puzzles that drive the inquiries of the authors in the chapters that follow.

Islamist parties are currently more important political players than ever before. In some countries they have competed in elections for many decades, such as in Malaysia where the forerunners of the Pan-Malaysian Islamic Party (PAS) began competing in the 1950s, or in Turkey, where the National Order Party (MNP) and National Salvation Party (MSP) ran for office in the early 1970s. Islamist parties subsequently emerged as important political competitors in more than half a dozen other countries by the 1990s, and continued to grow significantly during the 2000s. In the early 2000s, more than a dozen countries witnessed the electoral participation of Islamist parties; this number greatly expanded in the last half of the decade, with approximately twenty countries worldwide holding an election in which Islamist parties competed for legislative seats. Countries or territories that have seen Islamist parties or blocs compete in recent elections include

Afghanistan, Algeria, Bahrain, Bangladesh, Egypt, Indonesia, Iraq, Iran, Jordan, Kuwait, Lebanon, Libya, Malaysia, The Maldives, Mauritania, Morocco, Pakistan, Palestine, Tajikistan, Tunisia, Turkey, and Yemen. Since popular uprisings in the Arab world began to challenge regimes and attempt to overthrow long-standing leaders beginning in 2011, Islamist parties or blocs have dominated elections in Tunisia, Morocco, Egypt, and Kuwait, making them the most important political groupings in these countries. There has never been a more interesting time to study Islamist parties, and we believe that there will be opportunity to further test and refine the hypotheses presented here, as the political behavior of these newly competitive parties evolves.

In this volume, we define Islamist parties as political parties that seek to win votes in the electoral arena, and that articulate a political agenda derived in large part from an Islamic worldview. They are political parties that use Islamic religious narratives to make political claims on the state, which may include concerns for Islamic social and cultural norms, Islamic models of governance, or resource allocation toward religious institutions. Often, but not universally, Islamist parties articulate some degree of support for the application of Islamic law in their societies. Serious discussions of Islamic law are common in Malaysia, for example, while they have less resonance in Morocco, and are beyond the political pale in Turkey. While we use *Islamic* as an adjective to describe characteristics of Islam as a religious tradition, we confine *Islamist* to refer to political actors and activities that make reference to Islamic norms or ideals. In most cases, the parties under consideration in this volume self-identify as Islamist, and in all cases they are viewed as a comparatively Islamist choice when set against their domestic competitors (though they differ considerably from one another across country cases).

In many ways, Islamist parties are similar to other political parties, and one of the central themes of this volume is that they are subject to many of the pressures and incentives that other parties face, regardless of their ideological platform. We see substantial evidence that Islamist parties have a great many overlaps with other types of religiously affiliated parties, as well as parties that cater to a particular identity group, such as ethnically delineated parties. Indeed, Islamist parties may not be too different in their behavior from Jewish or Hindu religious parties, early Christian parties in Western Europe, or even Marxist-oriented or far-right European parties, which have sought to challenge the political status quo from a minority position. Ideologically, they may be very much at variance with this diverse set of parties, although we assert that their behavior in electoral politics may have substantial overlaps because they find themselves in similar positions vis-à-vis their competitors.

Islamist parties do have similar ideological affinities to one another, although they hold these political perspectives along a very wide spectrum that ranges from preferences for an exclusively Islamic state to a desire for government to foster greater social morality and religious devotion. On the surface there appears to be a wide political gap between more religiously conservative parties, such as the Jamaat-e Islami in Pakistan or Al-Nour (Light) in Egypt, and those on the modestly Islamist spectrum of the scale, such as Al-Nahda (Renaissance) in Tunisia or the Justice and Development Party (AKP) in Turkey. Indeed, the activities and behaviors of these parties might differ substantially in practice from one another, because of how they have defined themselves in their given political contexts.

Though Islamist parties may take very different political positions regarding the necessity of Islamic law (shari'a), the need for restrictions on public dress or consumption, or the organization of the religious establishment, they have a common ideological and institutional heritage that helps to distinguish them from non-Islamist parties. On the ideological side, they share a philosophical heritage that provides them with common assumptions of the value of Islam in the public sphere and the need for the greater Islamization of society (though their political strategies to accomplish this may differ). On the institutional side, they benefit from formal or informal connections to Islamic religious institutions, which may include institutions of worship (the mosque), education (the *madrasa* and Islamic universities), scholars and clerics (the *ulama*), social welfare (Islamic charitable organizations), proselytizing (*da'wa* or *dakhwa*) groups, or the Islamic media. These connections to religious society often give Islamist parties access to resources, constituents, and shared social and cultural assumptions that are unavailable to their non-Islamist competitors.

In some cases, Islamist parties have explicit ties to a broader Islamist movement whose goals extend beyond competition in the political arena. In the case of Lebanon, for example, Hezbollah competes as a party in elections, but its party wing is largely subsumed within the larger movement that has a diverse set of goals, including militant resistance, providing security and public goods, and delivering social and religious services outside the state framework. Parties with ties to a broader movement, such as the Prosperous Justice Party (PKS) in Indonesia or the Freedom and Justice Party (FJP) in Egypt, may find themselves at odds with the nonpolitical goals of the movement regarding religious, social, or economic issues, and be constrained in their political behavior due to their organizational ties to an Islamist movement with a broader set of objectives and incentives. Islamist movements, therefore, are not equivalent to Islamist parties, which are typically narrower political actors. Nevertheless, the overlapping goals and institutional ties between these two types of organizations often matter in explaining party behavior.

Islamist parties in the Middle East and Asia are embedded in the history and trajectory of party development in these two regions more generally, and should be understood within the context of party systems in the regions and countries where they participate. In the Middle East, party systems have historically been very weak, existing primarily in the context of authoritarian regimes. Israel, the principal exception to this rule, does not have sizable Islamist parties in its political system and is not examined in this volume. Turkey and Lebanon are other Middle Eastern countries with a lengthy history of party competition, with Turkey's system substantially more developed and institutionalized than that of Lebanon. Even in Turkey and Lebanon, however, political parties have been historically weak and elite-driven, without the kinds of ties to mass organization and grassroots support that are common in more developed party systems. In countries such as Morocco, Jordan, Algeria, and Egypt, most political parties have historically been either artificial constructions tied to a strong executive or personal vehicles for co-opted elites. In Iraq and Palestine, the political party system is new enough that it is not clear how and whether it will evolve and develop beyond the shadow of individual leaders. If these are the broad contours of Middle Eastern party systems, then Islamist parties and blocs within these systems are comparative exceptions to the rule. In many of the cases described above, the parties with the strongest organization, with the most grassroots outreach, and with the clearest political narrative (though often still murky) are the Islamists. This distinguishes them from their competitors as much as does their religious ideology.

In Muslim Asia, party systems are comparatively more developed than in the Middle East, although less so than in many other parts of the world. Pakistan has a history of vibrant, if highly personalized party competition, which has extended to Bangladesh for parts of its postindependence period. In both cases, political elites have used parties as personal vehicles to extend rivalries into the public sphere and competition can be fierce at times. Both systems have also been punctuated by military coups d'état and interregnums of military rule, which have prevented the natural evolution of parties and the party systems. Malaysia also has a long history of party competition, although the dominance of one party, the United Malays National Organization (UMNO), makes the Malaysian system unique in having a clear center of gravity around which a number of smaller competitors attempt to mount political challenges. Indonesia currently has one of the most dynamic party systems in Asia, although it was artificial and highly constrained under military leadership for three decades (with three designated electoral blocs beginning with the 1977 elections). After democratization began in 1998, the Indonesian party system has flourished in the context of three elections in 1999, 2004, and 2009. Indonesia's party system remains fragmented and personalistic, but has also become very vibrant and competitive. In these Asian systems, Islamist parties have often participated on the fringes of the large political blocs, seeking to distinguish themselves from the center rather than to explicitly capture it. In each case they act as important minority players in the party systems, and at times they can affect the balance of power between parties and in coalition governments. As in to the Middle East, Islamists in Asia are more likely to have active grassroots organizations and to maintain party discipline than their non-Islamist competitors.

The key questions examined in the volume, discussed at length in Chapter 1, are divided into several different categories, including questions about party platforms and constituencies, the effects of participation on Islamist parties, and the sources of the parties' electoral success. We also introduce and examine evidence for several arguments that predict changes in party behavior as these organizations participate in elections or in governments over time. These arguments are derived in part from existing scholarly debates regarding the behavior of Islamist parties, but they also move the discussion substantively forward by postulating relationships that have not previously been specified or tested.

We introduce a term that is not commonly associated with the scholarship on Islamist parties, but which we find descriptive of a process that we have observed in a number of cases: *normalization*. Normalization is a process by which Islamist parties increasingly accommodate themselves to the rules of the political regimes in which they operate; in other words, they become less unique and more *normal* political actors when compared with other parties in the competitive system. Normalization is related to a more common term in discussions of Islamist parties: *moderation*. Moderation can be ideological or behavioral, and has many similarities to a process of normalization. Whereas moderation is often associated with ideological change, we confine the term normalization to observed political behaviors. This is done to avoid confusion with ideological shifts, which are often very difficult to observe or measure from the outside. Classifying a party as moderate may also involve a value judgment, marking a set of beliefs or behaviors along a normative scale. Depending on the case, normalization or moderation may be a more useful descriptive term in describing the evolution of Islamist parties in the cases we examine, and the authors in this volume use both terms. Chapter 3 introduces a number of deductive arguments about the conditions under which Islamist parties may be expected to normalize their political behavior. These conditions include participation in electoral competition over time, lack of ties to a broader Islamist movement, and participation in political coalitions, including coalition governments.

This volume therefore seeks to push the boundaries of current knowledge about the behavior of Islamist political parties by proposing a number of hypotheses that extend our current understanding of party behavior, and then examining whether there is comparative evidence in support of those hypotheses in a number of diverse and prominent case studies. As we discuss in the conclusion, we find that some of the arguments examined here have much more support than others, and that (unsurprisingly) there remains considerable diversity in the experience of Islamist parties around the globe. In addition, we find that there are compelling reasons to examine the experience of Islamist parties in the Middle East and Asia together, as similar pressures and incentives can drive similar party behaviors across both regions, despite their geographical and cultural diversity.

What We Know About Islamist Parties

A significant amount of scholarly work has been done and continues to be done on Islamist political parties. The two most sustained research programs in this regard have centered on two interrelated themes. First is the extent to which Islamist parties are participating in formal politics.[1] Second, given that Islamists are participating, to what extent does the experience of inclusion encourage Islamist parties to "moderate" their behavior, rhetoric, and goals.[2]

In the Middle East, much of the initial research was done in response to political openings that occurred in the 1990s, where for the first time Islamist parties were permitted to form and, amid constraints, engage in formal politics. These studies examined how Islamist parties participated in their systems, the constrained political environment under which these parties operated, how they mobilized popular support, and whether they were committing credibly to participation in the democratic system.[3] In Asia, where Islamist parties had a longer history of participation in semidemocratic systems of government, research echoed similar themes.[4]

The most sustained research program on Islamist parties has been done on the "inclusion-moderation" hypothesis, which asserts that as Islamist parties participate in their political systems, their "radical" Islamist behavior begins to "moderate."[5] Recent studies by Carrie Rosefsky Wickham, Janine Clarke, Murat Somer, and Jillian Schwedler[6] have taken issue with certain aspects of the inclusion-moderation hypothesis, most notably the radical-moderate conceptual construction undergirding some studies and the basic assumption that participation inevitably leads to moderation. These scholars noted that it may not be simply the act of participation itself that is engendering moderation; certain experiences, incentives, and disincentives may in fact be driving the process. As a result of these concerns, these scholars among others[7] have endeavored to unpack the inclusion-moderation hypothesis further by introducing process into the discussion of moderation. In so doing, they are decoupling ideological moderation (wanting different things) from strategic or behavioral moderation (behaving differently). They assess the extent to which a particular Islamist party has been moderating and provide specific reasons for that moderation, and explaining the conditions under which participation does not, in fact, lead to moderation.

From this research program, two conceptual definitions of moderation stand out that were developed in response to the radical-moderate polarization. Schwedler defines moderation ideologically, as moving from a rigid and closed worldview to one that is more open and tolerant of alternative perspectives. Thus, it is not participation that encourages moderation but engagement and interaction that engenders transformation. In another treatment, Wickham's definition of moderation delineates between moderation of strategy and moderation of ideology, noting that some Islamist parties may moderate their strategies and tactics before they moderate their worldview. Wickham defines ideological moderation as "the abandonment, postponement or revision of radical goals that enables the movement to accommodate itself to the give-and-take of normal competitive politics," thus highlighting the process element within moderation as a phenomena that may occur in stages and on some issues before others.[8] Similar to Schwedler, Wickham notes that ideological moderation requires movement toward a substantive commitment to democratic ideas and principles, which include peaceful changes of power, ideological and political pluralism, and citizenship rights.

Scholars have proposed various factors that interact with one another to engender moderation, either of strategy or of ideological positions. These include strategic incentives, political learning, experience with political alliances, a need to obtain state resources, institutional constraints, and organizational change. In analyzing election results in Indonesia, Pakistan, and Bangladesh, Syed Vali Reza Nasr notes that center-right Muslim parties tend to win majorities, which suggests there is a vital center in Muslim nations that belongs to neither the secularists nor the Islamists.[9] In each of these cases, he contends that since no one party can dominate the political system, all parties are pressured to act pragmatically and move to the center to accommodate the median voter.

Wickham also attributes moderation to incentives, but she adds another variable—political learning—in her examination of the Al-Wasat Party in Egypt.[10] As Al-Wasat members interacted more with secular opposition leaders in pursuit of shared goals, as they traveled abroad interacting with Christians and Jews, and as they successfully organized and oversaw the Egyptian syndicate elections, they broke out of their insular networks and evolved toward an understanding that they did not possess a monopoly on truth. This realization, combined with rational calculations about the willingness of Egypt's authoritarian leaders to accommodate their original aims, resulted in a shift in Wasat positions on numerous sensitive issues, including women's rights, the status of the Coptic Christian minority, and relations with the West. Thus, in this view, Wasat moderated in response to the recognition of existing political incentives and political learning brought on by sustained interaction and political activity.

Studies examining the behavior of Islamist parties in Turkey also follow a similar trajectory, emphasizing strategic incentives for moderation as well as iterated periods of political learning through which the Turkish

Islamist movement was able to gauge the preferences of the voters and the "red lines" of the state.[11] However, they also highlight the importance of institutional constraints in making a shift to the center a necessary condition for political survival and continued participation.[12] Murat Somer notes, "the moderation of Turkish Islam in the example of the AKP did not result from simple, unrestrained participation in a democracy but from a complex mixture of incentives to participate and disincentives to accentuate Islam in a guided democracy."[13]

Scholars are also debating the organizational mechanisms through which moderation takes place. For example, cooperative alliances are frequently referenced as indicators of moderation taking place.[14] Clarke takes issue with the emphasis on cooperative agreements as a *key* indicator of moderation, contending that Islamists may only be cooperating on those issues where they see room for compromise, therefore, not experiencing any fundamental worldview reorientation.[15] In discussing Islamist-Leftist cooperation in the Arab world, Schwedler and Clarke endeavor to break the concept of cooperative alliances into three distinct levels:[16] (a) short-term tactical alliances convened on an issue-by-issue basis; (b) sustained midlevel strategic cooperation, where alliances encompass multiple issues, yet certain issues are "off the table"; and (c) high-level cooperation, where partners remain distinct entities, yet develop a common social, economic, and political vision for reform. In this last model, few issues are "off the table" and rigorous debate on contentious ideological issues may replace avoidance of the issue altogether. In so doing, one can assess whether an alliance is merely "shaking hands with secularists" or is indicative of greater transformational change at work.

In short, it is clear that scholarship over the past decade has endeavored to assess the inclusion-moderation hypothesis, highlighting the processes through which moderation takes place, the conceptual basis of moderation itself, and the factors that are taken to be indicative of moderation. While much of the evidence to date supports the broad outlines of the hypothesis, there are some important caveats, including the effects of internal party organization,[17] both moderating and radicalizing effects of repression,[18] and pressure to highlight ideological distinctiveness when competing against other Islamically oriented parties.[19] For example, Farish Noor notes how competition with the UMNO, the dominant party in government, over how to define the "meaning and content" of Islamism in Malaysia was a key factor in engendering radical swings within the PAS.[20] Thus, even as the

PAS participated in every election since its establishment, often in coalition with other non-Islamist parties, the Islamization race with the UMNO provided a clear incentive to highlight religious distinctiveness vis-à-vis its main competitor for Malay Muslim support. Similarly, in this volume, Ali Riaz notes that the Jamaat-e Islami and the Islami Oikya Jote (IOJ) in Bangladesh choose to highlight their ideological distinctiveness vis-à-vis each other to win the support of the Islamist constituency.

Within these two frames of reference, democracy and moderation, Islamist parties have been studied as examples of successful political mobilization, as in Egypt, Malaysia, Algeria, Morocco, Jordan, and Palestine,[21] or as unsuccessful or partly successful mobilization, as in Pakistan, Indonesia, Tunisia, Jordan, Lebanon, Senegal, and Iran.[22] Whether Islamist parties are successful or unsuccessful depends to a large extent on the expectations one has for their performance, and high expectations shared by both supporters and opponents are not often met.

It is important here to remember that Islamist parties are but one variety of political party that shares a number of characteristics with other party types, including right-wing parties, communist parties, or religious parties more generally. Islamist parties do have some unique characteristics that justify examining them as a category, but they have enough commonalities with other party types that one may learn a great deal about their behavior from the lessons of the Christian parties in Western Europe, communist parties, and parties of the radical right.[23]

Case Selection

While the results of the cases addressed in this book provide key lessons and insights for those seeking to understand the political openings and democratic developments occurring in post-2011 Tunisia, Egypt, Libya, and Yemen, the initial workshop for this volume took place in September 2010, several months prior to the outbreak of the Tunisian revolution. The initial impetus for the volume arose from what we saw as a pronounced gap in the literature with regard to Islamist parties. Namely, while there were articles on Islamist parties in the Middle East and articles on Islamist parties in South and Southeast Asia, these studies did not speak to one another. Yet, given the increasing political space for mobilization and competition in Yemen, Morocco, Malaysia, Indonesia, Bangladesh, and Turkey, such scholarship was not only eminently possible but also necessary, and the lessons derived from such a study could potentially speak to broader issues of Islamist parties in the Muslim world.

For example, there are clear bases of comparison between Turkey and Indonesia, where Islamist parties contest free and fair elections. Yet, while the AKP and the Welfare Party (RP) won elections in Turkey and were able to form governments, Indonesia's Islamist parties have had no such success. This raises the question why. An examination of Islamist parties in Malaysia, Yemen, and Bangladesh reveals that Islamist parties face not only incentives to normalize their participation and moderate their ideology and rhetoric but also countervailing incentives that promote a radical swing. A comparison of Turkey and Morocco can serve to highlight how Islamist parties compete in political systems where overt appeals to Islamism are constrained by the rules of engagement in those particular systems and yet manage to achieve victory.

In conceptualizing this edited volume, we selected six cases, which are widely viewed as among the most open and participatory cases in the Islamic world: Morocco, Yemen, Turkey, Indonesia, Malaysia, and Bangladesh. Thus, the volume is not simply a comparison of Middle Eastern with Asian cases but one that spans the entire Islamic world and speaks to issues cross-regionally. Morocco is historically one of the more politically competitive cases in North Africa, as Yemen is the most participatory case on the Arabian Peninsula, and Bangladesh in South Asia. Indonesia and Turkey are the most democratic states in the Islamic world, and semidemocratic Malaysia has one of the longest histories of Islamist party participation of any country in the Muslim world apart from Pakistan. Moreover, in each of these countries, Islamist parties are permitted to form and to participate in elections, and, apart from the case of Yemen, those elections have occurred on a regular basis.

Yet, within this universe of cases, there is significant variation. A brief look at Freedom House scores assessing civil liberties and political participation on a 1–7 scale ranks Indonesia as "free" with a combined average score of 2.5; Turkey as "partly free" with a score of 3.0; Bangladesh, Malaysia, and Morocco as "partly free" with scores of 3.5, 4.0, and 4.5; and Yemen as "not free" with a score of 5.5. Islamists contest reasonably free and fair elections in Indonesia, Turkey, and Bangladesh and heavily managed or gerrymandered regular elections in Malaysia and Morocco, while in Yemen the last parliamentary election was in 2003. The rules of the political system permit Islamist parties to make overt appeals to Islam and to Islamic law in their rhetoric and policy platforms in Indonesia, Malaysia, Bangladesh, and Yemen, while in Turkey and Morocco they are significantly constrained from doing so. Islamist parties appear to be moderating strategically and ideologically on specific issues, for example, on women's rights in Morocco, Malaysia, Indonesia, and Turkey, while in Yemen and Bangladesh they remain ideologically doctrinaire. Yet, in each case examined in the volume, Islamist parties form coalitions with non-Islamist parties in the legislature. This points to a broad normalization and acceptance of democratic institutions in all cases of the volume, with the possible exception of Bangladesh.

As the political revolutions associated with the Arab uprisings are ongoing, we have chosen not to include specific chapters addressing Islamist party behavior in Egypt or Tunisia. We made this decision because it seemed premature to comment, at this time, on Islamist party behavior before those parties had sufficient time to adapt to the new and evolving strategic environment. We speculate, however, on the lessons from this volume for recent developments in Tunisia and Egypt in the Conclusion, and believe the trajectory of Islamist parties in these cases will become increasingly clear in coming years. That notwithstanding, this volume represents one of the most comprehensive efforts to date to understand Islamist party behavior across the Muslim world, and we believe that this exercise will provide valuable lessons for Egypt, Tunisia, and other post-2011 revolutionary states.

Structure of the Book

Chapter 1, "Islamist Parties as Strategic Actors" by Quinn Mecham, sets up a framework and foundation to guide the subsequent case chapters. The chapter centers on four main themes: (1) platforms and constituencies; (2) how Islamist parties respond to the constraints and incentives found in different political systems; (3) how democratic participation affects Islamist parties; and (4) how Islamist parties may achieve success. Within these themes, Mecham articulates a number of arguments, which are empirically evaluated in the subsequent case chapters. These arguments are derived from both the scholarly literature on Islamist parties and the broader literature on party behavior. Each subsequent case chapter selects a subset of arguments that pertain to the particular case at hand and addresses the extent to which the predicted party behavior fits the reality of the case.

Chapter 2, "When Is Normalization Also Democratization?" by Murat Somer, uses the Turkish case to theorize what moderation or normalization means for Islamist parties and democratization. He argues that normalization can be conceptualized as a process whereby Islamist political actors compromise with mainstream values, institutions, and actors in a country, and contends that normalization can contribute to democratization only to the extent that normal politics has democratic characteristics in that country. The chapter illustrates how the evolution of Turkish Islamist parties was shaped by electoral incentives, nonelectoral constraints and interventions, and the changing nature of the country's social, political, and international context over time. It highlights how the ruling AKP owes its success to both "protest" voters and its successful discursive and behavioral normalization in response to domestic and international incentives. Using a systematic content analysis of the press, Somer maintains that the AKP normalization became more credible because it was embedded in broader discursive changes among pro-Islamic elites.

Chapter 3, "Patterns of Normalization" by Julie Chernov Hwang, examines how Islamist parties participate in the democratic political system of Indonesia, where there are multiple Islamically oriented parties; where Islamist parties do not gain significant votes vis-à-vis their competitors by asserting their religious credentials in election campaigns; and where "protest voting" is only one reason among many for party success. By analyzing the strategic behavior of the Prosperous Justice Party (PKS) and the United Development Party (PPP), the two most notable Islamist parties, this chapter argues that Islamist parties have become increasingly integrated into the Indonesian political system. However, this has not resulted in significant electoral gains, for nationalist parties have successfully co-opted moderate Islamic themes in order to compete for the median Muslim voter.

Chapter 4, Joseph Chinyong Liow and Wenling Chen's "Between a Rock and Hard Place," examines how the Pan-Malaysian Islamic Party (PAS) has engaged in coalition building behavior in response to the strategic incentives for coalition building in the Malaysian political system. As it has done so, it has been pushed to moderate its ideological agenda to appeal to a wider array of voters, including non-Muslims. However, the PAS is a party beset by internal factionalization between purists, who hold fast to the party's goal to bring about an Islamic state, and mainstream supporters who understand that the party must accommodate the multiethnic, multireligious Malaysian context that may require the postponement and reassessment of long-held goals. This chapter highlights the unique mix of challenges and incentives that faced the PAS in the 2012 elections.

Chapter 5, "Searching for Political Normalization" draws upon the themes of strategic incentives and constraints and democratic participation in order to explain how the monarchy as an institution has forced Islamist parties in Morocco to normalize and moderate their political behavior as a condition for political participation. Yet, within those parameters, the Party of Justice and Development (PJD) has been able to appeal to a wide array of constituents outside a narrow Islamist constituency and not only successfully contest elections but make significant political gains. Driss Maghraoui and Saloua Zerhouni conclude by addressing how the PJD has responded to the new political environment and incentives brought about through the Arab protests of 2011 and beyond.

Chapter 6, "Mapping the Terrain of Reform in Yemen" by Stacey Philbrick Yadav, examines the strategic behavior of the Islah party, including how it has engaged in a political system that is, at best, an electoral authoritarian state where there has not been a parliamentary election since 2003, and where coalition building with non-Islamist parties is a necessity for participation. This chapter analyzes how Islah has responded to regime constraints, achieved legislative victories despite the constrained political environment, and the extent to which the party has normalized its behavior. This chapter also examines Islah's response to the 2011 protests and analyzes why the party sided with the regime against the protestors and the implications of that behavior.

Chapter 7, "Islamist Parties, Elections, and Democracy in Bangladesh" by Ali Riaz, challenges several of the arguments presented in the theory chapter, illustrating what happens when Islamist parties decide they are content with a smaller share of the vote and a devoted constituency of core supporters. Rather than respond to the strategic incentives in the Bangladeshi political system that would encourage normalization, these parties oppose the democratic system even as they engage in it. Moreover, they exploit the divided nature of the system to play a kingmaker role, which enables them to achieve legislative goals despite winning less than 10 percent of the vote combined in any given election. This chapter highlights what occurs when Islamist parties decide to hold fast to their religious raison d'être at the expense of electoral success.

"The New Dynamism of Islamist Parties" by Julie Chernov Hwang and Quinn Mecham concludes the volume. It provides a synthesis of the volume's key arguments, examining the comparative evidence from the collective case chapters. This final chapter describes which arguments presented in Chapter 1 have the most plausibility based on the evidence presented here, and how the behavior of Islamist parties compares across different contexts. It highlights broader patterns of party normalization, along with a number of important exceptions and caveats raised in the cases.

We turn now to Chapter 1, which introduces the theoretical framework for the volume and guides the inquiry of the subsequent case studies.

Chapter 1

Islamist Parties as Strategic Actors: Electoral Participation and Its Consequences

QUINN MECHAM

Islamists are participating in their political systems more than ever before. Whereas electoral participation by self-identified Islamist movements was rather novel in many parts of the Muslim world in the 1990s (with the Islamic Salvation Front (FIS) in Algeria, Islamic Action Front (IAF) in Jordan, or Islamic Renaissance Party (IRP) in Tajikistan providing major challenges to their political systems), Islamist participation in elections has become the norm in a wide variety of countries, from Egypt to Indonesia, and Morocco to Pakistan. Though "participation" in these systems varies widely, and political freedom remains a concern in most Muslim-majority countries, Islamists now have an established track record of electoral participation. With caution (because of the real discrepancies in the level of regime constraints), we can now assess how Islamists participate, when they succeed and fail, how they affect their political systems, and how they change as a result of their participation. In the majority of cases, though not all, Islamists are participating in the form of legal political parties, or blocs of political independents that behave like parties.

While Islamist parties usually share a strong ideological orientation and anti-system orientation with parties of these other types, they are unique in the symbolic and institutional reference points that provide commonalities between these parties across vast geographies and large variation in political systems. In particular, Islamist parties speak a common language of shared references about what is right and wrong, share a mythical history of the glory days of the original Islamic community (*umma*), have common scriptural and linguistic (Arabic) referents, share some expectations on legal issues (through knowledge of the shari'a), and have a common understanding of the negative role of Western imperialism, with particular reference to perceived injustices in Palestine. In addition to this shared normative and cultural content, Islamist parties often have unique access to the institutional richness of Islamic schools, mosques, endowments (*awqaf*), and social networks, which are often the dominant form of social organization outside the family in the societies in which they operate. This access to the mobilizing potential of Islamic institutions is without parallel in the radical right or radical left, and is comparable only with other religious parties with similar institutional legacies (Jewish, Hindu, Catholic, etc.). These shared characteristics are what make a meaningful comparison of Islamist parties possible across such diverse geographies as Indonesia, Yemen, and Turkey.

This chapter proceeds as follows. First, I highlight some of the general characteristics of Islamist parties in two areas: their political platforms and their political constituents. In the process, I introduce several questions regarding the relationship between the parties, their platforms, and their constituents. This is followed by a brief discussion of the variety of political regimes under which Islamist parties operate, and some potential mechanisms by which regime type affects the political opportunities for these parties. I then turn to a discussion of the strategic incentives of Islamist parties, making assumptions about the parties' political objectives, and assessing how the pursuit of these objectives may play out in the context of strategic opportunities and constraints. I then hypothesize why some Islamist parties are more electorally successful than others, and also how the participation of Islamist parties affects both the systems in which they compete and the parties themselves. I conclude with potential implications for how the participation of Islamist parties may affect the future of political Islam.

Platforms and Constituencies

Islamist parties share Islam as a common reference point in formulating their political platforms, but they vary in how prominent and explicit Islam is in their political agenda. The Islamic content of political platforms ranges from the direct advocacy of an Islamic state based in shari'a to more general aspirations for communal morality based in Islamic principles (illustrated by the Justice and Development Party (AKP) in Turkey). Whether Islam is at the front and center or embedded within general principles of the political platform, it can be highlighted when politically useful, or downplayed as necessary, as political platforms are malleable in the process of politics.

The malleability of the political platform is often strategically useful, and many Islamist parties have shied away from too much detail in explaining their vision for governance. This allows them to avoid controversial or sensitive subjects while criticizing their competitors with, at times, sweeping generalizations. Even when they succumb to the temptation to write out the details, actual political behavior rarely mimics the written priorities. In Indonesia, for example, few would consider a written political platform an accurate roadmap for political decisions. Although the Muslim Brotherhood of Egypt was long criticized for ambiguity in its aspirations, when a draft, detailed platform was circulated in 2007, criticism mounted over several specific provisions,[1] with the result that the rest of the platform got lost in the shuffle of public debate. Additionally, even when a platform is subject to rigorous internal review and prominent publication, it can change from year to year in response to the political environment. The Justice and Development Party (PJD) in Morocco, for example, moved its focus on Islamic priorities further down in its platform over time to mirror its rhetorical strategy in political campaigns.

Despite these two main weaknesses in Islamist political platforms, their ambiguity and their inaccuracy, Islamist parties across geography do tend to focus on a number of similar political priorities. In general terms, these priorities often include: clean government, economic development (including support for Islamic finance), social and economic justice, health care and sanitation, religious and civic education, support for religious institutions, modesty and morality in public spaces, strong ties with other Muslim-majority countries, opposition to "Western" cultural, economic, and political influence, and concern for occupied Palestine. Depending on the regime context, Islamist parties may also prioritize democratic reform—particularly if it works to their advantage in a democratically constrained environment.

As Islamist parties increasingly participate in their political systems, the range of political issues on which they must speak or act increases. Especially if they participate in coalitions or governments, they are more likely to face difficult political decisions on budget priorities, economic development, and foreign relations. Increased participation may also necessitate higher levels of compromise with political actors who do not share their religious priorities. This leads to a key question regarding the relationship of political participation to political platforms: what happens to the religious content of an Islamist party's platform as it participates in the political system? I hypothesize that **as Islamist parties increasingly participate in their political systems, they choose to deprioritize the religious content of their platforms in favor of more mainstream political priorities**.

The logic behind this relationship is two-fold. First, more participation requires more competency and activity on a wide-range of political issues, so the religious content of the party platform gradually gets crowded out by necessity. Second, highlighting the party's competency on nonreligious issues becomes increasingly *politically* useful, as the party becomes more politically relevant. As the party demonstrates its constructive participation in the political system, the need to maintain its relevance becomes politically necessary. Showcasing the party's nonreligious credentials is one way to amplify the party's political relevance among the broader cross-section of voters. This does not mean that Islamist parties eliminate the religious content of their platforms over time, but only that they move religious issues down the priority list. The party can still reach for their religious credentials at any time it proves politically useful, and this happens with some regularity.

Related to a party's political platform is the constituency that the party seeks to attract. As with the wide variation in political platforms, these parties have constituencies that differ substantially from one another, ranging from narrow sectors of society to cross-cutting sectors and voters across the ideological spectrum. Parties that attract a high percentage of voters (like the AKP in Turkey) will naturally have a more varied constituency than parties that attract only a small percentage of the vote. However, in broad terms, Islamist parties are more likely to attract the young, the deeply devout (although general piety is not necessarily a good predictor of support), the educated but lower middle classes, and those who are weakly integrated into state patronage networks. Support may come from both urban and rural environments, although some Islamist parties see high levels of support from marginalized urban populations (who may have been recently rural). Likewise, support may come from all economic classes, but those with unfulfilled aspirations to advance in class seem to be particularly prone to support Islamist parties.

These are broad generalizations, however, and this raises an empirical question: who votes for Islamist parties? When one breaks down electoral support for Islamists in any given election, there are usually multiple constituencies that support them, and these constituencies may include voters who do not see themselves as Islamists. I argue, then, that it is useful to understand **Islamist parties as having a dual constituency: those who vote for them for religious reasons, and those who vote for them out of deep dissatisfaction with other political alternatives or as protest against the political system.**

If this hypothesis holds true, we would expect to find Islamists who consistently vote for Islamist parties because they best represent the identity of the voter, in ways not entirely different from ethnic voters who vote for an ethnic party because they believe it best represents the interests of their identity group. However, we also expect to find voters who vote for Islamist parties inconsistently, based on the current political climate, who have little or no identification as Islamists. In some cases, this non-Islamist constituency will be larger than the Islamist one, although it is likely to be fickle and may leave the Islamist party at any time. This non-Islamist constituency may be particularly prone to desert the party after the party participates in a governing coalition, as this vote is more likely to follow protest parties than those with ties to the government.

For Islamist parties with sizeable Islamist and non-Islamist constituencies, this leads to a potential tension in electoral strategy. Because their supporters vote for them for different reasons, they must maintain a balance in their appeal, remaining both Islamist enough to keep the party's core religious supporters and attractive to others for political reasons outside religious appeals. These nonreligious characteristics that attract voters may range from a strong anti-establishment platform, to a more mainstream or centrist platform that caters to basic political and economic concerns.

In some cases it may not be possible to please both sides of the party's constituency, and party leaders will be forced to make a choice about pursuing the Islamist or the non-Islamist choice. This may lead to a shift in the party's constituency over time, through either defection of core Islamists or deterioration of party support from non-Islamists. This threat of defection from constituents will be a key strategic consideration as parties weigh the consequences of their political choices.

Islamist Parties and Political Systems

Islamist parties operate under widely varying contexts that affect their behavior, in large part due to the diversity of political regimes under which they compete. Even within the set of cases that have competed many times in elections under reasonably free conditions, parties often face political obstacles due to restrictions on political behavior. Of the six countries included in this volume, levels of political freedom vary from mostly free (Indonesia) to free within boundaries set by unelected actors (Morocco, Turkey) to, at times, outright authoritarian (Yemen).[2] Within the scope of this study, that is, across parties that have competed multiple times in at least partly free elections, regime interference has sometimes been significant enough to alter a party's political strategy.

Regimes vary in at least three principal ways that may affect the political strategy of Islamist parties. The first is simply variation on the democratic to authoritarian continuum. Parties that face state interference in their political campaigns or their electoral results face a different set of constraints on their strategic behavior from those that do not. The second source of variation is in the religious orientation of the regime. Some regimes are overtly Islamic in orientation (Pakistan, Malaysia), and may even claim religious authority (Morocco). Others are overtly secular in orientation (Turkey), or multireligious (Indonesia). A third source of variation occurs at the party system level. Some party systems are highly fragmented in the Islamist choices available, with multiple Islamically oriented parties (Indonesia, Pakistan), while others have one dominant Islamist party that serves as the focal point for the Islamist electorate (Malaysia, Morocco, Yemen, Turkey).

Parties that operate under more authoritarian conditions are more likely to face regime pressure or even open repression, which may limit the party's political impact. However, under moderate levels of state-based interference, this repression can also extend a party's popularity and make it a focal point for the political opposition. Islamist parties, in particular, have the ability to survive state repression by taking refuge in religious society, and can attract opposition for normative reasons if the government is perceived as un-Islamic. As a result, I hypothesize that **Islamist parties that face opposition from the state will attract anti-regime supporters who see them as an opposition movement, not just as an Islamist party**. If the regime is perceived as secular in orientation, this effect may be particularly strong because of the contrast of the Islamist party to the existing regime. Similarly, state pressure when applied to multiple opposition parties has the potential to lead these parties to coalesce in challenging the existing regime. As a result, **Islamist parties that face opposition from the**

state may find it useful and important to build political alliances with other parties facing state opposition.

In party systems in which one dominant Islamist party competes against a field of non-Islamist parties, that party is likely to be seen as the Islamist challenger regardless of the extent to which it focuses on Islamist priorities. This is illustrated most dramatically in Turkey, where the AKP, despite its limited focus on religious issues, is seen as an Islamist political party by a large portion of Turkish voters who see it as distinct from all its main secular competitors. By contrast, in fragmented systems in which multiple Islamist parties may compete for the "Islamist" label, a label that is important if the party is to carry an identity-based constituency, Islamist parties have to work harder to convince voters that they are "the Islamic choice." This may lead to a pattern of competitive "outflanking," in which Islamist parties move increasingly toward Islamist rhetoric to demonstrate that they are the best representatives of their identity group. This is a similar process to that which has been observed in ethnic parties that radicalize to compete with one another to represent the same ethnic group.[3] How then do Islamist parties behave when they are competing in a party system with multiple Islamist parties? I propose that **parties that compete with other Islamically oriented parties will be more likely to emphasize the Islamic parts of their platform to highlight their distinctiveness versus their competitors.**

Taken together, these propositions suggest that Islamist parties will behave differently under different political regimes and party systems. As a generic statement, this should be intuitive; however, I have here tried to specify the direction in which different regime characteristics will lead to differential behavior from Islamist parties. Other regime characteristics not mentioned here, including the electoral system and the electoral threshold, will certainly impact party behavior as well, but should do so in predictable ways regardless of party type, and are beyond the scope of this theoretical discussion.

A Strategic Framework for Islamist Participation

Why do Islamists choose to participate in electoral politics and how do they strategically interact with the government, other competitors, and their diverse constituencies? I seek here to provide a theoretical framework for understanding why participating in electoral politics is both tempting and ultimately transforming for Islamist groups. I first outline several assumptions about the objectives of Islamist groups and then argue that they face a set of *opportunities* that allow them to realize those objectives, but also a set of *constraints* on how they can be realized. This interaction between pursuing opportunities and navigating constraints forms the basis of the strategic decision-making in this model. The end result is that Islamist groups are likely to become increasingly normalized in their political systems, although the degree of that normalization will depend on several factors. In developing the framework, I make assumptions throughout that do not apply to every case under consideration, but are designed to illustrate the logic of Islamist party behavior under a common set of circumstances.

What do Islamist groups want? I assume that these groups have three major objectives, and that their behavior is driven by their pursuit of these objectives. First, they seek to transform society. They want to change both individual and collective behavior within society, which will lead to social change in key areas. Society should be more moral, particularly as defined in an Islamic framework, meaning that people within society are more likely to live Islamic precepts in their daily lives and social interactions. Likewise, society should be more just, meaning that there is less poverty and corruption; more charity and equity. Finally, society should have more abundance, meaning wealth or development—more to go around economically.

Second, Islamist groups want the state to better support these social goals, including intervening in society to support them if it fails to achieve them on its own. The state should be a better advocate for growth and development, a better protector of the poor, and a better punisher of the unjust. It should also be modeled on (or at least consistent with) Islamic law, meaning that the civil and family statutes prominent in Islamic legal tradition are supported and enforced within society. Islamist groups may vary in their interpretation of Islamic law, or in their belief in the practicality of its enforcement, but I assume here that they want the state to be more active in supporting its principles.

In addition to transforming society and increasing state support for an Islamic society, I assume that Islamists want power—power to drive the social and political changes they envision. Their desire for power may come from a mistrust of those in power (after all, they haven't been successful in making the necessary transformation), and also from self-confidence that their religious background makes them uniquely well positioned to make good decisions about the transformation of state and society. While there are many other potential objectives driving Islamist leaders (including fame, wealth, revenge) that are common among political entrepreneurs of all stripes, for illustrative purposes I assume only these three here: social transformation, state support for social transformation, and power to drive the change.

To realize these objectives, Islamists must take advantage of some opportunities to create change that are present in their political systems. This study assumes that they are actors in political systems that allow for social mobilization and electoral competition, both of which present interesting opportunities for Islamists. These opportunities to realize their objectives include working outside politics as well as within it. However, each opportunity also has associated constraints, so that pursuing one opportunity may be limiting or even counterproductive in other respects. I highlight four opportunities below, and some corresponding constraints that limit a party's ability to fully meet its objectives while pursuing them.

A first opportunity that Islamists can take advantage of is to create a social movement. Many Islamist groups from the early days of the Muslim Brotherhood on have done this, often to great effect. A social movement need not be overtly political, and can thrive in otherwise hostile political environments if it stays far enough from the state to avoid direct repression. A social movement is designed primarily to meet the first objective of transforming society, and usually has greater potential to achieve Islamists' social aims than do political parties or otherwise overtly political groups that remain marginal within their political systems. The great strength of an effective social movement is in its ability to mobilize ordinary citizens for collective action, which can serve religious, social, or even political causes. For Islamists, a social movement usually serves several functions, including religious propagation (da'wa), providing charitable and relief services, supporting Islamic education, and as a demonstration of the power of Islamists either to influence social norms or as a latent political threat.

While many, though by no means all, Islamist groups use a form of social movement to achieve these objectives, a movement has its limitations. The main one is that in the state-heavy political systems common in the Muslim world, one can only have so much impact on society if one ignores the levers of state. In particular, two of our assumed objectives of Islamist groups (increase state support for Islamic concerns and obtain

power to drive change) are difficult to achieve only through a social movement if the state dominates decision-making or economic resource distribution. Movements may still be extremely influential, particularly in places
where they have served as a dominant form of organized civil society (the
Nadhlatul Ulama in Indonesia has membership exceeding 50 million), but
their ability to fully advance Islamist goals remains constrained if they fail
to engage the state.

A second constraint of social movements is that they can easily take on
a life of their own outside the broader Islamist vision of using the state for
Islamic purposes. This independence can be used either to avoid Islamist
objectives that require directly engaging the state, or to constrain Islamist
actors who want to pursue political opportunities. On one hand, the social
movement may develop its own interests, leadership, and internal promotion system that rewards Islamic, but not Islamist goals. For example, a
movement's leaders may become fiercely devoted to Islamic education or
charitable work, but fail to engage the state on issues of justice, development, or Islamic law, abdicating these goals in favor of less controversial
ones. This independence can also work the other way, however, if the
movement holds Islamist politicians tightly yoked to conservative Islamic
ideals and prevents them from making strategic compromises in favor of
broader political goals. For example, an Islamist party may see strategic
value in downplaying its Islamic objectives in favor of other political objectives in order to attract non-Islamist voters. If, however, it is closely tied to
an Islamic movement that does not share its political objectives, movement
leaders may object to any political focus that distracts from the dominantly
religious objectives of the movement. In this sense, an Islamic movement
may work to keep an affiliated political party in the religious corner despite
the political opportunities it may forfeit as a result.

A second opportunity Islamists may pursue to meet their objectives is
to enter the electoral system through the use of a political party. In each of
the cases of this study, Islamists have done this and have won a number
of parliamentary seats as a result. Given the social transformation potential
of a social movement, why would Islamists choose to enter electoral politics? By entering the political arena, Islamists can engage the government
directly on issues related to governance, which is core to Islamist objectives.
Additionally, entrance into parliament offers a number of benefits, including an opportunity to directly confront political opponents, heightened
media access, access to state patronage resources, or even immunity from

prosecution. Entry into parliament allows Islamists to propose legislation and directly participate in debates on political issues, both of which are likely necessary if they are to meet their objective of increasing state support for Islamic priorities.

Parliamentary seats come with a limited amount of political power (access and visibility), even if parliamentarians do not participate directly in government. However, minority Islamist parties in systems with modest parliamentary authority soon discover the limitations on their power and may acutely feel the political constraints of being a minority parliamentarian. Muslim Brotherhood affiliated Members of Parliament (MPs) in Egypt, despite being the largest opposition bloc, never successfully passed legislation through the People's Assembly prior to the 2011 revolution. The PJD in Morocco and the PAS in Malaysia, despite being regular participants in comparatively more powerful legislatures, have historically failed to obtain any meaningful political power on the national level through direct elections, although the PJD did ultimately win the post of prime minister in 2012. For most Islamist parties that compete as minority parties, the primary constraint of parliamentary participation is that without compromise or coalition with other, larger parties, actual political power to effect change remains uncomfortably limited.

A third opportunity thus emerges for Islamist parties who have some seats in the legislative assembly: they can work directly with those who hold power to promote their Islamist agenda. "Working with" others can range from political horse trading, to crafting political compromises, to serving as part of a coalition government and thus obtaining ownership of relevant ministries. By working with other powerful political actors, the party is more likely to accomplish elements of its social and political agenda. After all, many of what Islamists view as Islamically relevant priorities (clean government, economic development, poverty reduction) are similar to the political agenda of parties coming from other ideological backgrounds. In many cases Islamist priorities overlap with non-Islamist priorities, and compromise or coalition to serve a common objective is possible. Even in areas without overlap, powerful parties may be willing to give Islamists some leeway on what they perceive to be a minor or niche issue, in exchange for support in fending off their political competitors on core political issues.

The constraint associated with this opportunity, however, is that often traditional political parties do have very different goals from the Islamists and may find ways to ensure that an Islamist challenger is marginalized in core areas of its concern. Because Islamists must make some political compromises in order to secure support for their priorities, they run the substantial risk of "diluting" their platform in the process of obtaining power through political trades or coalitions. Diluting the platform in the process of political compromise is common across all experienced political parties, although Islamists may pay a higher price than others if they are perceived to be unfaithful to their founding principles. Straying too far from the party's Islamic priorities risks alienating the party's religious constituency, and becoming too close to mainstream or government parties risks alienating the party's protest-based constituency. The catch is that without such compromises, the party may risk accomplishing very few of its objectives, and thus be perceived as ineffectual over time.

A fourth opportunity provides an alternative approach to compromise or coalition-building with an Islamist party's political rivals. Rather than work with rivals in uncomfortable compromises, the party may seek to overcome its minority status and political impotence by going directly to the electorate and expanding its constituency over time. This, of course, is something most political parties would like to do, and is never an easy process. For Islamist parties, it means aggressively working to attract mainstream voters to secure an increasing number of legislative seats or other political posts. The best example of Islamists successfully pursuing this approach is the Islamist party tradition in Turkey, which after the election of the AKP in 2002 with a dominant plurality of the vote, demonstrated that Islamist parties can move into the mainstream with great political success, even in a fiercely secular state like Turkey. Likewise, in the 2011–2012 elections in post-Mubarak Egypt, the Muslim Brotherhood's newly formed Freedom and Justice Party (FJP) successfully attempted to capture many mainstream voters by focusing on a wide range of more traditional political priorities.

However, this process is not without its political costs. The key constraint on Islamist parties that seek to capture a large portion of the electorate is that most voters are not Islamists. This is certainly the case in Turkey, but it is likely the case in almost all Muslim-majority countries, where a minority of religious Muslims link their faith explicitly to a vision of Islamic governance. If an Islamist party chooses to expand into the mainstream electorate, it must do so by finding ways to attract many voters who do not consider themselves Islamists. As hypothesized previously, it can do this by attracting anti-regime or protest voters, although if it is successful and subsequently participates in government, it will not be able to maintain this support from protest voters over time. To maintain support from centrists in the electorate, the party must credibly cater to centrist concerns, and beyond the basics of good governance and economic prosperity, these concerns are not traditional Islamist concerns. Therefore, to take advantage of this opportunity, an Islamist party must also dilute the religious content in its platform, and will look less and less Islamist over time, as a result.

Taken together, **these four potential political opportunities (build a social movement, enter the electoral arena, work with more powerful political rivals, and attract centrist voters) are ultimately too tempting for most Islamist groups committed to driving social and political change to resist.** Not all Islamist groups pursue every opportunity, but pursuing a mix of these opportunities is the most likely way to achieve the objectives I have assumed Islamist groups share. Indeed, Islamists who pursue more of these opportunities are more likely to have greater impact in accomplishing their objectives, **but the constraints on achieving these objectives are real, and require compromises that may lead over time to unintended consequences.** The principal unintended consequence from pursuing these political opportunities in the face of constraints is that Islamist parties become increasingly normalized within their political systems. By normalization, I mean that they behave more like mainstream political actors in their given context over time, and less like distinctive, anti-establishment, religious actors. Normalization is not one of the Islamists' objectives at the beginning of our hypothesized political process, but it is an unintended consequence of pursuing Islamist objectives within a competitive electoral framework. This leads to a key proposition of this chapter: **Islamist parties are becoming increasingly normalized actors within their political systems, and become less distinct in their behavior from non-Islamist political competitors as they pursue their political objectives in the electoral arena.**

Not all Islamist parties will normalize to the same degree, or at the same rate, however. What factors affect how far an Islamist party will normalize its behavior within its political system? I argue that Islamist parties with ties to broader Islamist movements might be less likely to take full advantage of their political opportunities because the movement will constrain their strategic flexibility. The movement's interests will be more directly tied to Islamic social and religious objectives, and therefore movement leadership will push to keep party leadership from moving too far from core Islamic objectives even with the promise of political gain. This leads to a prediction that **parties with strong ties to outside Islamic movements are constrained in their strategic options in the political arena, and will be less likely to normalize through electoral competition than parties without such ties**.

By contrast, parties that participate in government through coalitions or as part of a broader alliance are subject to powerful incentives to compromise in order to obtain power to realize their objectives. In the process, the pursuit of these objectives may look less and less Islamist as the areas in which they are likely to receive support from partners are those that are furthest from their distinctive Islamist identity. Therefore, **as Islamist parties participate in coalition government, they are more likely to normalize their political behavior than those remaining outside government**.

A visual depiction of the strategic framework for Islamist participation is found in Figure 1. The figure depicts the pursuit of Islamist objectives in a democratic political process. Islamists can take advantage of multiple political opportunities to achieve their objectives, but are faced with associated constraints that set some limits on how far those opportunities will take them. After negotiating democratic opportunities and confronting constraints, the parties emerge at least partly normalized into their political systems, with the degree of normalization dependent on ties to outside movements, government actors, and the degree to which they must act in coalition.

Islamist Parties and Electoral Success

A brief examination of cases where Islamist parties have competed in multiple, sequential legislative elections demonstrates the high variability in electoral success both across Islamist parties in different geographies, and across time within the same Islamist party. Why are some Islamist parties ultimately more successful at the polls than others? How do we account for a party's relative success in one election and failure in another? These questions can be posed as interesting puzzles for all types of political parties, although I theorize that many Islamist parties have distinctive advantages as protest parties that may explain this high variability.

In some cases, Islamist parties have never been successful at reaching a critical electoral mass that makes them a credible challenger for state power.

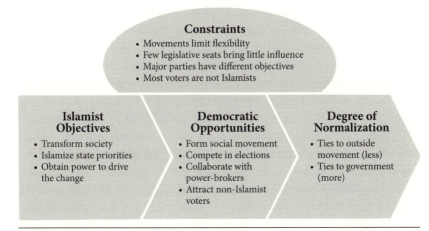

Figure 1. Strategic framework for Islamist participation.

In Indonesia, Pakistan, Bangladesh, and Malaysia, Islamists have become important political actors over time, but have failed to make sufficient inroads with the electorate to threaten the traditional sources of elected political power. This is not to say that they have been consistent in their electoral returns, however. In fact, each of these cases has seen variability in support for Islamists, but within a band that remains below the threshold for meaningful participation in government.

Other Islamist parties have seen wider variability in electoral returns, including spikes in their success that make them a dominant focal point for political opposition or a credible challenger for governance. In Morocco, Tunisia, Yemen, Jordan, Iraq, Kuwait, Egypt, and Turkey, Islamist parties have seen dramatic growth in support between one election and another, and most have also seen relative declines in support in subsequent elections. Only in regimes that have institutionalized democratic elections within an Islamist framework, Iran and the Sudan, have Islamist groups consistently dominated the electoral field; however, this is in many ways an artificial construction that fails to offer voters choice across the full political spectrum, and there is too much noise in these elections to adequately assess the reasons for Islamist success.

In each of the cases of electoral expansion, Islamist parties have been able to attract new voters within short periods of time. These include voters who have previously voted for other, non-Islamist parties, as well as citizens who may have abstained from participating in the electoral process. While the ranks of those who support Islamists due to religious conviction or identity association can and do grow in some cases, the growth in a core Islamist constituency takes time and occurs more slowly than the spikes in support between elections would suggest. Expansion in electoral support is more likely to come from the support of non-Islamists who vote for the Islamist party for reasons other than Islam. Building on the idea that Islamist parties have a dual constituency, **I suggest that Islamist parties are most likely to have electoral success when they are able to capture a large protest vote that is dominated by non-Islamist voters**.

If securing the party's objectives is most likely with electoral success, and electoral success is most likely through securing the support of non-Islamist voters who vote for Islamists in protest against the government or political system, then parties should be tempted to chase that vote. By going after that vote, Islamist parties are likely to focus on political concerns that are not directly relevant to Islam, but that Islamists and non-Islamist voters share. If they are opposition parties, these concerns will certainly include the inadequacies of the present government, and will likely include economic stability, unemployment, corruption, or even violence. By catering to the portion of their potential constituency that most needs convincing, and is most likely to help them succeed electorally, the party again finds that political incentives pull it away from its distinctiveness as an Islamist party and toward mainstream party politics.

Because capturing this protest vote is not guaranteed, it must be courted. In most systems, protest voters have several different options outside an Islamist party, including radical nationalists, leftists, or ethnic parties. Protest voters will support Islamists only when they are perceived to serve as the most effective channel for their grievances, and this will be reassessed in every election. Protest voters are therefore fickle in their support for the party over time, which leads to the problem of sustaining electoral success. On average, we should expect to see protest bumps in electoral support deflate in the next election, particularly if, as a result of its previous electoral success, the party has participated in (or become close to) government. Therefore, in order to maintain its enlarged constituency over time, an Islamist party must find ways of turning protest voters into regular supporters who vote for the party because of what it is, rather than what it is not. This is a difficult process, but again, is dependent on catering to the political issues most resonant with these voters, which are unlikely to based primarily in Islamic concerns. Turning protest voters into committed supporters requires fundamental changes in the party's appeal and increases incentives to dilute its Islamist character.

This raises an important question regarding what is lost in the pursuit of electoral success: does electoral success equate with party success? In the previous section I defined success for an Islamist party as the realization of three objectives: transforming society along Islamic lines, increasing state support for this social transformation, and obtaining power to drive these changes. When realizing electoral success by catering to non-Islamist voters, an Islamist party only partly realizes its initial objectives. It now has more power to drive the changes it would like to see, but that power is ultimately constrained by its political evolution and the internal organizational change that is likely to accompany it. In theory, it can better increase state support for Islamic interests from a position of greater political power, but in the process it may lose its ability to advocate openly for Islamist priorities. If it does so, it may risk alienating a portion of the supporters that have helped to craft its political success.

The Effects of Islamist Participation

To this point, I have argued that in reasonably democratic systems, Islamist groups are likely to use political participation through parties as a way to meet their primary objectives of state and social transformation. Electoral participation presents several tempting opportunities that can help them realize their objectives, despite the constraints and potential costs that may come from taking advantage of these opportunities. As Islamists compete in elections and secure seats in parliament over time, they are likely to see opportunities to expand their influence by compromising and collaborating with more powerful competitors, and may find opportunities to expand their electoral success by catering to non-Islamist voters. In doing so, Islamists can find greater electoral success, but they also become more normalized within their political systems and can lose much of their Islamic distinctiveness. The process of Islamist participation in electoral politics therefore affects how parties behave, and it also affects the political systems in which they participate. In this section I theorize about the effects of political participation on both Islamist parties and on their political systems over time.

How does democratic participation affect Islamist parties? The first way is in the gradual loss of Islamist distinctiveness, as I have discussed throughout the chapter. Note that this is related to, but different from, claims that Islamist parties "moderate" through democratic participation discussed in the introduction to this volume. The movement away from Islamist religious priorities in favor of more mainstream political priorities is theorized here as a strategic response to political opportunities in the face of constraints from political competitors and voters. It does not necessarily imply ideological moderation, which would include a change of belief among Islamist party leaders. This strategic response may be correlated with "behavioral moderation," to the extent that moderation is conceived of as new ways of interacting with competitors and potential constituents. Moderation, however, usually implies moving away from extremist positions, which is not necessarily reflective of the starting point of Islamist parties in the strategic framework discussed here.

A second way in which participation affects Islamist groups is organizational, changing the career trajectories and incentives of Islamist leaders. By participating in electoral politics, Islamist leaders take some risks in expectation of a measure of reward. These risks include the potential of electoral failure, as well as the potential to be seen by supporters as complicit in an unpopular governing regime. By moving into electoral politics, leaders must sell the idea to their religiously focused constituents that such a move will do more good than harm in meeting their objectives. This makes a successful foray into electoral politics critical to the credibility of Islamist leaders (increasing the reputational costs of failure) and they are likely to invest considerable energy into the process once the decision to participate has been made. This includes shifting organizational resources in the direction of electoral competition and using rhetorical energy to convert Islamist followers to the idea of a participatory strategy.

Once an Islamist party holds seats in parliament and begins to try out political compromise with opponents or attempts to expand its constituency, further organizational change is likely. New resources come into the party if it can gain access to state patronage networks and new party leaders emerge who may not have originally come out of the Islamist tradition. The party thus becomes increasingly tied to its participatory position, and may risk a loss of patronage resources or even some party leadership if it tries either to exit from the political process or to move back to distinctively Islamist political behavior. It is, of course, still possible to exit if political conditions deteriorate sufficiently that the benefits of political participation disappear. However, it becomes more difficult over time as the reputational and organizational risks of exit increase. I suggest, therefore, that participatory behavior can become path dependent and that **political participation by Islamist organizations makes exit from the political process increasingly improbable over time.**

The trajectory of Islamist groups toward normalization is not without its detractors both within the groups and among their core constituency. In fact, the process of party normalization is usually highly controversial for some party members, who fear that the principal mission of the group is at risk the deeper that the movement becomes involved in a compromised political process. As the Islamist party makes new political tradeoffs or becomes closer to its traditional political opponents, vigorous debates within party leadership are likely to occur about the wisdom of these choices. Most often, older party leaders who have been with the Islamist group for some time prior to these political developments are the most likely to resist change, as they have more personal history invested in the group's traditional positions. The younger generation of party leaders is likely to have a shorter record to defend, and may be looking for new opportunities to demonstrate political leadership. Younger members may also feel that their career opportunities are constrained by an older generation that does not easily relinquish internal party authority, particularly in parties with a strong internal hierarchy.

The combination of strategic incentives for party change with internal party divisions about the costs and benefits of that change, implies that Islamist parties are prone to splits during the process of political normalization. Sometimes these internal divisions can be contained without a formal rupture, but at other times the divisions prove irreconcilable and make the formal division of the party likely. When are divisions in an Islamist party most likely to emerge? I propose that **splits are more likely to occur around the period of major political transitions, such as first participating in elections, joining an alliance with traditional opponents, or newly participating in government.** I also argue that because parties face internal divisions over the choice of the degree of their Islamic identity, they are most likely to split over disagreements about the extent of their Islamic identity.

Although participation affects the parties themselves, there are also reasons to believe that it affects the political systems of which they are a part.

There are three main areas in which political systems are likely to be affected by the entrance and participation of Islamist parties into electoral politics. These include public renegotiation of the rules of the political system, appropriation of some Islamist priorities by non-Islamist competitors, and ultimately increased accommodation of Islamist parties in the political system as these parties normalize.

In systems where the appropriateness of political Islam is contested (Egypt, Turkey), or in which there is a public contest over who has the authority to speak on behalf of Islam (Morocco, Yemen, Pakistan) the political participation of Islamist parties is likely to trigger public debate regarding the role of Islam in the political sphere. This will happen to some degree in all systems where groups compete as Islamists, but the effect is amplified when there is public controversy regarding whether Islam has an appropriate place in the public sphere and who has authority to represent Islam within that sphere. In Turkey, and also in Egypt and Tunisia until very recently, political parties have been explicitly forbidden from organizing around Islamic identity. In Morocco, the king officially represents Islam, although he is not a cleric and is open to challenges regarding his religious authority. Likewise, in Yemen and Pakistan, sectarian divisions within the Islamic community make individual claims to represent Islamic interests very controversial within segments of religious society. The entrance and participation of Islamist parties, therefore, provides challenges to how political and social order is conceived, and forces a renegotiation of Islam's role in the public sphere. This can trigger some turbulence in the political system, as in Turkey, where institutions of state have openly challenged the ruling party because of its perceived Islamist agenda. In Egypt, the government historically used the threat of Muslim Brotherhood success at the polls to justify its intervention in an ostensibly democratic process, distorting political life. Islamist participation can also impact the relationship between religious communities, if one feels threatened by the exclusive nature of the claims of Islamist groups, as do Shi'a or Isma'ilis in Pakistan.

Despite the controversy that Islamists can bring into the political system, their appeal among important segments of society is noticed by their political competitors, and their participation is likely to bring change to the public sphere even without large-scale electoral success. Their successful appeals to religious identity and the preferences of many religious Muslims can be appropriated by competing opposition parties or by the government. This may be done either to benefit from the Islamists' successful political strategy, or to marginalize the Islamist opposition by taking away its distinctive appeal. When competitors appropriate elements of the Islamists' agenda, as the government has repeatedly done in Malaysia, the Islamists secure both a political victory, and a political loss. Their victory comes through having increased state or social conformity with Islamic priorities, a key Islamist objective. However, their own power to manage political or social change is likely to diminish as those who are better politically positioned articulate what is Islamically important in their list of political priorities. This appropriation of Islamist elements by more central political players forces Islamist parties either closer to their powerful competitors in shared objectives, or farther apart, as Islamists are forced to reassert their Islamic distinctiveness and argue for the religious illegitimacy of their competitors' positions. Either way, it is likely to weaken the Islamist parties' political appeal in the short run, even as it influences the political system in ways that may support Islamist objectives in the long run.

Although Islamist participation may initially generate some turbulence in the political system, the system is also likely to move toward greater accommodation of Islamists over time, thus normalizing Islamist participation in politics from a systemic, and not just a party perspective. This may occur for several reasons, each of which has been alluded to previously. As Islamist parties themselves increasingly accommodate the political systems in which they compete, responding to the political incentives already present in those systems, the gap between Islamist parties and competitors within the system narrows. This makes it easier for the political system to accommodate Islamist participation, with Islamist parties gradually becoming "normal" political actors that play by the system rules. Likewise, as the fortunes of Islamist parties wax and wane, they also appear to be less of a threat to system elites than they were initially. Often, their failure to take over the levers of state is comforting to those who hold those levers, and they become more tolerant of Islamist participation as Islamists' inability to dominate the system becomes apparent. Even when Islamist parties enjoy electoral success or win elections, they do so by catering at least in part to non-Islamist voters, engaging in the political issues that drive competition within the democratic system. Finally, if mainstream political parties appropriate aspects of the Islamists' platform, the gap between Islamists and other actors in the system becomes narrowed from the other direction. As the acceptable norms of the system become increasingly Islamic through appropriation, the political system also becomes more tolerant of Islamist political claims. Therefore, **despite the potential for political turbulence that Islamist participation in democratic systems often brings, those systems may increasingly accommodate Islamist parties over time as the political distance between Islamist parties and other parties narrows.**

Regardless of the apparent weakness of many Islamist parties as they enter democratic politics, their participation often has profound effects both on their own behavior, and on the behavior of the system in which they participate. The effects of their participation on the political system allow them to be more influential actors in shaping the overall behavior of political systems than their electoral support may indicate in isolation.

Conclusion

In this chapter I have introduced a diverse set of questions regarding the strategy and behavior of Islamist parties in democratic politics, as well as the outcomes associated with their political participation. I have also theorized about the mechanisms that drive behavior in Islamist parties and introduced a number of propositions regarding Islamist parties' platforms, constituencies, interaction with regimes, reasons for participation, sources of electoral success, and the effects of participation on the parties and political systems in which they compete. Collectively, these propositions tell a story about why Islamist parties enter the electoral arena, how they take advantage of political opportunities to achieve their objectives, the constraints and tradeoffs they face in pursuing these objectives, and why they are likely to lose their Islamic distinctiveness over time. I have argued that the normalization of these parties within their political systems is a rational but unintended outcome of pursuing their objectives in democratic politics. Some of these propositions have more empirical support than others, and their empirical accuracy is assessed through the detailed case studies in this volume and summarized in the conclusion.

To the extent that these propositions hold true, they paint a picture of a modern political Islam that responds to nonreligious political incentives, and is constantly evolving as a result of its interaction with political systems, political competitors, and voters. Islamist parties in this story engage in electoral politics for good, Islamically centered reasons, but are also constrained to make sacrifices in their religious objectives as they become more deeply entrenched in the political process. After repeated experience with electoral politics, the parties may look substantially different from those that first took the plunge into the democratic political arena. For parties embedded in a broader Islamic movement or whose core Islamist constituency is comparatively large, the tug of war between Islamist and democratic political incentives may be too much to endure and lead to a party split, or weakness and inconsistency at the polls.

This theorized pattern of Islamist evolution has implications for the future trajectory of political Islam. On the one hand, the increasing normalization of Islamist politics means that political Islam is in a position to influence more political systems than ever before, and that Islamist parties are becoming increasingly relevant within their political systems. They are likely to take advantage of more democratic opportunities over time and also find ways of capturing a larger portion of the electorate, either alone or in association with others. On the other hand, however, the way in which they influence their political systems over time may have less and less to do with traditional religious concerns. As the distance between Islamist parties and other parties narrows, many Islamist parties will begin to look much more like mainstream political actors than advocates of religious ideology.

Chapter 2

When Is Normalization Also Democratization? Islamist Political Parties, the Turkish Case, and the Future of Muslim Polities

MURAT SOMER

What does normalization mean in an electoral democracy with considerable majoritarian and authoritarian characteristics? This chapter examines what we learn from the Turkish case regarding how Islamist political parties behave and sometimes become normalized in response to electoral, competitive politics as well as secularist constraints. I also explore what kinds of changes their normalization might entail and how this might affect democracy. The relationship between democratization and the participation of religious actors in politics is multifaceted and contingent.[1] Thus, I will try to identify and conceptualize when and to what extent the normalization of religious politics might also contribute to democratization. I will do so through a cross-temporal examination of Turkish democracy and political Islam since the 1970s.

I contend that the transformation of Turkish Islamists since the 1990s illustrates how electoral incentives combined with nonelectoral, authoritarian interventions can bring about the normalization of Islamism. This normalization includes compromises with the country's mainstream politics, society, and international political and economic linkages. The Turkish case also shows the democratic implications of normalization if a country lacks the values, institutions, and relationships of a fully democratic "center" and Islamist and secularist actors fail to cooperate for democratic reforms.[2] Normalization has enabled Turkish Islamists to expand their constituency, find liberal and secular domestic and international allies, and rule the country since 2002 by winning three consecutive national elections and a crucial constitutional referendum in 2010. But the implications for democratization indicate a double-edged relationship between normalization and democratization in the context of a flawed democracy. On one hand, Turkish Islamists used these benefits of normalization to make Turkey considerably more democratic in many respects. In particular, they raised the income level, curtailed militaristic and judicial tutelage, and allowed pious Turks, who previously felt disadvantaged, more access to mainstream social and political life. On the other hand, democratization suffered as Turkish Islamists instrumentalized their "normalcy" for their own material and ideological purposes. They began to exclude secular rivals, became increasingly intolerant of opposition and secular freedoms, and embarked on Islamic social engineering, especially after liberating themselves from nonelectoral constraints.

In many ways, Islamists began to reproduce many authoritarian characteristics of mainstream Turkish politics and the state-society relationship in such a way that they now favor and serve Islamic-conservative elites, communities, and values at the expense of others. The inability of weak secular opposition to democratically check and balance the Islamists contributed to this outcome. Democratization is a multidimensional process and the normalization of Islamists generated progress in some dimensions while producing regression in others.

Islamism has been a dynamic and important social, political, and ideological current in Turkey since the nineteenth century.[3] Yet until recently secular republicanism primarily shaped what was considered "normal" or "mainstream" in Turkish politics and society. This is because secular nationalists oppressed and excluded the Islamist opposition when they unilaterally shaped the mainstream institutions and values of the republic during the 1920s and 1930s.[4]

Political Islam, which had previously found limited expression in center-right political parties, entered the political scene with the formation of the first explicitly Islamist parties during the 1970s. Since then, these parties have proved themselves to be shrewd political actors and modern electoral machines with a remarkable ability to embrace selective features of mainstream Turkish politics. At the same time, they gradually transformed mainstream politics by contesting elections, participating in governments, having their supporters enter the state bureaucracy, and politicizing new issues, identities, and values, which mainstream parties felt compelled to address. Hence, they simultaneously played a participatory-electoral and a "regime delegitimation" game with respect to mainstream politics.[5] They also invented new political and discursive strategies and adapted to changing domestic and external circumstances.

Nevertheless, until the 1990s these parties were relatively small with an antisystemic orientation and came to power only as junior partners in coalition governments. Thus, they were not perceived as part of "normal" politics and catered to a narrow ideological constituency. In 1996, the Welfare Party (RP) became the first Islamist party to win a national election and came to power as the senior partner of a coalition government. The short-lived RP government fell as a result of a vicious, military-induced secularist campaign.[6] In 2002, however, a breakaway party rooted in the same tradition, the moderate-Islamist Justice and Development Party (AKP) came to power in a single-party government and has managed to govern the country since then. As we will see, in addition to fortuitous circumstances, the main factor that explained the AKP success was its pragmatism. This enabled the party to embrace—or compromise with—the discursive and behavioral attributes that were normal and acceptable in the eyes of the mainstream domestic and external (Western) power holders. The AKP also adjusted to changing global political and economic conditions more aggressively and extensively than any of its predecessors. Thus, the party was able to expand its voter base beyond religious conservatives to a broad spectrum of centrist voters. It also enlisted the crucial support of major segments of the liberal-secular intelligentsia, media, and economic bourgeoisie. These strategic moves helped the party to secure the initial, contingent tolerance of the pro-secular military and judiciary, and the acceptance of Turkey's Western allies, most importantly the EU and United States. Thus, the AKP's willingness and ability to "look and act normal" in the perception of a wide variety of domestic and external actors explains many of its accomplishments.

But this normalization did not always make the party adopt more democratic attitudes and policies because normal Turkish politics harbored a great deal of authoritarianism to begin with. The party adopted many of these authoritarian norms and attitudes, such as impatience with criticism, opposition, and consensus-building and only grudging respect for moral and ideological pluralism, and freedom of expression. At the same time, during its decade-long tenure in government, the party has gradually remolded mainstream Turkish politics, sometimes in a more pluralist and other times in a more authoritarian direction, because its own ideological repertoire was a mixture of democratic and authoritarian values itself, especially but not exclusively in the social realm.[7] The methods that the party has employed to transform Turkish politics and society have included many practices that cannot be considered normal or legitimate in consolidated democracies. In the end, the AKP government has been very successful in advancing Turkish democracy in areas such as subduing military tutelage over civilian politics. But its impact in areas such as freedom of expression, government accountability, judicial neutrality and independence, and ethnic and religious pluralism has been disappointing, if not regressive.[8]

This Turkish experience helps envisage how Islamist political parties might behave after becoming dominant political actors and liberating themselves from secularist veto players. In recent legislative elections, Islamists gained about 70 percent and 41 percent of the seats in Egypt and Tunisia, respectively. Thus, Islamist political parties may become the predominant players in some of the emerging Muslim-majority polities following the Arab Spring. Many of them such as the Egyptian and Syrian Muslim Brothers and Tunisian Al-Nahda have declared the AKP as partial examples for themselves. Likewise, major portions of the public in Arab countries see Turkey "as a good model."[9]

In the case of the Turkish AKP, it is useful to conceptualize "normalization" as a process whereby the party selectively adapts to the mainstream social, political-economic, and international contexts in which it operates, which can be called a country's "center."[10] I discuss the evolution of Turkish Islamist parties' normalization process by examining consecutive chronological periods when these parties were faced with both opportunities and constraints in the Turkish political system. In doing so, I evaluate how the arguments presented in Chapter 1 of this volume play out in the Turkish case.

The Emergence of Turkish Political Islamism: 1971–1983

From 1946, when Turkey transitioned to multiparty politics, until the 1970s, religiously inspired ideas were represented within center-right parties. The first explicit and short-lived Islamist party was established in 1970 by a group of dissidents from the center-right Justice Party. These dissidents were led by a charismatic Ph.D. in engineering, Necmettin Erbakan (1926–2011), who founded the National Outlook (Milli Görüş) (MG) movement and ideology. From then on for three decades, the MG became the primary ideological and organizational basis of a series of political Islamist parties.

Turkish Islamists sought to establish an independent political party distinct from center-right parties mainly in reaction against mainstream Turkish politics and society. Thus, one would need to refer to the attributes of the Turkish social and political "center" in order to fully grasp its roots and nature.[11] The institutional and ideological features of the center were shaped by top-down secular-modernist reforms during the 1920s and 1930s. These radical reforms were anticlerical and secularizing but also continued the late-Ottoman tradition of employing and instrumentalizing Islam for modernization as well as the goals of the state.[12] The leading actor of this era was the Republican People's Party (CHP) founded by Kemal Atatürk (1881–1938), which established an authoritarian single-party regime.[13] After completing Turkey's secular-nationalist transformation, the CHP partially moderated its secularist policies and allowed the transition to multiparty politics in 1950. This reflected the intra-elite divisions within the CHP, a compromise with Muslim-conservative median voters, and a willingness to integrate with the Western world in the post-World War II international context.[14] But despite this transition to electoral democracy and the institution of a formally liberal-democratic constitution in 1961, authoritarian state policies and military praetorianism remained deeply ingrained attributes of the Turkish state-society relationship and normal politics.

The main features of the political center thus became Turkish nationalist; semidemocratic (an electoral democracy with an illiberal state and military tutelage); secular but with state control of religion and instrumentalization, even promotion of Sunni Islam (*laiklik*)[15]; a vision of modernization encouraging political-economic as well as social-cultural westernization; and, especially after the end of World War II, a foreign policy firmly based in Western alliances such as NATO membership. The mainstream socioeconomic context was a predominantly Muslim-conservative and secularizing society, with a state-dominant, urban-centric developing economy.

Against this background and compared with center-right parties, the establishment of Islamist parties represented a moment challenging political normalcy. This is because Islamist parties differed from the center-right parties through their explicit and unwavering objection to some features of the political center such as Turkish state-controlled secularism, sociocultural Westernization, and pro-Western foreign policy. In the view of the MG, most of Turkey's socioeconomic ills and international weakness could be attributed to the country's pro-secular and pro-Western orientation.[16] The MG movement was founded in defense of "Islamic values," proposing an indigenous (*milli*) developmental path as an alternative to the extant parties "imitating the West." At the same time, the MG parties embraced electoral democracy and made efforts to run on a diversified political platform including religious as well as secular issues.

What led to the formation of the MG parties? Sufi brotherhoods, disenchanted with the performance of center-right parties, were instrumental. Therefore, the transformation of the Sufi orders into social and political-economic movements can be seen as a crucial causal process.[17] However, the MG parties remained sensitive to the support of but organically separated from Sufi movements. The same can be said for the relationship between the MG parties and other Islamist groups and the Islamic movement in general, which the former tried to mobilize as well as control.[18] In terms of grassroots organization and ideology, the MG parties drew their support from the MG movement.

Another important development was the shifting interests of the small and medium size businesses in central Anatolia, which were diverging from the interests of big business in large urban centers and coastal Turkey.[19] When center-right parties failed to reconcile these two groups' interests, the MG developed a program and discourse to represent the interests of small business in Anatolia.

All this should not lead us to underestimate the role of ideas and ideological trends. Social and economic developments only created political opportunities for the formation of Islamist parties. By themselves, they do not explain why and how some Islamists responded to these opportunities with a particular Islamist frame of reference. The MG movement was developed by Erbakan in a particular historical and intellectual milieu. This milieu reflected the thinking of Turkish Islamic intellectuals that had been changing through domestic experiences and debates as well as interactions with global ideas. The latter included third world developmentalism and revolutionary Islamism.

The first MG party was short-lived, shut down by the Constitutional Court soon after the 1971 military coup. It was soon replaced by the

National Salvation Party (MSP). During the 1970s, this party managed to become a junior partner in a series of coalition governments including one with the mainstream CHP, with an average voter support of 10.18 percent.

The Rise of Turkish Political Islam: 1984–1997

This period witnessed the weakening of pro-secular political parties and the ascendance of political Islam, especially during the 1990s. The average voter support of Islamist parties increased to 17.89 percent in the national elections during the 1990s. In local elections, they were even more successful. While Islamists thus increasingly became major players in electoral politics, this did not necessarily mean that they made less use of religious discourse and ideology. In fact, Table 1 shows that religion and the discourse of national-religious authenticity became more prominent in the program of the RP.

Normal politics in Turkey became more Islamic-conservative and nationalist during this period. Arguably, this reflected the intended and unintended consequences of authoritarian and ostensibly secularist state interventions in politics, the policies of Islamist and center-right political parties, and global developments. The military regime of 1980–1983 embraced the "Turkish-Islamic synthesis ideology" as an antidote against the "Marxist threat." This ideology was developed by some Islamic intellectuals and adopted by the military, echoing the Brzezinski doctrine of establishing a "green crescent" surrounding the Soviet Union's southern belly. The military regime promoted Islamic discourse and identity, introduced mandatory religion courses in primary and secondary schools and constitutionally tasked the colossal state agency regulating Islam, the Directorate of Religious Affairs (Diyanet), with promoting "national solidarity and unity." The self-identified preferences of median Turkish voters thus began to grow more nationalist and conservative.[20]

At the same time, even though the military targeted all movements it deemed subversive, including the Islamists, its crackdown was most effective against the leftists. Islamists took advantage of both the Turkish-Islamic synthesis ideology and the gap in Turkish politics vacated by the leftists after the 1980 military coup.

The AKP's main predecessor, the Welfare Party (RP), was founded in 1983 by the leadership of the MSP. After a less than impressive electoral

Table 1: Frequency of Discourse of Religion and Authenticity in Programs of Turkish Islamist parties (per 1,000 words)

	MNP-Program (1970–1971)	MSP-Program (1972–1980)	RP-Program (1983–1998)	FP-Program (1997–2001)	SP-Program (2001–)	AKP-Program (2001–)
Religion (din)	0.15	3.33	3.61	3.33	2.58	1.88
Spirituality (maneviyat)	2.75	2.78	3.89	0.66	1.92	0.27
National (milli)*	5.11	3.33	7.78	2.33	1.00	0.67

*In MG ideology, "national" (milli) has strong religious overtones as the MG believes Islam to form the main and crucial ingredient of Turkish national identity.

performance in 1987 (7.16 percent of the national vote), which fell short of the 10 percent threshold necessary to enter the parliament, the RP significantly increased its votes to 16.88 percent in the 1991 elections. A successful electoral coalition with two other far-right parties contributed to this increase. In 1994, the RP raised eyebrows in local elections by capturing 19.14 percent of the vote and winning the mayorships of major cities like Istanbul and Ankara. This foreshadowed the party's remarkable success in the national elections a year later. Following its emergence as the winner of the 1995 national election with 21.38 percent of the vote, the RP became Turkey's first Islamist party to rise to power as the dominant partner of a fragmented coalition government.

The RP embraced electoral, competitive politics and saw significant rewards for doing so. In the process, it developed a political platform and used frames of reference that extended far beyond the use of religion. It was able to effectively address nonreligious issues such as economic development and displayed considerable ideological and discursive innovativeness and flexibility. This contributed to the party's electoral successes. Compared to the MSP, the RP managed to mobilize a larger segment and broader cross-class coalition of voters. In addition to small town merchants and small businesses, it appealed to "recently migrant urban slum-dwellers, a growing group of Islamist professionals and intellectuals, and the rapidly rising Islamic bourgeoisie."[21] The RP was a modern party and built an efficient grassroots organization that synthesized traditional idioms and modern methods of mobilization. It promised rapid and equitable economic development and prosperity.

The RP also benefited from the weakening of the center-right and center-left parties. These parties were marred by internal struggles, endemic corruption, and failure to develop new electoral strategies beyond clientelism.[22] The festering Kurdish conflict and economic instability were also undermining their credibility and legitimacy. As a result, the RP was able to capture a significant segment of protest voters who felt alienated from the existing options on the center-right and center-left.

All this did not necessarily mean, however, that the RP was becoming a mainstream party. Tuğal argues that in some ways the RP radicalized (while the more radical Islamist fringe groups moderated) during the late 1980s and early 1990s.[23] Despite its discursive and political flexibility and dynamic efforts to attract a broader segment of voters, the RP remained a mainly antisystemic party,[24] highly critical of Turkey's Western political and cultural orientation. Its understanding of democracy was majoritarian rather than pluralist. It sought to revive an authentic Islam that the party's supporters believed to be central to Turkey's social and political identity.[25]

The RP respected the general principle of secularism but was highly critical of *laiklik* (Turkish secularism). It emphasized religious freedoms while disregarding the separation of state and religion.[26] While sympathetic to private business, it envisioned a state-led, fundamental transformation of the economic system. The party pronounced the idea of a new and just order (*adil düzen*), which would be accomplished through such practices as ending the charging of interest in economic transactions. It advocated ending Turkey's pursuit of EU membership, long-standing pro-Western foreign policy, and membership in international organizations such as the International Monetary Fund (IMF). Overall, Buğra argues, the RP sought "to establish religion as the cultural basis of a comprehensive reorganization of social, economic, and political life."[27]

Lacking sufficient power to reorient Turkey's economic and political system, the party focused on culture and foreign policy. These policies—such as a widely publicized first visit by Premier Erbakan to Libya, plans to build a mosque in Istanbul's central Taksim square—which symbolized secular culture and lifestyle—and efforts to allow public servants to wear headscarves in government offices—proved deeply alienating to the pro-secular state elites and civil society. Consequently, a public campaign led by the military and backed by major pro-secular media, business and labor organizations rapidly eroded the party's ability to govern.

The final blow came on February 28, 1997, when the military-dominated National Security Council publicly criticized the government and effectively demanded that it implement a number of secularist reforms. The subsequent "February 28 process," which mainstream political parties openly or tacitly endorsed, turned into a "post-modern coup" and compelled the RP government to resign. A crackdown on actual and perceived Islamist political and economic actors followed, along with a series of reforms, particularly in the educational realm, ostensibly aimed at stemming Islamization. The Constitutional Court ultimately closed the RP in 1998.

The Moderation of Turkish Political Islam: 1998–2001

The authoritarian intervention of 1997 became the main trigger that led to the decisive normalization of Turkish political Islam.[28] After a brief period in which the Islamists competed under the banner of the Virtue Party (1999), the Islamist party split into two factions, with the reformist faction forming the Justice and Development Party (AKP). Thus, the AKP was the product of the reformers (*yenilikçiler*) within the MG, who decided to compromise with mainstream actors through significant discursive and organizational changes.

Early elections were called soon after the financial crises of 2000 and 2001, the worst in the country's history, and the AKP won the 2002 elections decisively. Turkish voters had decided to punish the mainstream parties, which they blamed for the crises, in favor of a new and "clean" party. Protest voters flocked to the AKP, lifting it to more success than it would have achieved through the normalization process alone. In a period of greater political stability, the reformist Islamists who formed the AKP would likely have been less successful.

But the party was able to use these circumstances because its founders had decided to normalize to avoid the RP's fate of closure by the Constitutional Court. In particular, the AKP's normalization entailed discursive and behavioral change in five areas: an organizational split from the MG tradition to highlight its distinctiveness from its predecessors; avoiding the discourse of religion and authenticity to minimize conflict with mainstream secularist actors and to appeal to a wider array of centrist voters; adopting the discourse of liberal as opposed to majoritarian democracy both to secure more protection from the authoritarian state and to reconcile with EU standards; embracing Turkey's Western alliances; and embracing economic globalism.

Table 2: Positive Evaluations of Electoral and Liberal Democracy
in Pro-Islamic Press (%)

	1996–1999	2001–2004
Electoral democracy	65	71 ↑
Liberal democracy	69	76 ↑

The formation of a new party and organization signaled that the AKP would be more independent from the MG movement than the RP was. Table 1 illustrates that the AKP program deemphasized religion more than any of its predecessors had done. The AKP's strong discursive emphasis on liberal democracy was somewhat surprising for actors that had emerged from a tradition that had been suspicious of liberal values in politics. While embracing democracy in general and often embracing economic liberalism, many Islamists had traditionally viewed the extensive pluralistic and individual rights and freedoms that liberal democracy entails as a potentially divisive and corrupting influence.[29] However, the AKP's normalization in this realm was embedded in broader discussions among Islamic circles. Many Islamists had concluded that they needed liberal democratic rights and standards as an instrument to protect themselves from secularist interventions.[30]

One way of assessing Islamist opinions of liberal democracy, as well as how the AKP fits within the broader context of Turkish political opinion, is by examining the ideational patterns in the Turkish press. Turkish elites writing in the press comprise a wide spectrum, from activist journalists to academics and politicians, and are closely connected with the political field.[31] Based on a systematic content analysis of the pro-Islamic press, Table 2 compares the share of supportive views about liberal democracy in the four years from 1996, when the RP came to power, to 1999, with supportive views in the period from 2001, the year the AKP was founded, to 2004.[32] Pro-Islamic elites discussed both electoral and liberal democracy more positively in the second period, even though the overall findings (not shown here) indicate no change in the evaluation of democracy in the pro-secular press. As a result, the positive evaluation of democracy in the pro-Islamic press began to converge during this period with that in the pro-secular press. Arguably, this linkage to these broader discussions among the Muslim-conservative intelligentsia made the AKP's normalization more credible.[33] Similar figures summarized in Table 3 reveal that the pro-Islamic

Table 3: Changing Image of the West

		1996–1998	1999–2002	2003–2004
	Positive	10% (42)	16% (69)	12% (45)
Pro-Islamic press	Negative	72% (314)	55% (240)	60% (230)
	Neutral	19% (82)	29% (125)	28% (106)

Table 4: Image of EU

		1996–1998	2000–2002	2003–2004
	positive	14% (24)	45% (274)	38% (235)
Pro-Islamic press	negative	57% (98)	30% (180)	36% (225)
	neutral	29% (49)	25% (154)	25% (157)
	positive	13% (30)	26% (170)	19% (77)
Pro-secular press	negative	42% (99)	40% (260)	45% (186)
	neutral	45% (105)	34% (219)	36% (150)

elites' image of the West improved drastically. The numbers in parentheses indicate how many times a positive, negative, or neutral reference was made to the West. The years 2003–2004 are treated separately as the war in Iraq, which the Turkish public predominantly saw as an unjust occupation of a Muslim country, had a negative impact on coverage of the West. More striking findings summarized in Table 4 concern the image of the EU. In the second period in the religious press, the EU became a much more frequently discussed subject (receiving three times as many references), with a considerably more positive coverage. In fact, it became more positive than in the secular press. This is remarkable considering that pro-secular elites had previously been the frontrunners of Turkey's EU ambitions.

Secular Skepticism and Unsustainable Democratization: 2002–2007

The period 2002–2006 was a major democratic-reformist period for Turkish democracy, in addition to rapid economic recovery.[34] From the beginning, the AKP government gave its priority to the "twin objectives" of democratization and Turkey's EU membership.[35] Major constitutional amendments expanded the formal freedoms of expression, association, press, and religion, while expanding minority rights and civilian authority over the military.[36]

Notably, this was a period of significant interparty cooperation. In general, the reforms were legislated with cooperation across Islamist-secularist ideological fault lines. EU conditionality for membership undoubtedly facilitated cooperation. At first, it is also tempting to inter-pret this as a welcome product of normalization. One might think that, as the AKP normalization narrowed the political distance between them and the secularists, the latter embraced cooperation with the Islamists This may indeed be part of the story for optimistic pro-secular actors. In fact, AKP's normalization divided pro-secular elites between skeptics and optimists. Major segments of the pro-secular military were particu-larly concerned; it became public later that some military commanders planned, or at least considered waging a coup against the government in its early years.

Nonelectoral constraints such as secularist veto players and the EU might have enabled skeptical pro-secular elites to cooperate with the AKP despite their misgivings about the latter's intentions regarding secularism. Skeptics' fears were curbed by the presence of a pro-secular president elected earlier, the EU anchor, and the ever watchful and still popular army. By using his powers to their utmost legal limits, president Ahmet Necdet Sezer—a staunchly secularist former judge—vetoed the government's appointments and laws. The military and the EU pronounced strong warn-ings whenever the government attempted to pursue a religious-conservative agenda such as a short-lived draft law criminalizing adultery in 2004.

But democratization was unsustainable with this role of nonelected veto players because their interference weakened democracy, kept religious-secular distrust intact, and undermined the incentives for pro-secular polit-ical parties and civil society organizations to reform themselves. The latter were in disarray because of internal fissures, corruption, discursive-ideolog-ical inertia, and AKP-skepticism.[37] The CHP reversed its earlier attempts to develop a more liberal secularist ideology such as the so-called "Anatolian left" project of the late 1990s, adopting instead a more radical-secularist orientation with a view to confronting the AKP.[38] Meanwhile, the AKP was gradually consolidating power through its economic performance and bureaucratic recruitments.

Things changed in 2007 when a showdown occurred between the AKP and the military and secular political and civil society over the AKP's election of Abdullah Gül to the presidency. As the military issued an ultimatum, pro-secular mass rallies protested aganist the government.[39] In the end, the AKP both elected Gül and won the parliamentary elections. This tipped the balance of informal power between the party and the secularists in favor of the former.[40]

Power Consolidation and the Question of Democracy: 2008–2011

In this period, the AKP consolidated its power and position in normal Turkish politics by winning a crucial referendum in 2010. In the 2011 national elections, it won almost half of the votes and became the first party in the country's history to win three consecutive national elections with increasing support each time. In addition, it wrested more autonomy from secularist nonelectoral constraints by effectively bringing the military under its control. In 2009, the Constitutional Court convicted the party of "being a focal point of anti-secular activities" but, in contrast to its decisions on earlier pro-Islamic parties, the court ruled not to ban the party, according to one author due to "the [overwhelming] economic, political and international costs of dissolving the popular governing party."[41] Meanwhile, a series of sensational trials convicted hundreds of civilians and military officers of plotting coups against the government. While these decisions were "milestones in civilian control over the military," a key disappointment was that they failed to "represent progress toward holding (state officials) accountable for their actions in a way that will resonate with the public across the political divide, and that (they) did not (necessarily) serve to promote a more democratic culture."[42]

Political stability and expanded autonomy for elected governments can be expected to advance democratization. But the actual impact on democratization was ambiguous because they made the AKP more complacent and less tolerant of opposition. The domineering reorientation of the AKP combined with the weak and distrustful opposition undermined interparty cooperation for the reforms that were necessary for further democratization.

Three more factors seem to have contributed to this outcome. The external support for Turkish democracy waned as Turkey's EU membership prospects became increasingly moot for reasons on both sides. Electoral victories emboldened the government to express its conservative and authoritarian values in such areas as social pluralism and freedom of expression. And, even though the government made unprecedented attempts to resolve Turkey's festering democratic problems such as the Kurdish conflict, ideationally it was insufficiently prepared to generate specific policies and institutional solutions to address these problems.[43]

The pro-EU and pro-liberal democratic zeal of the AKP gave way to an increasingly majoritarian, religious, and social-conservative rhetoric and practice. Parliamentary attempts at writing a new constitution based on cross-party consensus were stalled at least in part because of the AKP's initiatives to replace the parliamentary system with a presidential or semi-presidential system that would give Prime Minister Erdoğan extensive powers. The AKP's earlier emphasis on developing civil society in general was transformed into the promotion of a religious-conservative civil society and the vilification of the rest, whether secularist, leftist, Kurdish, or Alevi.

Instead of working to construct a state apparatus more respectful of popular dissent and human life, the AKP began to reinforce the "normal" Turkish state orientation focused on controlling society and suppressing difference. The police forces grew in size by 72 percent in the period 2003–2012.[44] New laws and regulations gave the police, which lack transparency and accountability, extensive and often arbitrary powers to tap private communications, suppress protest, and monitor citizens' daily lives.[45]

In summer 2013, the government did not hesitate to fully and indiscriminately employ these powers against the anti-government "Gezi" protesters. According to available official reports, the Turkish police used more than 130,000 canisters of tear gas during the first twenty days of the protests; 8,000 people were injured and 5 people died during the clashes. Amnesty International maintained that at least three deaths occurred for reasons related to police brutality and the government's "attempt to smash the Gezi Park protest movement involved a string of human rights violations on a huge scale."[46]

Between 2007 and 2013, Turkey's score of press freedoms declined by about 49 percent. Between 2002 when the AKP came to power and 2007, Turkey's ranking was more or less stable (101 in 2007, 100 in 2002). By 2013, however, its ranking fell to 154 of 179 countries.[47]

A new educational bill overhauled the primary and secondary school system and allowed for more religious education. Use of religious discourse became more frequent. Erdoğan declared abortion to be murder and new regulations made its practice very difficult. A 2013 law restricted sale and consumption of alcohol and transferred authority to issue licenses from elected mayors to government-appointment governors. Vice-prime minister Bülent Arinç opined that the new constitution should retain the unchangeable principle of republicanism but make the principles of democracy, secularism, and social state alterable by a supermajority.[48]

Rather than advocating for a fuller separation of religion and state, for example, by dismantling, downsizing, or decentralizing the state agency Diyanet, the AKP seemed to have embraced Turkey's state-controlled secularism for its own goals.[49] The Diyanet promotes an official version of Sunni Islam at the expense of other faiths and interpretations through such practices as employing imams (Muslim preachers), subsidizing building Sunni mosques but not shrines of other sects, and publishing religious material. Diyanet personnel increased 33 percent between 2002 and 2013, from 74,374 in 2002 to 84,195 in 2007 and 98,555 in 2013. Its share in the total state budget rose more than twofold, from 0.54 percent in 2002 to 0.82 in 2006 and 1.2 percent in 2012.[50]

Conclusions

The Turkish case lends substantial but qualified support to the arguments articulated in this volume and invites us to further theorize the relationship between normalization and democratization. As they participated in electoral politics, Turkish Islamist political parties indeed became "normalized" in many ways. They increasingly accommodated themselves "to the rules of the political regime" in which they operated and became "less unique and more *normal* political actors, when compared with other parties in the competitive system," at least when compared to center-right parties. The Turkish case is consistent with the thesis that parties without strong ties to Islamic movements will be more likely to normalize. The AKP became more flexible by disassociating itself from the MG organically and ideologically, even though the MG was more a social-political movement than a religious movement. Second, the experience of the AKP lends support to the argument that Islamist parties are more likely to be successful when they can attract a significant segment of protest voters whose preferences are not religiously based.

However, the rest of the story draws a more complicated picture invit-
ing further theorization about the relationship between electoral participation and religious politics, as well as about the process of normalization
and democracy. First, while participation in electoral politics made Turkish
Islamist parties prioritize and develop policies on nonreligious issues such
as economic development, this did not necessarily translate into less
emphasis on religious content. During the 1990s, religious and moral issues
found more expression in the RP's program when compared to its predecessors of the 1970s, even though the RP enjoyed more electoral support.
This apparent reversal of normalization cannot be explained without analyzing the changing profile of Turkish voters, who had simultaneously
become more religious-conservative in their orientation, the altered international environment in which Islamism was a rising political-ideological
trend, and Islamist parties' continuous efforts to rearticulate non-religious
issues within an Islamic discursive framework, and vice versa.

Furthermore, the AKP, which had sharply deemphasized religious issues
at the time of its election in 2002, began to reemphasize them after 2008
when it felt more secure and shielded from nonelectoral constraints in
mainstream Turkish politics. This also happened in a period when the AKP
was not facing serious competition from another Islamist party. Thus, one
should not underestimate how deeply Islamist political actors desire to
transform what is normal in society, while they also face strong incentives
to gain acceptance as normal actors in the political process. Even when pro-
Islamic parties are in opposition, Islamist actors who cooperate with pro-
secular opposition do not always make concessions from their religious
goals. Instead, they tend to focus on other, more practical goals by keeping
religiously sensitive questions shielded from criticism and reconsidera-
tion.[51] Islamist political parties may strategically reprioritize Islamic issues
depending on their electoral and political strength. This also means that the
strength of rival pro-secular political parties, as well as the ability of pro-
Islamic and pro-secular actors to challenge and cooperate with each other,
are crucial factors in predicting to what extent and when an Islamist political party will deemphasize religious content.

Second, normalization in the Turkish case was far from a linear, continuous, inexorable process resulting from political participation. Rather, it
occurred discontinuously, entailed reversals, and resulted from nonelectoral constraints and interventions as well as from competition with pro-
secular political parties.[52] The most decisive leap of normalization with the

emergence of the AKP resulted from a major clash with the secularist political center.

Third, it would be incomplete to analyze what normalization entails with reference to domestic politics alone. Normalizing Islamist political parties need to consider how external allies perceive and react to their politics. A major dimension of the AKP's normalization comprised its successful efforts to convince Western governments and business communities that it embraced Turkey's Western alliances, favored integration with the global economy, and would present a valuable example of "Muslim democracy" in the post-911 world.[53]

Fourth, Turkish Islamist parties have had a dual constituency, and many supporters vote for them not for religious reasons but out of a "deep dissatisfaction with other political alternatives or as protest against the political system." But relative credibility and performance of Islamist parties are crucial factors that determine to what extent nonreligious voters will support them. Most recently, the AKP increased its votes in the 2007 elections partly because many voters were protesting the military-induced secularist campaign against the party prior to the elections, and because the party had proved itself since 2002 by securing impressive economic growth and the start of EU accession talks. However, voters did not necessarily lend more support to the Islamists after a more vicious campaign against them in 1997, when the Islamists in government had much less to show in terms of successful governance.

Finally, all these observations mean that the impact of normalization on democratization depends on what is normal in a country, that is, the normative, behavioral and institutional qualities of that country's "center." Normalization can be a double-edged sword for democracy because it may lead an Islamist party to embrace democratic as well as authoritarian qualities of the mainstream politics in a country. In authoritarian or semidemocratic contexts, democratization requires pro-Islamic and pro-secular political actors to transform what is considered normal in their country by building the institutions, norms, and relationships of a more democratic center either together or unilaterally.[54]

Chapter 3

Patterns of Normalization:
Islamist Parties in Indonesia

JULIE CHERNOV HWANG

Indonesia stands apart from the other countries examined in this book as arguably the most democratic. Since the fall of the authoritarian New Order regime in 1998, it has experienced three cycles of free and fair elections. Of the countries in this volume, only Indonesia was ranked by Freedom House as "Free." In 2010, Freedom House gave Indonesia a combined score for political rights and civil liberties of 2.5, while Malaysia received a 4.0, Turkey 3.0, Pakistan and Morocco 4.5, and Yemen lowest at 5.5.[1] Indonesia is the largest Muslim nation in the world, with an estimated population of over 240 million, of whom over 88 percent are Muslim.[2] It is home to the two largest Islamic mass organizations in the world, Nahdlatul Ulama (NU), with a membership estimated at 50 million, and Muhammadiyah, with approximately 30 million.[3] Islamic civil society is active and lively, with myriad Islamic organizations at the national, provincial, and district levels ranging from progressive Islamic organizations, which campaign for the rights of women and minorities, to hardline Islamist organizations that advocate the reestablishment of the Caliphate. Moreover, there are parties at nearly every point in the politico-religious spectrum from parties that are largely secular in orientation to those with roots in Islamic communities to those seeking the implementation of shari'a. Recognizing this variation is important for understanding the unique position of Islamist parties in Indonesia vis-à-vis other Muslim nations. Unlike Malaysia or Turkey, there are no institutional or structural constraints on the ability of Islamist parties to contest and win elections. The only constraint on Islamist party success is the preference of the Indonesian voter.

Thus, Indonesia represents an interesting contrast to the other cases in this volume. Using the Indonesian case, we can analyze how Islamist parties behave in a democratic political system, where there are multiple Islamically oriented parties contesting free and fair elections; where Islamist parties do not gain significant votes vis-à-vis their fellow Islamist parties by asserting their religious bona fides in electoral campaigns; and where "protest voting" is one reason among many for party success.

At the same time, we find Islamist parties in Indonesia possessing several similarities to other cases in this volume. First, Islamist parties have become increasingly normalized and integrated in the political system. This manifests itself in several ways including the common practice of building coalitions at the national, provincial, and district levels with secular and nationalist parties; Islamist party participation in the governing coalitions of the administration of president Susilo Bambang Yudhoyono in 2004 and again in 2009; a deemphasis on Islamist themes in their electoral campaigns; and a reassessment and revision of the plan to struggle for the formal acknowledgement of shari'a in the constitution.

Second, as this normalization process is occurring, Islamist parties are becoming less distinct from their political competitors. This is a result of two interrelated factors. First, most Islamist parties are "moderating" their agendas, postponing and reassessing those aspects of their platforms where their goals are not widely shared by the populace and diversifying their basket of issues.[4] Second, nationalist parties have also sought to appeal to voters on religious grounds, especially around election time, resulting in a mainstreaming of political Islam. Thus, there is movement toward the ideological center from both directions. This chapter seeks to assess the extent of and patterns of normalization among Islamist parties in the Indonesian political system.

Before proceeding further, it is necessary to give a brief overview of the electoral and party systems. The Indonesian party system is a highly fragmented multiparty system with no dominant party. Over the course of the 1999, 2004, and 2009 elections, between 40 and 48 parties competed, between 5 and 11 of them Islamist in orientation. Parties seldom breach the 10 percent threshold. Only two nationalist parties, Partai Golkar (Functional Groups) and the Partai Demokrasi Indonesia-Perjuangan (Indonesian Democratic Party of Struggle; PDI-P), have garnered more than 10 percent of the vote in three consecutive elections.[5] When Partai Democrat (Democrat Party; PD), a nationalist party formed in 2004, won 20 percent of the vote in 2009, it was referred to as a "tsunami."

Islamically oriented parties in Indonesia can be divided into two categories: pluralist Islamic parties and Islamist parties. The two pluralist Islamic parties of note, Partai Kebangkitan Bangsa (National Awakening Party; PKB) and Partai Amanat Nasional (National Mandate Party; PAN), have their cultural roots in Nahdlatul Ulama and Muhammadiyah respectively, but take the Indonesian national ideology of Pancasila[6] as their foundation and eschew calls for implementation of shari'a law. By contrast, Islamist parties take Islam as their foundation, actively proclaim an Islamic identity, and seek to varying degrees to implement shari'a law. While seven Islamist parties participated in the 2009 elections, only two passed the newly implemented 2.5 percent electoral threshold: the Partai Keadilan Sejahtera (Prosperous Justice Party; PKS) and the Partai Persatuan Pembangunan (United Development Party; PPP).

In 2004, two others succeeded in gaining seats in the Dewan Perwakilan Rakyat (People's Representative Assembly; DPR): the Partai Bulan Bintang (Crescent Moon and Star Party; PBB), which was inspired by the modernist Masyumi party of 1955 and has made implementation of shari'a the cornerstone of its campaign, and the Partai Bintang Reformasi (Reform Star Party; PBR), a breakaway faction of PPP. However, both parties failed to pass the electoral threshold in 2009.

This chapter highlights the two Islamist parties that have played the most significant roles in defining political Islam in the party sphere: the PKS and PPP. Other Islamically oriented parties will be referenced as points of comparison, as will nationalist parties, specifically, Democrat, Golkar, and PDI-P, which have all engaged in "soft Islamic politics" to attract the elusive median Muslim voter.

The chapter first examines the roots, platforms, and approaches to political Islam of the PKS and PPP. Second, it analyzes the constituencies of the two parties and how the PKS has made gains at the expense of the PPP, and how the PKS is affected by its dual status as social movement and political party. Finally, it assesses the extent to which Islamist political participation has become normalized and why Islamist parties have not been more successful in their pursuit of electoral gains.

The PKS is rooted in the Gerakan Tarbiyah (education movement), which was popular on public university campuses during the New Order era. As a result of the limitations on student activism put in place by the New Order regime, student dissent was channeled through mosques and faculty-level prayer rooms, with students focusing their attention on improving personal piety. Gerakan Tarbiyah was a notable and popular example of a widespread phenomenon taking place on university campuses throughout Indonesia—the proliferation of religious study clubs catering to Muslims and Christians.

It is important to emphasize, during this period, the great variety of study clubs available for Muslim students, from progressive to Salafi. Tarbiyah took its particular inspiration from the ideals and organizational training methods espoused by Hasan al Banna, founder of the Muslim Brotherhood, including his writings on politics, the state, and personal behavior.[7] Like al Banna, they believed Islamization of the state necessitated a long-term strategy, a four-stage gradual process that must begin with increased education and development of an Islamic personality among individual Muslims.[8] To that end, Tarbiyah activists met regularly in small groups for weekly *halaqah* (study circles) for studying the Qur'an, Hadith, and the writings of such notable scholars as Yusuf Qardawai, Sayyid Hawwa, Sayyid Qutb, Mawdudi, and Ali Shariati.[9]

During the New Order era, Tarbiyah was a closed movement insofar as its members only interacted with one another. With the fall of Suharto, however, Tarbiyah leaders decided the time had come to move to the third stage—"political penetration"—in the movement's strategic plan, and to that end, formed Partai Keadilan (Justice Party; PK). Of the Islamically oriented parties that participated in the 1999 elections, only the PK had a clearly articulated platform and cadre structure. Since the party failed the 2 percent election registration requirement,[10] however, it reconstituted itself as the PKS in 2003. In the 2004 elections, the PKS was the only Islamically oriented party to increase its share of the vote, gaining 7.34 percent, after deemphasizing Islamist themes and campaigning on its commitments to clean government, socioeconomic equality, and social justice. As other parties were perceived as corrupt and elitist, the PKS succeeded in winning the "protest vote" among disgruntled voters seeking an Islamic or Islamist party to advocate for their interests.

In examining the the PKS approach to political Islam, it is important to understand that the PKS is the political wing of a mass-based Islamic movement with a specific religious mission of *dakwah* (propagation), *tarbiyah* (education), and service to the community, the nation, and the global

Islamic community.[11] While the primary goal of the PPP and PBB is to win
elections, the raison d'être of the PKS is to educate Muslims about Islam.
According to PKS cadre, most Muslims have a poor understanding of
shari'a and must be educated to see how Islam offers comprehensive solutions to the challenges of daily life. In contrast to the PBB and PPP, which
sought formal recognition of shari'a in the constitution in 2000 and 2002,
PKS strategists advocated gradualism through socialization of Islamic values among individuals and families. To that end, the PKS adopted a hybrid
strategy—a top-down structural approach (what it terms vertical mobilization) and a bottom-up, grassroots-driven cultural approach (horizontal
mobilization).

This "two-level" process is explained in detail in *Memperjuangkan
Masyarakat Madani,* the 634-page text illustrating the party's philosophy,
program of struggle, and platform. Through the structural approach, PKS
cadre enter the institutions of the executive, legislature, judiciary, and
bureaucracy in order to translate Islamic concepts and values into public
policies.[12] Through the cultural approach, *dakwah* cadre work through
organizations and foundations to serve the Muslim community in various
capacities—social, economic, cultural, environmental, agricultural—to pre-
pare the people to accept the Islamic *manhaj* (method) and the products
of Islamic policy.[13] To that end, PKS cadre conduct year-round activities
including holding *majlis taqlim* (Qur'an study groups) and prayer meetings
targeting university students, housewives, and students of all ages; establishing Islamic schools; and publishing books, bulletins, magazines, and newspaper articles as well as a host of social welfare activities to show how shari'a
has universal applications. PKS cadre are required to act as exemplars to
show how shari'a can be applied in a nondiscriminatory and inclusive manner so that Muslims and non-Muslims can become comfortable with it.[14]

In these public endeavors, the PKS couches its message in religiously
neutral language in order to raise awareness of and support for shari'a-
based policies without necessarily labeling them as such. Mutammimul Ula,
a former representative of the DPR from the PKS and a founding member
of Gerakan Tarbiyah, explains,

> We don't speak about shari'a in concept but we practice it in the
> field. For example, if you see party activists and how they build
> their families, observe that. And how the party activists [among] the
> Islamist parties give out zakat. That does not mean we do not fight

for legislation about Islamic teachings. But we do not do so using language that points to shari'a. For example, in fighting for budgetary rights for *pesantren* (Islamic boarding school) education, this was a fight for justice, but the fight for justice is also a fight for shari'a. We emphasize the substance of Islamic teachings.[15]

The sum total of the PKS activities is geared toward several interrelated goals: teaching Indonesian Muslims about Islamic values; encouraging Indonesian Muslims to implement those values in their daily lives; familiarizing voters with the PKS so that they will support the party; and gradually transforming Indonesian society into one with more Islamic flavor.[16]

While the PPP may have similar goals as the PKS, the two parties differ dramatically in their origins, strategies, and capacities. The most significant challenge for the PPP is its historical roots as an artificial construction, created by the New Order in 1973, when the Suharto regime forced the amalgamation of the four Islamic parties, Parmusi—the New Order sanctioned successor to Masyumi—Nahdlatul Ulama, Perti, and PSII, into a single official "Islamic" party by the New Order regime. As these four parties represented different streams within Islam, the party was plagued by infighting and power struggles between the modernists, represented by Parmusi, and the traditionalists[17] in Nahdlatul Ulama, a reality exacerbated by the gamesmanship of the Suharto regime. In 1984, the marginalized NU faction would formally withdraw from the party and return to its founding mission of providing education and social welfare services for its members, although members who had devoted their careers to the party remained in. While the withdrawal of the NU caused the party to lose a significant measure of support, for NU voters were no longer constrained in vote choice by the movement's affiliation to the PPP, the party remained marked by infighting among its factions.

During the New Order era, electoral support (in *heavily* managed elections) for PPP, as the officially designated Islamist party, varied from a high of 29 percent of the vote in 1977 to a low of 16 percent in 1987, when the party was adversely impacted not only by NU's official withdrawal but also by its decision to adopt Pancasila as their *asas tunggal* (sole foundation) in 1985. This required the party to remove direct references to Islam from its charter and Islamic symbols from its flag and materials, effectively "abandoning" Islam. When Suharto resigned in May 1998, many thought the PPP would dissolve itself, but instead it reclaimed its Islamic identity, readopting the Ka'bah, Islam's holiest site, as its symbol and Islam as its foundation. In the 1999 elections, it garnered 10.72 percent of the vote, the best performance among the Islamist parties. However, its aspirations to be the leading party for Muslim interests have not been realized, as the faction-alism that impeded its internal coherence during the New Order continues to constrain its capacities in developing its cadre as well as, organization, promotion, and mobilization. Over the past two election cycles, the party has seen its share of the vote decrease to a new low of 5.01 percent in 2009, with disgruntled former PPP supporters choosing the PKS instead.

As Platzdasch explains, "being a compulsorily formed federation of modernists and traditionalists, the PPP was never able or even willing to sustain a full ideology."[18] Given the differing historical and intellectual tra-ditions between traditionalists and modernists within the PPP, including differing methods of exegesis, sources of law, and interpretation of specific aspects of shari'a, it is not surprising that the PPP has difficulty in develop-ing an original party Islamist ideology.[19] According to PPP chairman Faisal Baasir,

> PPP is more flexible than others, for example the PK(S). They [the PKS] have their ideological concepts. They have a record of forming cadres. The system of their caderization is like the system of the Muslim Brotherhood and this is different from the PPP because PPP consists of the NU camp and Parmusi. These two groups unite their shared political interests. But they differ on religious doctrine and on the political concepts that are based on religion. In PPP, these two camps have made this compromise. The result of this compro-mise is there is no firm position.[20]

In practical terms, as a result of this compromise, the party no longer speaks of the formal implementation of shari'a but instead of the inculca-tion of religious norms and values. Since the party also aspires to be a big tent party to advocate for the interests of all Muslims regardless of religious ideology, it endeavors to appeal to both the ideologically minded and plu-ralist Muslims.[21] This necessitates a "flexible" approach.

The party's platform and policy advocacy illustrate this flexibility. With great frequency, party documents concomitantly highlight the themes of the need to inculcate Islamic values, the universality of those values, and the need to implement them in a manner reflecting the plurality and socio-cultural and religious diversity of the Indonesian polity. The PPP platform emphasizes

(1) the need for the organization of Islamic societal life [via] the princi-ple of *amar ma'aruf nahi mungkar* (enjoining the good and discour-aging the bad);
(2) the important role of Islam as a moral guide and resource for inspi-ration of the life of the nation;
(3) the paradigmatic relation between Islam and the state characterized as symbiotic, synergistic as well as mutually needing and nourishing that holds to the principles of harmony between the universality of Islam and the locality of Indonesianness; and
(4) commitment to the principles of tolerance between religious com-munities.[22]

However, flexibility, it must be noted, is not coterminous with moderation. This party remains an Islamist party; it is not seeking to remake itself as nationalist-religious or pluralist Islamic. It has no plans to open the party to non-Muslims any more than the law requires. Instead, it assesses market sentiment of what moves might be likely to win votes. For example, in weeks prior to the 2009 election, the PPP swung hard right, campaigning on the banning of the controversial Ahmadiyah movement. This not only included public statements at their rallies and in the media but also a mod-est participation in anti-Ahmadiyah demonstrations held by Hizbut Tahrir and the Islamic Defenders Front (FPI).[23] As Ahmadiyah was an issue mean-ingful to ultraconservative and radical Muslims, the PPP may have hoped such moves would enable the party to win their support. By contrast, dur-ing that same period, the PKS avoided discussion of the Ahmadiyah issue in its rallies and did not join the anti-Ahmadiyah demonstrations.

There are several notable similarities between the PKS and PPP. In terms of their long-term goals, they are quite similar. Like the PKS, the PPP seeks to inculcate individuals, Indonesian society, and the state. Both par-ties advocate the adoption of shari'a-inspired legislation in those districts and municipalities where there is popular support. Ideologically, both par-ties endeavor to reconcile Pancasila and Islam as well as commit to working for their goals through the democratic political system. However, there are several distinct differences in their approach. When PPP refers to shari'a in its party documents, the emphasis tends to be the creation of the best possible climate for the performance of worship and religious activities according to shari'a.[24] The party does not attempt or have the capacity to conduct PKS-style *dakwah* activities. Instead, it endeavors to achieve its goals, not by educating individual Muslims about how to apply shari'a to their daily lives but by advocating for specific Islamic policies. During the New Order, the party led the opposition to the 1973 Marriage Law and the 1978 Kepercayaan Law (Belief Law),[25] both of which it viewed as running counter to the interests of the Muslim community. In the democratic era, it has been a leading force advocating for increased funds for religious education and the banning of the Ahmadiyah sect. "PPP never endeavored to achieve sweeping societal change by thoroughly Islamizing community and state, nor did it train its cadre to achieve this goal."[26]

Constituency-Building: Refuting the Dual Constituency Argument

As political participation in democratic elections has become a regular feature of Indonesian politics, Islamist parties have realized they have the potential to appeal to voters outside their core base. In fact, all parties have attempted to identify and court the median Muslim voter. Thus, in Indonesia, the dual constituency argument is an oversimplification; it is far more complicated than Islamist parties drawing support from either Islamically oriented voters or voters protesting the status quo alternatives as they exist in other states in the Muslim world. The PKS is simultaneously benefiting from voter disgruntlement with alternative Islamic parties; its own Islamic image; and its extensive network of community welfare programs. Other Islamist parties, by contrast, are suffering from their inability to compete effectively against the PKS.

In 1999, the PKS (as PK) had a small, narrow, devoted support base, concentrated largely among members and alumni of the Tarbiyah movement. Since then, the party has expanded into new segments of society. Its core base can be described as young, urban, educated, pious middle classes and students. In 2004, it made inroads among working class voters in urban areas, who benefitted from the PKS social service and community welfare programs.[27] In 2009, it made further inroads into rural communities in the provinces of Central and East Java. In 2008, it declared itself an open party and invited non-Muslims to join. In majority non-Muslim Eastern Indonesia, most notably the provinces of Papua and Papua Barat, it runs non-Muslim candidates for provincial level (DPRD I) and district level (DPRD II) elections, albeit not for the national level DPR.[28] According to Anis Matta, PKS secretary general, opening the party in this manner was necessary for the PKS to combat perceptions that it was exclusive and enable it to become one of the top three parties in Indonesian politics.[29] However, there is no evidence to date that non-Muslims are joining the party in significant numbers.

Of all parties in Indonesia, there is a higher rate of loyalty among PKS voters compared to supporters of other parties. According to a survey conducted by the Center for Strategic and International Studies in Jakarta, over 75 percent of PKS supporters remain loyal to the party in iterated election cycles, a loyalty rate considerably higher than its nationalist party or Islamist party counterparts, whose loyalty rates range from 32 to 61 percent.[30] The party's territorial base is in Jakarta, West Java, and Banten and in those areas in cities with large public universities such as Depok, Bogor, and Bandung, where the Tarbiyah movement was strong. It also made small inroads into several outer island provinces, netting more than 10 percent of the vote in West Sumatra, Riau Archipelago, South Kalimantan, and North Maluku in the 2004 elections.[31] However, in 2009, the party suffered declines both in its territorial base and in West Sumatra, South Kalimantan, and North Maluku. By contrast, the party made its most significant gains in Central Java and East Java, picking up 136,677 and 260,043 votes respectively, the largest increase in any provinces for the PKS in the 2009 elections.[32] The party's gains in these two provinces, however, were due to a combination of factors, most notably the political infighting, which paralyzed the PKB, whose stronghold was in those two provinces, in the run-up to the 2009 elections and PKS activities targeting rural farmers. If the PKS is able to maintain its inroads in Central and East Java, the party could potentially become a Java-dominant party insofar as the majority of its supporters would be on Java. This is not to say that the PKS is targeting Java more than the outer islands or that the PKS is unsuccessful in picking up seats in the outer islands. Instead, it points to the paralysis of other Islamically oriented parties who were formerly strong on Java and the PKS ability to make gains at their expense. That phenomenon is not happening to the same degree in the outer islands.

Although PKS strategic behavior, particularly its campaign strategy, is aimed at incorporating voters from all segments of society, the PKS remains a party popular with those voters seeking a political role for Islam. According to a PKS internal party survey, 75.2 percent of respondents chose the PKS for its Islamic image.[33] Moreover, in examining those districts where the PKS won seats, 12 of 14 were won at the expense of other Islamically oriented parties. Of those, 8 were won at the expense of Islamist parties—PPP, PBB, PBR—while the other four were formerly held by PKB.[34] By contrast, each time the PKS lost a seat, it lost to nationalist parties, most notably the Democrat Party.[35] In effect, the PKS is consolidating the support of Islamist voters even as it is attempting to win the support of other segments of society.

In contrast to the PKS, the PPP has been unable to expand its voter base. It is a common perception both inside PPP and among observers of PPP that both the party and its voter base are dying. According to party Secretary General Irghan Mahfidz, "if we look at the results of the 2004 and 2009 elections, [our constituents] are more in the old people in the villages, those who knew the history of PPP. Young people are not interested in PPP."[36] The voter base is highly fragmented among elderly Muslim men scattered throughout rural and urban areas both on Java and outside of Java. During the Suharto era, PPP was popular among young male Muslims between seventeen and thirty. However, that segment of society has since left it and formed the core constituency of the PKS.

During the Suharto era, prior to the withdrawal of NU from the party, the PPP had several strongholds, in West Java, Central Java, East Java, Aceh, South Kalimantan, and South Sulawesi. In 1999, the party netted more than 15 percent of the vote in Jakarta, West Java, and Banten, the very areas that today constitute the territorial base of the PKS as well as Aceh, West Sumatra, South Kalimantan, Maluku, and North Maluku.[37] By 2004, party support had dropped dramatically in all of these provinces apart from South Kalimantan.[38] In 2009, according to Mahfidz, one cannot speak of provincial-level strength, only district and city level in areas like Tasikmalaya in West Java, Pandeglang in Banten, Jepara in Central Java, and Situbondo in East Java.[39] This loss of voter base has resulted in the party slipping from the largest Islamist party, third ranked in the DPR in 1999 to sixth place in 2009, with its voter share dropping from 10.72 to 5.32 percent.

The party has attributed its floundering support to several factors. First, it lacks the opportunities for upward mobility found in the PKS. According to Husnan Bey, "We are managed by relationships, not by merit. If I want to become an MP, I have to be close to the leadership of the party. If I am an intellectual or a manager, I may enter the party and work for the party, but parliament is closed because I am not close to the right people."[40] Other party elites echoed this sentiment, referring to the party as "closed," "unresponsive," "slow to change its internal culture," and "unwilling to accommodate younger leaders."[41] As a result, it has been unable to compete effectively with the PKS for the support of Muslim students and intellectuals.

This, then, raises the question why the PKS has been successful in recruiting former supporters of other Islamist parties, particularly among young Muslims, who once formed the core of the PPP base. While one could interpret the shift as a protest vote against the PPP, it would be better to consider it a measure of the effectiveness of the PKS. First, in stark contrast with the PPP, the PKS has a tradition of merit-based recruitment and advancement, and the party values commitment, qualifications, and grassroots support over nepotistic ties, personal loyalties, and money in determining opportunities for upward mobility within the party as well as entry into politics and the bureaucracy.[42] Second, the party markets itself as youth-oriented: it runs seminars on young leadership; it runs young candidates for parliament, mayor, and governor; and the majority of the party leadership itself are under age fifty. This stands in contrast with PPP party elites, 80 percent of whom were between fifty-eight and seventy in 1998.[43] Thus, if pious young Muslims wish to join the bureaucracy or legislature, their interests are best served by joining the PKS. Additionally, the PKS successfully marketed itself as the "clean government" party in 1999 and 2004, which led some voters to choose the PKS as a protest against the gross levels of corruption in the other parties. However, by 2009, the PKS had been afflicted by its own set of corruption scandals, made somehow worse because of the party's longstanding reputation as the "clean" party. This was probably one factor in the party's decline in core base areas.

Movement-Party Dynamics: Opportunities and Constraints

Among Islamically oriented parties, the PKS stands apart for it is both a religious movement and a political party. While other parties may have cultural or historical links to Islamic movements or draw inspiration from prior Islamic movements, none are movement parties. For example, although PKB and PAN are culturally rooted in the Nahdlatul Ulama and Muhammadiyah respectively, it is not incumbent on either NU or Muhammadiyah members or leaders to support, campaign for, or vote for PKB or PAN. In fact, NU and Muhammadiyah members are high-ranking officials in Golkar, Democrat, the PPP, and the PKS. Likewise, although PBB sought to channel the spirit of Masyumi, it is not bound to a preexisting Masyumi "movement." In fact, in 1999 and 2004, other parties claimed the mantle of successor to Masyumi, including Partai Masyumi Baru (New Masyumi Party; PMB), and Partai Bintang Reformasi (Reform Star Party; PBR). The PPP has sought to emphasize its Islamic pluralism—a legacy from its status in the New Order era—as the home for all Indonesian Muslims regardless of movement affiliation.

By contrast, the PKS is the political wing of an Islamic movement. The embedded relationship is explained using the Arabic statement, '*al-jama'ah hiya al hizb wa al hiz hwa al jama'ah*' (the party is the movement and the movement is the party).[44] That the PKS functions as both movement and party provides it with both unique opportunities and constraints vis-à-vis its competitors. On the one hand, the party can tap human resources, organizations, and networks unavailable to other Islamically oriented parties. The movement (*harokah*) constitutes the party's core base and plays a vital role in the party's electoral strategy and membership recruitment through running PKS-affiliated social institutions (schools, hospitals, research institutes), all critical to the network of social welfare and community development activities that the PKS conducts and refers to as its "soft campaign."[45] Furthermore, all party cadre share a vision for societal transformation, which contrasts with the lack of common vision in PPP.

On the other hand, pragmatic party elites are often constrained by the larger movement in their capacity to commit the party to a sustained shift to the center, for the *harokah* is ideologically purist. As a political party endeavoring to govern the country, it must be pragmatic to attract new voters and that necessitates making difficult compromises that ultimately disappoint *harokah* members. Thus, there is a built-in tension within the PKS. Greg Fealy explains the central crux of the purist pragmatist cleavage in the following manner:

> The primary issue is a dispute between ideological purity and political expediency. In broad terms, [purists] argue that PKS must uphold the center elements of its Brotherhood derived teachings

because these provide guidelines for the struggle to create a new type of society in Indonesia. Compromising these teachings imperils the very mission that Tarbiyah and PKS were established to undertake. For the pragmatists, the PKS exists to bring change to Indonesia and this can only happen if it has power. To have real power, the PKS needs to be one of the two or three largest parties and this cannot be achieved without gaining support from the political mainstream. Ideological inflexibility hinders the party's prospects of reaching out to these voters.[46]

It is important to note that purist-pragmatist cleavage is both between movement and party and intra-party. While pragmatist elites at the apex of the party leadership, Hilmi Aminuddin, head of the Syuro Council, and Anis Matta and Fachri Hamzah, PKS secretary and deputy secretary general, have been the driving forces behind rebranding the PKS as inclusive, purists, including Mutammimul Ula and Abdi Sumaithi, are concerned that the party is compromising its raison d'être in pursuit of power.[47] The majority of the party elite can be positioned in the middle—"balancers"—recognizing that the pragmatist strategy is in the best interests of the party, while acknowledging the real concerns of the purists.[48]

Many of the disputes between the purists and pragmatists revolve around the open party strategy and the manner in which the party endeavors make inroads into new segments of the voting public. As noted earlier, in 2008 the PKS declared itself an open party and invited non-Muslims to join. It is important to state at the outset that legally all parties are obliged to be open to all Indonesian citizens. Purists do not oppose the law per se. In fact, in interviews purists expressed no qualms about the party running non-Muslim candidates for DPRD I and DPRD II positions in majority non-Muslim regions, a policy that has been in effect since 2004, predating the openness strategy, and is still the most visible element of the openness strategy at this time. Instead, they expressed concerns about the party decision to actively recruit non-Muslims as a key component of their strategic agenda for the future. In their view, to be a member of the PKS necessitated loyalty to Islam.[49] One former member of the DPR who advocates a purist position explained his perspective: "I think we should respect each other. People of other beliefs feel free to establish the party of their own religion; feel free to be fundamentalist; and we respect that."[50] However, there are limits even among pragmatists on openness. Purists, pragmatists, and balancers alike concurred that it was impossible for non-Muslims to become members of the Majlis Syuro or other central leadership bodies, at the very least, at this time.[51] The extent to which active targeted recruitment of non-Muslims is being conducted outside majority non-Muslim areas remains to be seen.

A subcomponent of the openness strategy that drew fire from PKS purists and supporters in urban areas was the decision to run controversial campaign ads in the run-up to the 2009 elections. The Great Indonesians ad listed Suharto, the dictator who ruled the country for thirty-two years, as one of Indonesia's founding fathers. This evoked the ire of purists who recalled the repression that Islamists faced during the Suharto years. According to Anis Matta, PKS secretary general, the ad was targeted to win the support of military families, even at the risk of alienating core voters in Jakarta. "I believe that our structure in Jakarta, the party in Jakarta, is already strong so they can [address] these problems. . . . In TNI areas it's very positive."[52] Nursanita Nasution, a former DPR member and candidate for election in Jakarta's third district in 2009, countered,

> [The ad] affected PKS votes because the Jakartans are critical. Earlier, they did not know about the PKS and they voted for the PKS because they thought that the PKS was a new party and pro reform. . . . The ads of Suharto, I think that was not wanted by public. We know that Suharto had contributions to our nation, but the pro reform youths did not like him. The ads were not a DPP [Central Board] decision; and it was initiated by some PKS members who used trial and error in their efforts to reach the target of 20 percent of the votes.[53]

The Partai Kita Semua (Party for Everyone) ad also alienated purist cadre and supporters because it portrayed women without headscarves. These ads are believed to be, in part, responsible for PKS declines in core base areas of Depok, Jakarta, and Bandung in 2009 as supporters of the party in 2004 took them as evidence that the party had changed. Moreover, the ads themselves, particularly, the Great Indonesians Ad, point to a haphazard strategy of constituency-building in the 2009 elections, where party strategists were attempting to make inroads with various segments of society to obtain the 20 percent of the vote sufficient to run a presidential candidate, without considering how it might affect their base. Effectively, the strategies that may have appealed to small segments of new voters had the effect of alienating core voters.

Not surprisingly, the pragmatists and purists have differing interpretations of the 2009 election results. The pragmatists see the results as a vindication of the openness strategy. According to this view, all Islamically oriented parties declined in 2009 apart from the PKS. This is a direct result of its embrace of pluralism and advocacy of a clean DPR. Thus, although they did not reach the target of 20 percent of the vote, they prevented PKS votes from declining. Purists counter that the 2009 election results indicated the pragmatists' strategies have failed because votes for the PKS did not increase.[54] In fact, the total number of votes actually decreased by 119,065 vis-à-vis 2004.[55] In the territorial base areas of Jakarta and West Java, the party's votes decreased by 330,990 and 343,476 between 2004 and 2009.[56] Only enforcement of the 2.5 percent electoral threshold led the PKS vote percentage and number of seats to increase over 2004.

According to multiple scholars close to the party, "purist" elites have effectively been marginalized in recent years and no longer have significant influence on the party's central board.[57] However, they constitute a fundamental channel between the party elites and the *harokah*, and thus, their views cannot be ignored. It is important to note that the very pull from the *harokah* enables the PKS to peel votes away from other Islamist parties by ensuring the party continues to assert its Islamic bona fides. At the same time, the need to satisfy both the movement and potential party supporters leaves the party vulnerable to accusations of inconsistency. Indeed, the party still regularly makes news on issues of Islamic morality, including former PKS president and minister of information and technology Tifatul Sembiring's tireless campaign to filter all pornographic websites by the first day of Ramadan, and the ban on alcoholic beverages championed by PKS legislators in Bandung. This threatens to put the PKS in a position of being at once too Islamist for the moderates and too moderate for the Islamists.

Islamist Party Performance: Normalization amid Declining Support

Over the past three election cycles, political participation by Islamist parties has become increasingly normalized and there has been a convergence toward the center by both the Islamist parties and the nationalist parties in the zeal to identify, court, and win the support of the median Muslim voter. This has manifested itself in several ways. First, cross-ideological coalition-building by Islamist parties has increased significantly since 1999. Islamist parties have increasingly participated in legislative and electoral coalitions with nationalist parties at the provincial and district levels. The PPP and PKS joined in the 2005 and 2009 coalition governments of President Yudhoyono, a move that evoked considerable ire among the PKS base. The PBB and PBR also participated in the first Yudhoyono government.

Another clear indicator of normalization can be found in election strategy. The majority of Islamist parties realize that, if they wish to gain a measure of support, they must "play it ideologically safe," emphasizing universalist themes and downplaying shari'a-based ones in election campaigns to appeal to as many segments of the voting public as possible.[58] Ideologically driven campaigns do not net votes. The lessons of the PBB are instructive. In 2004 and 2009, the PBB attempted to draw Islamist voters away from the PKS and PPP by campaigning on an explicitly pro-shari'a platform.[59] However, this strategy failed to win the party significantly more votes, and arguably, with the introduction of the 2.5 percent electoral threshold in 2009, cost the party its DPR seats.

There is also evidence of ideological normalization. This normalization has been gradual and ongoing. One ideological shift has been the effective abandonment by the PPP and postponement by the PBB of efforts to insert language formalizing shari'a into the Indonesian constitution. In 2000 and 2002, during MPR sessions, the PPP and PBB submitted proposals for revision of paragraph 29 to amend the current wording, "the state is based on the one all-powerful god" to add the seven-word clause (in the original Indonesian) from the 1945 Jakarta Charter,[60] "with the obligation for Muslims to carry out shari'a." Interestingly, as a member of Fraksi Reformasi, a joint two-party caucus, PK refused to support their initiative, instead advocating the "Madina Charter," based on the Constitution of Madina during the Prophet Muhammad's time, where each religion lived according to the laws of their particular faith, and each tribe retained its own identity, customs, and internal relations.[61] In reality, adoption of the Madina Charter would have also required Muslims to live by Islamic law. However, the overall message it sent was more pluralist and accommodating of religious difference than the PPP or PBB.

Since 2002, however, no further proposals for the revision of paragraph 29 have been submitted as all Islamist parties have eschewed calls for the formal top-down enshrinement of shari'a in the constitution in favor of advocacy for piecemeal shari'a-inspired initiatives at the provincial and district levels. In 2008, Irghan Mahfidz, secretary general of the PPP, expressed his support for the Madina Charter, stating that the Jakarta Charter issue was "outdated" and "no longer relevant to the current era."[62]

Despite increased normalization, electoral support for all Islamically oriented parties has been steadily dropping since 1999, apart from the vote for the the PKS. The PK won 1.52 percent of the vote in 1999 and after reforming as the PKS, the party increased its share of the vote to 7.34 percent in 2004 and more or less maintained its total in 2009, with 7.88 percent of the vote. By contrast, PPP's share has declined from 10.72 in 1999 to 8.15 in 2004 to a new low of 5.32 percent in 2009. The totals for PBB and PBR have also decreased—albeit slightly—from a height of 2.62 and 2.4 percent in 2004 to 1.8 and 1.2 percent in 2009. Taken together, support for Islamist parties has varied from 14.18 percent in 1999, rising to 20.5 percent in 2004, on account of the increase in support for the the PKS, and dropping to 16.2 percent in 2009. When combined with support for all Islamically oriented parties, support has fluctuated from 33.9 percent of the vote in 1999, to 37.5 percent in 2004, and a low of 27 percent in 2009 (see Table 5). By contrast, support for nationalist parties has remained over 50 percent.

There are several reasons why Islamist parties fare poorly in Indonesian elections. These include the priorities of Indonesian voters and perceptions of voters about the ability of Islamist parties to deliver on those priorities; the attempts by "nationalist-religious" parties to make inroads into Islamist party voters through symbolic gestures; and the 2009 "tsunami" of the Democrat Party. First, according to surveys conducted by the respected Indonesian Survey Institute (LSI), an overwhelming 76 percent of respondents believed the government should prioritize improving the economy and the prosperity of the people.[63] By contrast, only 0.8 percent believed morality and religion should take precedence.[64] This highlights the need for Islamist parties to address bread-and-butter themes if they wish to win the support of the voters. However, in the run-up to the 2009 elections, voters saw nationalist parties as more sympathetic to the needs of the common people. LSI surveys in 2008 and 2009 asked respondents which party had "the best programs for the people" and which "cared the most about the

Table 5: Indonesia's Election Results Compared: People's Representative Assembly

Party	Votes 1999	Seats 1999	Votes 2004	Seats 2004	Votes 2009	Seats 2009	Pancasila/ Islamist
Indonesian Democratic Party-Struggle (PDI-P)	33.73	153	18.53	109	14.0	93	PS
Golkar	22.46	120	21.58	128	14.5	106	PS
Democrat Party (PD)	—*	—	7.45	57	20.85	150	PS
Greater Indonesia Movement Party (Gerindra)	—	—	—	—	4.45	27	PS
People's Conscience Party (Hanura)	—	—	—	—	3.77	18	PS
National Awakening Party (PKB)	12.66	51	10.57	52	4.94	28	PS
National Mandate Party (PAN)	7.12	45	6.44	52	6.01	48	PS
Prosperous Justice Party (PKS)	1.52	7	7.34	45	7.88	57	IS
United Development Party (PPP)	10.72	58	8.15	58	5.32	38	IS
Reform Star Party (PBR)	—	—	2.4	13	1.2	—**	IS
Star and Crescent Party (PBB)	1.94	13	2.62	11	1.8	—**	IS
Other parties	9.85		14.92		15.28	—**	
Total	100		100		84.72		

Sources: Compiled from Leo Suryadinata, *Elections and Politics in Indonesia* (Singapore: ISEAS, 2002), 103; R. William Liddle and Saiful Mujani, "Indonesia in 2004: The Rise of Susilo Bambang Yudhoyono," *Asian Survey* 45, 1 (2005): 120; Stephen Sherlock, "Consolidation and Change: The Indonesian Parliament After the 2004 Elections," *Center for Democratic Institutions*, July 2004, 5–6; People's Representative Assembly (DPR) website, www.dpr.go.id; Indonesian Election Commission (KPU) website, http://mediacenter.kpu.go.id/images/mediacenter/berita.
*Democrat and PBR did not exist in 1999, Gerindra and Hanura did not exist in 1999 or 2004. **In 2009, an electoral threshold of 2.5 was enforced. No party receiving less than 2.5% obtained seats.

people."[65] On these issues, 24 percent of respondents viewed the nationalist Democrat Party as having the best programs and 22 percent perceived them as caring the most, compared to 11 and 10 percent for the nationalist Golkar.[66] The PKS averaged 5 percent on both measures, and PPP ranked lower still, averaging 2 percent on both. The pluralist Islamic PAN and PKB also averaged between 2 and 3 percent respectively over the same two years. The PBB and PBR were not listed.

Fealy notes that there is an inverse correlation in these surveys between perceptions of "Islamicness" and ability to provide for community welfare:

Results for PKS provide the most glaring example of this. 20 percent of respondents rank it as "Islamic" but only 6 percent credit it as having "community welfare programs," despite the fact that the

PKS is the only party with extensive welfare activities and a detailed economic policy emphasizing equality. Overall, the four big Islamic parties [PKS, PPP, PKB, and PAN] had a combined Islamic score of 56 percent but a mere 12.5 percent for "community welfare." By contrast, the combined community welfare score for the four main non-Islamic parties was 43 percent.[67]

From these data, it would be a mistake to assume that Indonesian voters are rejecting Islamically oriented parties outright for reasons of religion. Instead, we can ascertain that Islamist parties have been more successful in communicating their religious identities and the religious components of their agendas than their social welfare initiatives at the grassroots level. Even for the PKS, which has an extensive network of community development activities down to the neighborhood level, this is not surprising. According to a study by Burhanuddin Muhtadi between 1980 and 2006, 62.2 percent of PKS collective action events (demonstrations; public statements, calls, demands and appeals; public prayers; social work; etc.) had an "Islamic" essence focusing on religiously centered morality reform or transnational Islam, while only 25.8 percent had a "non-Islamic" essence.[68] Moreover, the PKS makes news on overtly Islamic issues such as its campaigns in 2006 and 2008 for passage of the Anti-Pornography Bill far more frequently than for its community welfare programs or the universalist components of its agenda.

Second, nationalist parties are also competing to define the "Islamic mainstream" in efforts to appeal to the median Muslim voter. The Democrat Party, PDI-P, and Golkar have supported popular Islamic legislation at the national and local levels to show that they are friendly to Islam. In 2003 and 2004, mayors and district heads from the Golkar party adopted shari'a-inspired legislation in districts in South Sulawesi, Banten, and West Java. Although the legislation was supported by the Islamist parties, it could not have been implemented without the approval of nationalist district heads, mayors, or governors. PDI-P, Golkar, and Democrat have Islamic wings and have engaged in Islamic institution-building within their own parties. For example, the PDI-P, arguably the party most closely identified with secularism, set up a Bait al Muslimin Indonesia (House of Indonesian Muslims), which conducts Islamic education and assists PDI-P members seeking to make *haj* to Mecca. Yudhoyono's Democrat Party, which refers to itself as "nationalist-religious," established Nurussalam Dhikir Council

(Light of Peace), which has organized a series of *dhikir bersama* (collective remembrance of God) devotional events, which include speeches by high-ranking officials, collective recitation of the ninety-nine names of Allah, and supplications and aphorisms from the Qur'an or Hadith.[69] Moreover, the nationalist parties adopted a strategy of "soft-selling" Islam by using Islamic symbolism and language in their campaigns. One 2009 Democrat Party campaign ad highlighted how Islamic values were instrumental to the party's anticorruption campaign, while another celebrated the anniversary of the Prophet Muhammad's birth. This co-optation policy, together with nationalist party perception advantage on economic policy, has enabled nationalist parties, most notably the Democrat Party, to peel off some voters from Islamist parties.

Finally, it is important to note that all parties suffered declines in support this year due to the surge of the Democrat Party. In the years prior to the 2009 election, the Yudhoyono government had succeeded in attracting foreign investment, reducing corruption, improving access to health care, and reducing school fees. The results of an LSI survey in February 2009, two months prior to the elections, showed that 83 percent of respondents classified government performance in the education and health care sectors as "good" or "very good"; 80 percent approved of government efforts to combat corruption; and over 80 percent believed the government was working hard to combat the negative effects of the world financial crisis.[70] As a result, Yudhoyono and his Democrat Party were viewed as the most capable channel for the aspirations of the people.

This then raises the question why the PKS alone among Islamically oriented parties increased its share of support between 1999 and 2004 and maintained it in 2009. The result can be attributed to several factors. First, the party has a devoted network of cadre who conduct year-round activities and marshal support for the party around election time. The party holds regular community welfare activities micro-targeting specific segments of the population. For farmers, there are programs conducted through the Ministry of Agriculture, which the PKS holds, where farmers are educated about how to increase outputs and productivity. For women, there are approximately 2,500 Women's Justice Posts around the country offering programs on health care, nutrition, and maternal health. There are anti-mosquito fogging programs, microfinance programs for entrepreneurs, and programs for fishermen. The *harokah* has a network of Integrated Elementary Muslim Schools (Sekolah Dasar Islam Terintegrasi; SDIT), which, although not formally affiliated with the PKS, are often staffed by PKS families. Every PKS branch at the provincial level has a division to anticipate natural disasters. Together, these programs assist the PKS in increasing its number of votes. According to Muhammad Razikun, head of the PKS campaign team, "These programs don't just happen during the campaign period, but every day. It is not a hard campaign but a very very soft campaign. Even if there is no election, we campaign. This is not because we are going to face elections, but because it is the culture of the PKS cadre. It is part of our tradition. This is the strength of PKS."[71]

The sum total of these programs indeed aided the PKS in making gains among farmers in Central and East Java in the 2009 elections, where the party made inroads into communities that were formerly the stronghold of the PKB, which was paralyzed by an internal leadership struggle. No other Islamically oriented parties conduct community development activities on the scale and with the consistency of the PKS. While there is no explicit linkage between participation in PKS programs and voting for the PKS— the programs are not restricted to PKS supporters—these activities have a positive impact on how voters perceive the PKS. Zulkielfimansyah explains, "We set up activities for the people and this way, we build [their trust]. Then, they will vote for us because they are close to us."[72]

Second, for voters who seek an Islamist party, the PKS is widely identified in surveys as the most Islamic of the political parties and PKS cadres have a reputation for their piety.[73] Moreover, although the PKS does not emphasize overtly religious themes in its election campaigns, PKS candidates do use religious flavoring in their individual campaigns. For example, an Islamic singing group performed at a rally for Zulkieflimansyah in Banten; Yoyoh Yusroh distributed prayer attire and Sarah Handayani passed out krudung (short headscarves) to prospective voters in Banten and West Java, respectively; and Anis Matta extolled voters of Selayar to choose him because he was "a religious man" and they should "vote for religious people."[74] These methods allow the PKS to gently assert its religious bona fides in a manner that contrasts starkly with PPP's anti-Ahmadiyah rhetoric in the last days of the 2009 campaign.

Finally, as has been widely noted, the PKS adopts universalist campaign messaging around election time, focusing on issues like clean government and a just economic system that appeal to Islamist and non-Islamist voters alike. That the PKS maintained a firm stance on corruption served it well in the 2004 elections, as disenchanted young voters chose the PKS as a protest vote against corrupt party alternatives. Since 2006, however, it must be noted that several PKS legislators have been investigated on corruption charges. In 2010, Mohammed Misbakhun was sentenced to two years in jail for forging documents to obtain a loan from Bank Century. Though only the Misbakun investigation resulted in an arrest, the scandals have adversely affected the PKS reputation. Saiful Mujani, a professor at the State Islamic University (UIN) Syarif Hidayatullah in Jakarta explains, "PKS is seen as a clean party. If they're [investigated] for corruption, the fallout is greater because people expect them to be clean. If they're arrested . . . , people lose faith."[75]

Conclusion

This chapter has endeavored to highlight the patterns of normalization among Islamist parties in the Indonesian political system. In contrast to other countries featured in this study, Indonesia is a multiparty system with parties at every point in the politicoreligious spectrum, including multiple Islamist parties. The chapter has highlighted the ideology, behavior, and strategies of two Islamist parties, the PPP and PKS, although other parties, including the Islamist PBB, the pluralist Islamic PAN and PKB, and the nationalist Golkar, Democrat, and PDI-P, have been referenced. After analyzing the platforms, constituencies, movement-party relationships, changes in party behavior, and degree of electoral success, several conclusions can be drawn.

First, while the PKS and PPP have the same goal of the incremental Islamization of society, only the PKS has a plan for how to achieve it. The parties use differing methods. While the PPP chooses to focus on advocating for specific pieces of legislation, the PKS is engaged in a comprehensive effort to structurally and culturally infuse the political system and society with Islamic values. Apart from the PBB, Islamist parties have deprioritized top-down initiatives such as enshrining an obligation for Muslims to obey shari'a in the constitution in favor of bottom-up efforts to pass piecemeal shari'a-inspired legislation in districts and regencies where there is a measure of popular support. In doing so, it must be reiterated, they are often aided by sympathetic mayors or district heads from nationalist parties seeking to assert their own religious bona fides. While Islamist parties have indeed diversified their agendas compared to 1999, they still make news most frequently on Islamic issues.

Second, constituency-building among Islamist parties in Indonesia is more complicated than in other countries in this volume, for there are multiple Islamist parties competing against each other for the same constituents. Whereas in other cases Islamist parties have had a dual constituency, Islamically inclined and protest voters, the story is more complex in Indonesia. Protest voters do not comprise a meaningful portion of PPP or PBB voters. In fact, the very voters that constituted the core of PPP support during the New Order, young pious Muslim men, have now shifted allegiance to the PKS. However, it would be a mistake to say the PKS has a dual constituency, for not all supporters can be classified neatly into Islamic voters and protest voters. According to PKS internal surveys, a majority of PKS voters polled chose the party because it was Islamic. This indicates that the PKS religious identity is of prime importance for its constituents.

The significant 2004 hike in support for the PKS from 1.52 percent to 7.34 percent can, in part, be explained by voter disenchantment with corrupt and elitist alternatives. This is evidenced by the fact that all major parties that had participated in the 1999 elections suffered declines in 2004. However, a new nationalist party, the Democrat Party, led by Yudhoyono also made gains, winning 7.4 percent of the vote. Thus, the protest vote was split between a nationalist party and an Islamist party. The PKS success in 2004 and 2009 must also be attributed to its year-round "soft campaign" of social welfare and community development activities, which micro-target specific communities including farmers, fishermen, young entrepreneurs, and housewives. Thus, unlike Turkey, where Islamist parties only gain a significant share of the vote when voters choose them for reasons other than Islam, PKS voters choose the party for reasons often including, but not restricted to, Islam.

Third, of the Islamically oriented parties in the Indonesian political system, only the PKS is both movement and party. The PPP endeavors to be a big tent to represent all Muslims, irrespective of movement affiliation. The PKS, however, is unique as the party is a political wing of a larger mass Islamic movement. That the PKS is both movement and party provides it with a unique set of resources and opportunities vis-à-vis its Islamist counterparts and constrains it vis-à-vis nationalist parties. On the one hand, through the movement, the PKS is able to tap into resources, organizations, cadre, and networks that assist it in bringing out the vote around election time. On the other hand, the more purist movement constrains pragmatist party elites from truly moving the party to the center, and in doing so, effectively competing with nationalist parties as becoming a mass-based party itself.

Fourth, in Indonesia, Islamically oriented parties do not succeed in elections when they run ideologically driven campaigns. Thus, in elections, Islamically oriented parties do not compete by trying to out-Islamize one another, as occurs in Malaysia. Asserting Islamic bona fides in elections does not lead to victory, even if it highlights distinctiveness. In 2004 and 2009, when the PBB campaigned on a shari'a platform, it was unable to breach 3 percent of the vote. When the PPP swung hard right in Jakarta in the waning weeks before the 2009 election and included anti-Ahmadiyah rhetoric in its rallies, it did not help the party to stave off the decline from 8.15 to 5.32 percent. The PKS, however, has been more mindful and cautious in how it competes against other Islamist parties and how it portrays itself vis-à-vis its Islamist and its pluralist Islamic and nationalist competitors. Frequently, on contentious Islamic issues, the PKS charts a middle path between the position espoused by the PPP and PBB, on the one hand, and the nationalist parties, on the other. This seems to be the party's strategy since it proposed the Madina Charter in lieu of the Jakarta Charter. In adopting a middle path approach, the PKS endeavors to avoid alienating potential voters or appearing divisive or exclusive. However, the party also regularly asserts its religious distinctiveness not only through its *dakwah* and *tarbiyah* activities, but also through legislative efforts at the national and local levels outside campaign season. For example, the party activities on behalf of the Anti-Pornography Bill in 2006 and 2008 were important to the bill's eventual passage and a significant success for PKS legislative abilities.

Finally, political participation by Islamist parties has become increasingly normalized, even as the percent of the vote attained by those parties in free and fair elections has declined. There are several indicators of Islamist normalization. All Islamist parties participate regularly in elections at the national, provincial, and district levels, often forming electoral and legislative alliances with nationalist parties to increase the likelihood of winning elections and to leverage their influence in the legislature. In 2005, the PKS, PPP, PBB, and PKR joined the governing coalition of President Yudhoyono, with the PKS in particular doing so despite protests from purists and its support base. In 2009, the PKS and PPP again joined the governing coalition. In election campaigns, the PKS adopts universalist messaging, highlighting bread-and-butter themes, while at the same time maintaining a religious flavor in rallies and constituent meetings. Moreover, such Islamic flavoring has itself become normalized as nationalist parties have used Islamic institution-building, Islam-themed ads, and support for moderate Islamic legislation to appeal to religiously inclined voters. To date, despite declining voter support, neither PPP, PBB, nor PBR show any signs that exit from the political system is a viable option. Instead, they are reassessing their strategies and readying themselves for the next round of elections in 2014.

Chapter 4

Between a Rock and a Hard Place: Reform, Reticence, and Realignments of the Pan-Malaysian Islamic Party

JOSEPH CHINYONG LIOW

WENLING CHAN

The Islamic Party of Malaysia (PAS; Parti Islam Se Malaysia) has been somewhat of an enigma for scholars of Islamism and Muslim political movements. On the one hand, the party leadership remains steadfast in its insistence that its ultimate objective is the formation of an Islamic state in Malaysia, complete with shari'a and its attendant penal codes. Arguably, this objective holds even for the more moderate "professionals" in their ranks. On the other hand, however, PAS is also demonstrably increasingly comfortable with discourses on democratization, justice, accountability, rights, and transparency—the benchmarks, as it were, of Western understandings of democracy. In addition to that, PAS has also repeatedly declared its commitment to mainstream political processes, in spite of the significant obstacles the Malaysian political system has placed in its way, and has deepened cooperation with non-Muslim parties and civic groups. This presents an intriguing puzzle: how has PAS managed to reconcile its political aspirations to be a national party with broad appeal with its ideological aspirations, which sees it promoting an Islamist agenda where the ultimate objective is the establishment of an Islamic state in Malaysia? How tenable is this balance that PAS has hitherto managed to strike between the two seemingly diametrically opposed objectives of normalization on one hand, and the preservation of Islamic distinctiveness on the other?

To be sure, these conundrums are not unique to PAS. Indeed, this collection of essays demonstrates how a host of Islamic political parties, operating in different social, cultural, and economic milieus, are being confronted with similar challenges. Nevertheless, the aim of this chapter is to unpack this enigma in the case of Malaysia's Islamist opposition, and to reflect on broader trends and themes introduced by the editors of this volume.

In order to critically examine the political ideology and strategies of PAS against the backdrop of Malaysian political realities and constraints, four themes highlighted by the editors will be explored following a brief introduction to the party and its history: (1) the place of Islamic distinctiveness in the party's engagement with mainstream politics, (2) its appeal to protest voters which effectively creates for it a dual constituency, (3) its rationalization of political alliances toward the ends of achieving its objectives, and (4) the internal divisions that inevitably arise as PAS grapples with the tension between Islamist fundamentalism on one hand, and pluralism and pragmatism on the other. These themes have been chosen not merely because they resonate with the conceptual framework presented in this volume; they get to the heart of the conundrums facing PAS as it seeks to realize its political aspirations. The chapter argues that having played an integral role in the Malaysian reform movement of the late 1990s, which belatedly bore fruit in the general elections of March 8, 2008, PAS is now confronted with the realities of power and incumbency (at least as a state government). These challenges include what steps to take in terms of furthering the commitment to a pluralist opposition coalition without diluting the commitment to the Islamist agenda and how to maintain internal party unity and cohesion in the wake of pressures arising from political change and transformation in Malaysia. To the extent that its resolution remains elusive, this tension between normalization and distinctiveness will define the party's internal politics as well as engagement in national affairs for the foreseeable future.

Background: Malaysia's Islamist Opposition

PAS has long been the primary Malay-based opposition in Malaysian politics.[1] As a political party, PAS emerged from the United Malays National Organization (UNMO), the dominant Malay-based political party in Malaysia, when members of the latter's Religious Bureau broke away in

1951 as a result of disagreements over the party leadership's commitment to Islam and Muslim interests.[2]

Yet notwithstanding the party's origins and overtly religious character and motivation, a cursory glance at the party's evolution will reveal that PAS politics and ideological predilections have in truth been far more ambiguous than is often portrayed (especially in the media). Through the 1950s and 1960s, the party under the leadership of eminent Muslim social-ist intellectual Burhanuddin al-Helmy demonstrated strong Islamo-socialist leanings and was influenced by the anticolonialism of Nasser and Sukarno. After the May 1969 race riots and intensification of communal politics, PAS under Muhammad Asri Muda moved right on the ideological spectrum and transformed into a pro-Malay ethnonationalist party that contested UMNO's claim to leadership of the Malay community. In fact, UMNO and PAS were so ideologically aligned at this point that the latter even joined the UMNO-led BN or Barisan Nasional (National Front) coalition in the period 1974–1977, in what proved eventually to be an ill-fated attempt at reconciliation.

Paradoxically, membership in the BN set in motion a chain of events that culminated in PAS's loss of its power base in the state of Kelantan for the first time since independence (at the 1978 elections). This in turn led to an internal coup at its 1982 annual assembly that purged the party of its old-guard nationalists led by Asri Muda, and brought into power clerical leadership bent on returning Islam to the party's political agenda.[3] Of course, the reorientation of PAS in 1982 cannot be attributed solely to the failure of Asri Muda's strategy of allying the party with UMNO. The early 1980s witnessed key global events transpire in the Muslim world such as the Afghan mujahideen struggle, the Iranian revolution, the introduction of Islamic government in Pakistan, and the intensification of Islamism in the political realm in Egypt, Tunisia, and Turkey, all of which promoted greater religiously referenced political assertiveness among Muslim popula-tions, including a large segment of Malaysian Muslims. Indeed, the events of the day gave rise to an increasingly active Muslim civil society sphere from which political parties like UMNO and PAS drew support. Malay-Muslim civil society groups proliferated, and across tertiary education insti-tutions the phenomenon of *dakwah* (propagation) took root that sought to heighten piety and Islamic consciousness of Malay-Muslim youth.[4] Efforts to tap into these constituencies by showcasing Islamic credentials heralded an Islamization "race" between UMNO and PAS, in which both sought to "out-Islam." This Islamization "race" witnessed not only both parties attempting to demonstrate their religious credentials, but also each condemning the other as "un-Islamic."[5]

The increasing salience of religious referents to Malay politics afforded PAS an opportunity to expand its support base, which it did in the northern states of Terengganu, Kelantan, and Kedah as well as in universities across the country.[6] At the same time, under clerical leadership the party's outlook was buttressed by its unyielding belief that the Islamic state is both a viable and necessary alternative to the UMNO-dominated secular state. Since 1990, when it was returned to power in the state of Kelantan, PAS has presented draft proposals to the parliament for the introduction of *hudud* (criminal law) in Kelantan. Similar efforts were made after the PAS electoral triumph in Terengganu in 1999. However, as criminal law falls under the jurisdiction of the federal and not the shari'a courts, the motions have been withdrawn on both occasions. This however, has not stopped UMNO politicians from periodically goading their PAS adversaries to proceed with implementing *hudud* in PAS-governed states.

While PAS leaders have been unwavering in their claims that the Islamic state anchors their political aspirations, what is striking about the party's behavior and political engagement strategies over the past two decades is its evident willingness to embrace a more pluralist brand of politics that among other things includes collaboration with non-Muslim political parties and civil society organizations as well as the induction of non-Muslims into the party. PAS understood that electoral success would give the party a better chance at securing its political objectives, and electoral success was more certain if the party went beyond appeals to its core constituency and courted the non-Islamist vote, which for the most part were protest votes. Although PAS had previously attempted to corral non-Islamist, and in particular non-Muslim support, it was in the late 1990s that this strategy came to the fore, when PAS joined the nationwide reform movement that mobilized against corruption and the mistreatment of popular former deputy prime minister Anwar Ibrahim. Equally telling was the fact that PAS's all-out embrace of a campaign strategy that stressed reform and democracy coincided with its best ever electoral performance when it went on to win an unprecedented twenty-seven parliamentary seats at the 1999 elections.

If the 1999 election results sent tremors through Malaysia's political landscape, then the 2008 results were indeed the "political tsunami" they have come to be described. That year saw PAS join with two other parties—

the Democratic Action Party (DAP) and the Parti Keadilan Rakyat (PKR; Peoples' Justice Party) to deny the incumbent a two-thirds parliamentary majority for the first time in Malaysian history. A key feature of the PAS campaign in 2008 was the party's deliberate move to distance itself from the Islamic state objective and to leverage the consternation of Malaysia's ethnic minorities in the wake of the UMNO rallying call of Malay supremacy.[7] In an obvious effort to woo non-Islamist votes, PAS leaders made clear that their election campaign at the national level would focus on a manifesto that held out the promise of a welfare state system, known as *negara kebajikan*, accessible to all Malaysians.[8] Not only did the welfare state concept dull the edges of its Islamist agenda, in the larger scheme of things it enhanced the appeal of the party across the electorate. Moreover, campaign rhetoric replaced the Islamic state and shari'a with references to meritocracy, the rights of religious minorities, and the importance of the presence of non-Malay ministers in the Malaysian cabinet. This repositioning of PAS disarmed non-Muslims especially of their traditional concerns toward the Islamist opposition, and in fact secured not a small measure of non-Islamist votes on their behalf as well.

By way of this survey of the different phases (and faces) of PAS over the last six decades, the chapter now moves to unpack underlying themes and dynamics of the Islamist opposition's engagement in Malaysian politics.

PAS, Piety, and Pragmatism

If media reports are anything to go by, the religious content of the PAS political agenda has been a source of some consternation for Malaysia's non-Muslims. Foremost in the list of concerns is the party's strident commitment to the implementation of an Islamic state, together with Islamic law and the *hudud* penal code. Despite attempts to demonstrate a more egalitarian, inclusivist, and democratic approach to politics, the fact remains that PAS has not waivered in its insistence that the Islamic state remains its ultimate objective. Indeed, even reformists (often also called "professionals," denoting that, while they are party leaders, they are not clerics, or "Erdoganists" for their support of Turkish prime minister Recep Tayyip Erdoğan's brand of Islamic governance) in the party abide by this position. Where differences exist between them and more conservative elements over this issue, it has for the most part been over the manner in which the Islamic state would be brought into being in Malaysia rather than the more rudimentary question whether the Islamic state should be an objective at all. In brief, while conservative elements favor a top-down approach based on the declaration of the party's Islamic state objective and codifying Islamic legislation whenever and wherever possible, the professionals believe in the gradual education and socialization of Malaysian Muslims on the virtues of an Islamic state as a means to greater social justice and equality through *dakwah* and *tarbiyah* (education).[9]

The Rise of the Pragmatists

Though fully committed to decidedly Islamist objectives, PAS also demonstrates pragmatism in how it is aware of its dual constituency and clearly cognizant that insofar as the ballot box is concerned, its political ambitions and objectives cannot be realized through reliance on party cadre and supporters alone—they need to take into account those that vote for the party for nonreligious reasons. Concomitantly, the party has endeavored to appeal to a broader electorate, either through participation in political coalitions (a matter for closer scrutiny later in this chapter) or, more recently, by an attempt to appeal directly to a wider audience, which includes non-Muslims. As Chapter 2 intimates, these two strategies reflect the normalization of Islamist parties—in this instance, PAS—as they pursue their political objectives through elections amid constraints within the political system. The party has done so by deliberately downplaying its Islamic state agenda, particularly during election campaigns, and diluting its Islamist message to focus instead on more resonant themes such as corruption, welfare, justice, and human rights to tap into an expanding pool of protest voters. This was clearly evident in the 1990s, when PAS campaigned on a platform of welfare and social equality in the mid-1990s, and later in the buildup to the 1999 election when the party articulated an agenda centered on political reform and democracy as it rode the waves of the Reformasi (reform) movement that had taken root after prime minister Mahathir Mohamad's unceremonious dismissal of his hitherto heir and deputy Anwar Ibrahim.

The manner in which PAS positioned itself in preparation for the 1999 election is particularly instructive of how the party deprioritized issues of Islamic distinctiveness in its political agenda to "mainstream" its appeal.

By the late 1990s, a combination of external shocks such as the Asian financial crisis and internal crises within UMNO led to increased public disenchantment with the BN government and created fertile ground for a potentially significant protest vote swing. PAS seized on this opportunity to enhance its stature by adroitly skirting dogma and presenting itself as a voice for reform of the existing social, economic, and political architecture that rested on UMNO's dominance, which the Islamists challenged as corrupt and moribund. In so doing, PAS was ahead of the curve inasmuch as appealing to the protest voters in the Malay community was concerned. Events of the day led to major calls for political change that overshadowed traditional communal themes (especially among the Malays) and coalesced into a reform movement now known in the Malaysian political lexicon as Reformasi. As Case and Liew argue, the political upheaval drove "large numbers of Malays, often urban-based and middle class, into the arms of PAS. In this way, as new members percolated up through the party apparatus, purists in PAS were joined by new cohorts of pragmatists."[10]

As alluded to earlier, the election itself never centered on the party's Islamist distinctiveness, even though religious issues did predictably feature. Rather, the gains by PAS were a consequence of its ability to ride the waves of reform and appropriate language and terminologies to appeal to its dual constituency. Underlying this tactical shift was the influx of professionals and pragmatists mentioned earlier—many of whom were close allies of deposed Deputy Prime Minister Ibrahim—who flocked to the Islamic party, and to the newly formed Parti Keadilan Rakyat (PKR), in droves. Many among them immediately assumed the role of campaign strategists in PAS. They orchestrated not only the shift in PAS discourse, but also masterminded the alliance with DAP under the auspices of the BA or Barisan Alternatif (Alternative Front), the first time the two parties were united under the same umbrella. With these shifts, the party managed to capture large swathes of non-Islamist voters on its way to becoming the largest opposition party in the Malaysian parliament.

While the creation of the BA was instructive of PAS's willingness to place its Islamist aspirations on the backburner in order to enhance its appeal, the manner in which the PAS-DAP leg of the BA unraveled was equally telling of the constraints that Islamist parties face when they attempt such balancing acts. Indeed, the success of 1999 and the BA was short-lived. Soon after the 1999 elections, the DAP-PAS alliance began fraying over the Islamists' insistence on the implementation of an Islamic state agenda, which by then had taken on greater urgency when the newly formed PAS-led state government in Terengganu moved to formulate *hudud* penal legislation in the state. Unlike PAS, whose political fortunes were not dented by its participation in the BA, DAP suffered major electoral setbacks, winning only 10 of 193 parliamentary seats in a performance that included loss of seats held by party heavyweights Lim Kit Siang and Karpal Singh.[11] The postmortems following the results revealed that DAP decision to work directly with PAS, as opposed to 1990 when cooperation took place via an intermediary, was unpopular with large segments of the Chinese electorate. Despite several attempts at dialogue at the highest levels in the BA, the differences between DAP and PAS over the Islamic state could not be resolved. On September 22, 2001, DAP officially left the BA.[12] The failure of the DAP-PAS alliance and the costs the former had to bear hid another salient fact—in the 1999 election the bulk of the opposition vote came from disgruntled quarters of the Malay-Muslim population, meaning non-Muslims for the most part remained staunchly behind the BN. What this translated to in PAS's case was that while deemphasizing its Islamist ambitions and agenda significantly enhanced its prospects among the Malay-Muslim community, it had minimal impact insofar as appeal to non-Muslim voters was concerned.

Aside from illustrating the strategic opportunities and constraints that confront Islamists who attempt to enhance their appeal by diluting their religious agenda, the point of the above discussion is also to establish that PAS's best electoral performances have resulted from a deliberate downplaying of their Islamist agenda in order to speak to more resonant popular concerns, so as to have a broader audience. Conversely, PAS's worst electoral showings in recent years coincided with the party's attempts to promote a decidedly Islamist agenda, where the focus was on maintaining its core constituency. This was evident in 1986, the party's most dismal general election performance ever, which followed closely after Abdul Hadi Awang's *kafir-mengafir* attacks on UMNO, which he denounced as apostates, and in 2004, when PAS's campaign was anchored, much to the chagrin of party moderates, on the controversial Islamic State Document, which the party launched in late 2003.[13]

The Islamic State

For the longest time, PAS had avoided articulating the party's understanding of what constituted a functional Islamic state in the Malaysian context.

The party's ambiguity on this issue proved to be a double-edged sword. On one hand, this ambiguity afforded PAS a strategic advantage as it allowed it to use the Islamic state clarion call for political leverage. Keeping matters ambiguous allowed the party to criticize UMNO policies as "un-Islamic" and suggest that its own position on matters would accord more closely with Islamic strictures once the party came into power. On the other hand, it was also a liability as it opened the party to criticisms that they were Islamic only in rhetoric. Moreover, publicly declaring a blueprint for its vision of Islamic government would open the party to criticisms of being "un-Islamic" on any particular issue on close scrutiny, and could in turn ignite divisions within the party while undermining its religious credentials in the eyes of its core constituency.[14]

When Prime Minister Mahathir publicly proclaimed on September 29, 2001, that Malaysia was already an Islamic state and further challenged PAS to stake its own claim, PAS was compelled to act to regain the initiative as the chief proponent of Islamic government in Malaysia. At the same time, within the party there were those, especially among the conservative ulama, who interpreted the 1999 success as precisely the signal they had been waiting for to return the Islamic state to the heart of the PAS agenda.[15] As a result, internal divisions over revival of the Islamic state issue escalated, causing friction between those intent on picking up Mahathir's gauntlet and those who sought to preserve the close but tenuous political alliance with other opposition groups to advance the party presence in national affairs.[16]

Not surprisingly, when PAS finally decided it was time to draw up a concrete blueprint based on their understanding of an Islamic state, they ended up with four drafts that were in effect a reflection of the divisions in the party. According to Liew, "a two-year intra-party conflict, between September 2001 and November 2003, over the constitution of an Islamic state preoccupied and divided its leaders and its members, much to the detriment of PAS."[17] This struggle over drafting an Islamic state blueprint was an early manifestation of the tensions between the conservatives (mostly but not exclusively ulama) and professionals (which eventually also had in their camp a number of reformist ulama).

Given their close association with late PAS president Fadzil Noor, the professionals presided over the initial deliberations over an Islamic state document, which carried the title "Memorandum to the Malaysian People: Islamic Governance in the 21st Century." According to Liew Chin Tong, for the professionals the move to define the party's version of an Islamic state was seen as an "opportunity to move the party to the middle ground so that the party could secure support beyond the Malay heartland. They intended to ensure that the Islamic state PAS called for would appeal to—or 'at least not instill fear in'—most Malaysians, Muslims and non-Muslims alike."[18] Furthermore, the memorandum also presented an opportunity to defuse Mahathir's claim that Malaysia was already an Islamic state, while at the same time asserting the compatibility of Islam with democracy, a move undoubtedly informed by the need to maintain close relations with its coalition partners.[19]

The conservative ulama, however, entertained an entirely different set of reasons for pushing the articulation of the tenets of an Islamic state. For them, this was a chance not only to stake the party's religious credentials, but also to prevent their professional colleagues from sacrificing these credentials at the altar of political expediency. The fact that the professionals were not cadre grounded on the party's historical struggles but rather mostly members who joined at the height of the 1998 Reformasi movement further strengthened the resolve of the conservatives to make clear the party's Islamic distinctiveness.

The tension between conservatives and professionals over the matter of party identity was captured most profoundly in the very titles of the documents that were drafted. Whereas the document prepared by the professionals was innocuously titled "Memorandum to the Malaysian People" with allusions to Islamic governance, clearly an attempt at a conciliatory approach to non-Islamist constituents, the ulama-led conservatives' document was cryptically titled "Islamic State Document." Needless to say, differences between the two documents did not stop there. While there were undoubtedly many points of convergence, one of the major distinctions was the presence of the freighted terms *hudud* and shari'a in the document but not in the memorandum. Moreover, while the memorandum stressed that Islamic governance respected different cultures, faiths, and the rights and will of the people, and was premised on consultation and democracy, the Islamic State Document, while recognizing the freedoms and rights of citizens in accordance with the Universal Declaration of Human Rights, nevertheless maintained that these rights could not contravene shari'a law. For these reasons an author of the memorandum described the Islamic State Document as "antagonistic" (*berlawanan*) to the original proposals found in and the spirit of the memorandum.[20]

Following the death of Fadzil Noor in June 2002, the Islamic State Document was officially published on November 12, 2003, and became the cornerstone of PAS's 2004 election campaign. Tellingly, the 2004 elections proved to be a dreadful episode for the political fortunes of PAS. Terengganu was lost, as were a large number of parliamentary and state seats, as UMNO experienced a new lease of life with the transition from Mahathir Mohamad to the more consensual Abdullah Badawi. From the election results, it was clear that the Islamic State Document cut little ice with the Malaysian electorate. That said, the losses suffered by PAS cannot be attributed solely to the Islamic State Document. More important was the fact that, as a new prime minister, Abdullah Badawi proved a welcome change from more than two decades of mostly authoritarian rule under Mahathir.[21] His more consultative approach and demeanor enhanced the appeal of the incumbent, and together with an improved economic climate, many of the protest voters who abandoned the BN in droves in 1999 swung back to the ruling coalition in 2004. This being the case, the question arises as to the fundamental nature and premises of PAS's constituency—do people vote PAS because they are Islamists, or because they are not UMNO? It is to this issue of party appeal that we now turn.

Platforms and Constituencies

When PAS was formed, it was primarily a Malay-Muslim political party. For much of its existence, the party has also largely been confined to the Malay-dominated states in the north of the peninsula. Indeed, in the PAS stronghold of Kelantan, Malays make up as much as 95 percent of the population. Under Fadzil Noor, however, PAS began to harbor aspirations to expand its footprint and become a national party. To do that, it had to find new bases of support beyond its core constituency in the Malay heartland.

In recent years, the party has paid particular attention to improving its image among the non-Muslim community and projecting sensitivity on gender issues. To be sure, garnering support from Malaysia's demographically significant non-Muslim community has been a longstanding challenge for PAS, despite earlier attempts such as the creation of a Chinese Consultative Council in 1985 As we noted previously, even at the height of the party's success in 1999, its support base remained almost exclusively Malay-Muslim. Having attracted urban, professional, middle-class Malays, the challenge from then on (a far greater one) was to endear itself to non-Muslims.

Attempts to engage non-Muslims took on urgency immediately after the 2004 elections as PAS worked to disarm them of their latent concerns, which were evoked by the party's release of its Islamic State Document. For instance, the party conducted tours for ethnic Chinese to PAS-led Kelantan and Terengganu and defended the rights of Chinese to consume pork to demonstrate how the lives of the Chinese residents of these two states had not been negatively affected by PAS rule. Additionally, the party roped in PAS members of Chinese descent to serve as unofficial ambassadors to the Chinese community.

Much in the same vein, PAS has tried to better integrate women, who account for roughly half the party's members, into leadership positions. While PAS leaders often highlight that the first female member of the Malaysian parliament was from the party, women have in truth never held the very highest leadership positions in the party. Yet the party also organized a rare public debate between one of its highest-ranking female members, a member of the feminist group Sisters in Islam, and a prominent non-Muslim lawyer to discuss Islamic law and its implications for women.[22]

New Constituencies: From Non-Muslim Supporters Club to Supporters Congress

To further advance the party's engagement of non-Muslims, PAS took the step of forming a PAS Supporters Club (Kelab Penyokong PAS) just prior to the 2004 elections, and subsequently upgraded the club to an official wing of the party, the PAS Supporters Congress, on May 23, 2010.[23] The launch of the Supporters Congress was an attempt to appeal to non-Muslims, dispel their fears toward the Islamist party, and acknowledge the labors of non-Muslim sympathizers, especially in assisting the party machinery during the 2008 general election and subsequent by-elections.

Hu Pang Chaw, chairman of the PAS Supporters Congress and co-founder of its precursor, the PAS Supporters Club, revealed in an interview that after twenty years in MCA (Malaysian Chinese Association—the largest non-Malay component party in the UMNO-led BN), he chose to join the

Islamist party because of its well-organized structure and friendly and humble leaders and members, and its message of equal treatment for all races under Islam, which he found more palatable than UMNO's emphasis on *ketuanan Melayu* (Malay lordship or supremacy).[24] Articulating a view that encapsulates an increasing number of non-Muslim opinions of PAS, Hu noted: "I accept the reality in Malaysia that Malay politics will be dominant. The choice between UMNO and PAS is obvious. UMNO divides people but PAS is more sincere about treating people fairly." As for PAS's Islamic agenda, Hu pointed out that "They say that in Islam, there is no racial superiority. And there is no mention of setting up an Islamic state in the PAS Constitution. I have studied the Constitution and there is nothing there that is against any other religion."

During the 2008 general election, PAS Johor announced bank officer R. Kumutha, chief of the Johor PAS Supporters Club women's division, as its candidate for the Tiram state seat, albeit on a PKR ticket. Kumutha explained that PAS's Islamic agenda that included corporal punishment did not worry her as it was intended only for Muslims.[25] She also pointed out that there were no demolitions of Hindu and Chinese temples in PAS-controlled Kelantan, unlike in other states under the UMNO state government.[26]

Hu and Kumutha are archetypal examples of anti-regime supporters who have been deeply dissatisfied with incumbent parties and have chosen PAS as their platform. Significantly, they have switched allegiances to PAS not because of its ideology, but rather because of its image as a party genuinely concerned for the challenges faced by Malaysians, including non-Muslims. According to Dzulkefly Ahmad, former director of the PAS Research Centre, the party managed to attract non-Muslim votes in 2008 because "PAS was able to allay their fears and anxiety about both the Islamic state/*hudud*. Our 'Inoculation Strategy' of the party's think-tank worked well to break down the prejudice and negative stereotyping, which was demonized by the mainstream media and, sometimes, admittedly reinforced by our own 'misdoings'—like the launching of the ill-understood Islamic State Document (ISD) in 2002 that invariably caused the breakup of the Barisan Alternatif when DAP left the opposition coalition."[27]

Even so, amid calls to further woo non-Muslims and work closely with the Islamist party's multiracial coalition partners, warnings that the core Malay-Muslim voter base was in danger of being neglected were never far from the surface. Speeches of delegates at PAS assemblies since 2008 have warned of both the danger of losing the Malay-Muslim and the risk that pandering to non-Muslim concerns might not eventually translate to significant gains in non-Muslim support. Others also stressed that the Islamic agenda may be watered down if the focus is mainly on gaining votes.[28] In fact, dark clouds were already looming, for amid the euphoria of March 2008 few have noted that despite winning more seats the PAS percentage of overall votes actually dropped by about 1 percent compared to 2004.

Late 2011 saw the issue of *hudud* brought back under the spotlight, and in so doing returned attention to the constraints the party faces as it becomes increasingly normalized in the political system, and less distinctive as an anti-establishment religious actor. The resurfacing of the *hudud* issue is a clear indication that this movement of the party toward normalization is not without detractors both within the party and among its core constituency. The episode began when former prime minister Mahathir Mohamad challenged PAS spiritual leader Nik Aziz Nik Mat to enact Islamic law in Kelantan.[29] The latter dismissed the suggestion and instead challenged prime minister Najib Tun Razak to remove obstacles to Kelantan's plans to implement Islamic law.[30] Needless to say, this elicited disapproving reactions from the PAS Supporters Congress as well as the party's coalition allies. DAP secretary-general Lim Guan Eng announced that the party's top leaders would resign en masse if *hudud* were allowed into the PR's common policy framework.[31] Hu laid out the potential political costs for PAS if it pursued the implementation of *hudud*: "I have never disputed that *hudud* is part of Islamic justice, but is PAS willing to lose support in other states, especially from voters in the west coast, by talking about *hudud* now?"[32] His other grouse was that the congress had not been consulted or briefed by the Kelantan PAS on implementation of *hudud* laws, to which Nik Aziz had replied that *hudud* had nothing to do with non-Muslims and they need not worry themselves over the matter.[33] Conversely, Kelantan PAS Supporters' Congress chief Lim Guan Seng said the state-level congress backed the implementation of *hudud* in the state and would be involved in the party's efforts to explain shari'a to the people, especially non-Muslims.[34] On the other hand, Kelantan UMNO chief Mustapa Mohamad claimed that more than three hundred PAS members had applied to join UMNO following the *hudud* controversy, stating that many of them were unhappy PAS was more concerned with the *hudud* law than with the economic well-being of the people.[35]

By-Elections and Malay-Muslim Sentiments

An important litmus test of PAS's ability to retain its core constituency—the Malay-Muslim vote—even as it intensifies its engagement with non-Muslims and deepens cooperation with its allies in the multiethnic, multi-religious opposition coalition is the trend and result of by-elections the party has contested since March 2008.

PAS began the by-election "season" well enough, winning comfortably in the four by-elections it contested in 2009, no doubt capitalizing on the opposition's "honeymoon" period. Yet by the end of 2009 the tide had well and truly turned. On October 11, 2009, the party suffered its first by-election loss when its candidate was soundly defeated in Bagan Pinang. This was followed by an alarming string of four consecutive by-election defeats in 2010, including a particularly exasperating loss in the seats of Galas and Manek Urai in Kelantan, PAS's stronghold. What do these losses mean for PAS, and what do they tell us about the party's ability to retain core Malay-Muslim votes?

First, it is likely that a large number of Malay-Muslim votes won by PAS in recent years have been protest votes. This is evident when we consider seats such as Kuala Terengganu, which PAS won in a 2009 by-election. The point about this example is that the voters of Kuala Terengganu have shifted allegiances on numerous occasions over the past two decades—the seat passed from BN hands to Semangat '46 (Spirit of 46, referring to the year UMNO was formed) in the early 1990s, back to BN in 1995, then PAS in 1999, returning to BN in 2004 and 2008, and finally back to PAS in the 2009 by-election. Such fluctuating loyalty is illustrative of the fact that votes like those in the Malay-dominated seat of Kuala Terengganu are determined on issues rather than ideologies. This point is reinforced when we consider PAS's performance in the seat of Manek Urai in July 2009, which it retained in a by-election by a razor-thin margin of 65 votes. The nature of this victory is telling on two counts: the constituents in this seat are 99 percent Malay-Muslim, and PAS was the incumbent, having won the seat a year earlier in the general election with a 1,352 vote majority. Clearly, there was a Malay-Muslim vote swing away from PAS. The fact that this particular by-election took place at the height of controversial PAS-UMNO unity talks (to be discussed in detail later in this chapter) might also have to be taken into consideration. While some argued that the results were a warning to PAS not to flirt with UMNO, because it was a Kelantan seat and the

Kelantan based leaders of PAS were opposed to the unity talks, others have suggested that the result was in fact a protest vote against PAS's Kelantan-based leaders for their rejection of cooperation with UMNO in the name of Malay unity.[36]

Second, PAS has been more successful in mixed constituencies than in Malay-Muslim dominated constituencies. The by-election in Permatang Pasir is instructive in this regard. While PAS retained the seat with a strong majority of 4,551 votes, it was, unlike Manek Urai, a mixed seat where the electorate was not taken in by UMNO's provocations regarding PAS's weakening Islamic credentials.[37] In other words, it would appear that PAS wins big in mixed seats, while they lose in others where the electorate is predominantly Malay-Muslim. This indicates that when the party appeals to its dual constituency of religious supporters and protest voters, they are more likely to succeed in elections, whereas when they attempt to emphasize their Islamic distinctiveness at the provocation of UMNO, their Malay-Muslim competitor, they tend to lose out. As Dzulkefly Ahmad suggested, even if PAS plays up issues of race and religion, they will not get that many votes as that will be "playing into the hands of UMNO."[38]

Alliance Politics as Normalization

Belying portrayals of the party as fundamentalists, a curious and often over-looked aspect of PAS's participation in mainstream Malaysian politics is its vast experience in political alliances. Indeed, apart from the Alliance coalition (the precursor of the BN), PAS has been a member of just about every other political alliance that came into being in Malaysia's postcolonial history, directly or indirectly. It was a member of the ruling BN coalition (1973–1977), the HAK or Harakah Keadilan Rakyat/People's Justice Movement (1986–1987), the APU or Angkatan Perpaduan Ummah/Muslim Unity Movement (1990–1996), the BA (1999–2004), and the PR or Pakatan Rakyat/Peoples' Alliance (since 2008). All but one of these alliances entailed formal collaboration with non-Muslim, non-Malay parties.[39]

At first glance, there are several reasons why these formal political alliances have proved beneficial for PAS. First, PAS's alignment and cooperation with other opposition parties allows it to mitigate threats or capitalize on opportunities by leveraging the resources and strengths of partners to take a collective stand against mutual political adversaries. Second, a coalition arrangement allows PAS to "protect its lot," particularly if such arrangements include other Malay-based parties. Third, coalitions, particularly with non-Muslim parties, are strategic because they allow the party to benefit, if indirectly, from any non-Muslim protest vote swing to the opposition. Fourth, non-Muslim partners are instrumental as they play a pivotal role in convincing non-Muslim voters that supporting PAS (directly in head-to-head encounters with UMNO or indirectly through an opposition coalition) would not compromise their minority freedoms and interests.

On the other hand, political alliances carry potential costs that are equally weighty. For instance, scholars have drawn attention to the need for "ideological connectedness" in coalitions, averring that while coalitions are often formed between likeminded groups, when parties align with others who do not share the same political or ideological viewpoint they risk alienation from their constituents.[40] Similarly, coalitions need to manage the tension—inherent in coalition politics—between simply winning electoral battles on the one hand and forming a viable government on the other. Finally, coalitions will require conflict resolution mechanisms so that, as differences invariably arise, there are institutions that can function to mediate and mitigate them.

PAS as a Coalition Partner

Looking at how PAS has rationalized its commitment to various political alliances and how many of them have unraveled in the past illustrates (1) the dilution of Islamist distinctiveness as the party shifts toward normalization in the political system as a result of political alliances, and (2) the consequences of such identity dilution in terms of internal divisions.

PAS's foray into the waters of alliance politics began, ominously enough, with an ill-fated partnership with UMNO in the early 1970s. Against the backdrop of rising interethnic tension in Malaysia, especially between the Chinese and Malays, both UMNO and PAS sought to strengthen the Malay lot against the perceived political assertiveness of the Chinese community in the wake of the 1969 elections, when Chinese opposition parties made significant inroads. PAS leaders themselves rationalized cooperation with UMNO as "assisting the cause of Islam." Indeed, a PAS leader suggested that it was only after the UMNO-led government had demonstrated sufficient commitment to place Islam squarely on the state's agenda that PAS agreed to cooperation.[41]

Membership in the BN offered PAS its first taste of federal power, with several of its key leaders given positions in the cabinet and senior posts in federal ministries. Be that as it may, in PAS circles the decision to join the BN was highly controversial, and pockets of resistance remained. The youth wing of PAS, in particular, voiced misgivings and continued to do so even after the alliance was formed. Likewise, the ulama wing rejected explanations that the Islamic agenda of the party could be further advanced through cooperation with UMNO.[42] The severity of these internal divisions eventually led to cracks in the UMNO-PAS alliance, and PAS was expelled from BN in 1977. To some extent, the expulsion contributed to the emergence of clerical leadership in the early 1980s as it discredited party president Asri Muda, who had brought the party into coalition with UMNO. By 1982, Asri and his supporters were forced to surrender leadership of the party to the ulama.

Clearly cognizant of non-Muslim suspicions and the potential impact they would have on the party's political prospects, in 1985 the ulama leaders of PAS founded the CCC or Chinese Consultative Council (Majlis Perundingan Cina) as a unit in PAS.[43] Although the CCC existed as an entity within PAS, it was unique by virtue of being the Islamist party's first attempt at formal cooperation with the Chinese community. The initiative was very much driven by PAS Muslim Chinese members such as Kamal Liang, Kamal Koh, and Ridhuan Daniel Onn. Through the CCC, a number of programs were launched in order to draw PAS closer to the Chinese community.

Together with three other parties, PAS and the CCC combined on July 14, 1986, to form HAK.[44] The parties aligned their objectives through a twenty-two-point Memorandum of Understanding, which included establishment of an Islamic state and defense of the principle of religious freedom.[45] Notwithstanding PAS's attempt to appeal to non-Muslims and shed its image as an extremist party, it suffered major electoral setbacks in the 1986 general election, winning only one parliamentary seat. The experimental outreach to non-Muslims failed. Non-Muslim misgivings toward the clerical leadership of PAS remained, in part a result of UMNO's successful demonization of the Islamist opposition through the government-controlled media but also because of the caustic rhetoric that PAS leaders such as Abdul Hadi Awang—who openly called for a jihad against UMNO—engaged in during the buildup to the elections.[46] Meanwhile PAS leaders themselves surmised that significant numbers of Malay votes were in fact lost as a result of the party's attempt to court non-Muslims through the CCC and HAK.[47] This subsequently led PAS to dissolve its relationship with the CCC in 1987.[48]

In 1989, PAS joined Semangat '46, Berjasa, and Hamim to form the APU coalition (Angkatan Perpaduan Ummah). The immediate rationale for the formation of the APU was shared opposition to UMNO as well as a quid pro quo arrived at between the two main parties PAS and Semangat '46, where PAS agreed to lend its support to Semangat '46 leader Tengku Razaleigh at the federal level in return for Semangat's support of PAS ambitions to return to power in Kelantan.[49] To further enhance the prospects of unseating the UMNO-led ruling coalition, a separate election pact was formed between Semangat and DAP, known as the Gagasan Rakyat (Peoples' Might). It was the link between APU and Gagasan Rakyat provided by Semangat '46 that allowed PAS to work with a major non-Malay party. While the Gagasan Rakyat failed in its attempt to unseat the BN nationally, PAS did manage to return to power in Kelantan through this vehicle.

Not long after the 1990 general election, further efforts were made by members of this coalition to institutionalize their loose electoral pacts. For example, in early 1991, Tengku Razaleigh initiated the reorganization of Gagasan Rakyat to include PAS, DAP, PBS (Parti Bersatu Sabah; United Sabah Party), and Semangat '46 under a single opposition umbrella with a common symbol and manifesto. The effort to form such a BN-type multiethnic coalition, however, floundered mainly due to conflicting ideologies and political interests among the opposition parties. PAS refused to participate as it was concerned that the other opposition parties, particularly DAP and PBS, might block its Islamist aspirations.[50] The coalition eventually fell apart when Semangat '46 disbanded and most of its members followed Tengku Razaleigh back into the UMNO fold in October 1996. While both the CCC and APU ultimately dissolved, their significance lies in the fact that they signaled the first attempts of the Islamist leadership of PAS to work with non-Muslims, which for the Malaysian Islamist opposition was not inconsequential to the nature of its normalization and moderation strategies. Not only that, these attempts at coalition politics also laid the ground for later, more sustained attempts that took the form of the BA and PR.

The unprecedented electoral victories secured by PAS at the 1999 elections were achieved in large part through the vehicle of the BA coalition. The coalition was formed in October 1999 when four parties—PAS, DAP, PKR, and PRM announced a joint manifesto. For PAS, the coalition allowed it to leverage on the campaign machinery of non-Muslim partners to project a more moderate image of the party even as party leaders deliberately downplayed the Islamic state and Islamic law in their electoral messages. The result was the party's most successful election campaign. Not only did the party win more seats than ever on the back of the Reformasi wave, its membership also increased as its appeal extended to hitherto reticent segments of the Malay community, in particular the urban-based middle class. The significance of this cannot be overemphasized, for these urban-based middle-class Malays would form the bulk of the "progressive" and "professional" party leaders, who in turn would work to further transform the discourse and profile of PAS.

The success of the 1999 alliance between PAS and DAP was short-lived. Soon after the elections, the alliance began fraying over the Islamists' insistence on the implementation of an Islamic state agenda, which, as the chapter demonstrated earlier, had by then taken on greater urgency when the newly formed PAS-led state government in Terengganu moved to formulate *hudud* penal legislation in the state. Despite several attempts at dialogue at the highest levels in the BA, differences between DAP and PAS over the Islamic state could not be resolved. On September 22, 2001, DAP officially left the BA.

By 2008, the Malaysian political landscape had changed yet again. While prime minister Abdullah Badawi won with a landslide in his maiden general election in 2004, four years of unfulfilled promises culminated in a groundswell of discontent against the incumbent. This time, it was the non-Muslims who were especially disenfranchised as they witnessed an increasingly Islamist UMNO whittle away at their religious freedom through a number of high-profile rulings on apostasy and religious conversion. Ironically, PAS was one of the biggest gainers of the blowback against UMNO's assertion of a restrictive brand of religious conservatism. PAS not only strengthened its control over Kelantan, it also made headway in the states of Kedah, Terengganu, and Perak. The triumphant electoral gains for PAS were a significant improvement from its performance in the 2004 elections, but fell short of its 1999 result.

What was noticeable about PAS's political platform in 2008 was the absence of any reference to its Islamist ambitions in campaign literature or election speeches. Indeed, in the wake of the dismal 2004 showing, PAS leaders prudently softened the party's stance on the Islamic state, so much de facto opposition leader Anwar Ibrahim assured Malaysians that "PAS's intention to establish an Islamic state is no longer an issue."[51] Echoing the party's strategy from 1999, at the 2008 election PAS consciously distanced itself from its Islamic state objective as progressives and professionals it recruited in the late 1990s injected vitality into the party and the opposition coalition at large. PAS sought to leverage on the consternation of Malaysia's ethnic minorities in the wake of the UMNO rallying call of Malay primacy. In response to the Malaysian government clampdown on protests staged by Hindraf (Hindu Action Force) in defense of non-Muslim rights, PAS moved quickly to criticize the heavy-handed response of the government and fanned the embers of discontent by charging that UMNO discriminated against ethnic minorities. In a move clearly calculated to capitalize on the ethnic Indian opposition to the government, PAS made public claims to have won ethnic Indian support in some of its constituencies and that demolition of Hindu temples—a major grievance articulated by Hindraf—was unheard of in Kelantan.[52] In a striking departure from 1999, though, in 2008 PAS managed to capture support from segments of non-Muslim and urban Muslim voters while at the same time retaining its traditional support in the rural Malay heartlands. Again, much of this was attributable to the campaigning of its coalition parties. This time, however, its supporters' club also played an instrumental role in "selling" the PAS message to non-Muslim constituents.

To be fair, it should be noted that the PAS response to matters of religious rights of Malaysia's minorities is not purely a matter of pragmatic politics. Since the religious turn in the party in the early 1980s, party leaders have labored to separate religion from ethnicity, a relationship enshrined in the Malaysian Constitution that stipulates that all Malays must be Muslims, de facto implying that the notion of Malay primacy necessarily meant Muslim primacy as well. To that effect, PAS has regularly condemned UMNO's brand of racial politics as *assabiyah* (tribalism), deemed un-Islamic in mainstream Islamic thought for how it contravenes the universal virtues of Islam. It is in this manner that PAS claims to be more tolerant of non-Muslim rights to build places of worship such as temples and churches.

Logic and Dilemmas of Political Alliances

As an expression of normalization, participation in political alliances forces Islamist parties such as PAS to question the extent of their commitment to, and readiness to compromise on, objectives that are roundly rejected by the broader electorate, such as the Islamic state and implementation of shari'a law. To that end, their rivalry with DAP, whose leaders have been and remain vehement critics of PAS's Islamist objectives, remains the most controversial and difficult to manage in opposition politics, to the extent that even today, at the height of opposition cohesion, certain senior members of DAP (as well as PKR—the other party in the opposition coalition) are privately labeled as "anti-Islam" in some more conservative quarters of the PAS rank and file.[53]

In addition, membership in a coalition that demands some measure of ideological restraint and compromise might have the further impact of generating and reinforcing factionalism and widening divisions within the party over the substance and expression of its Islamic identity. In the case of Islamist parties such as PAS, these tensions often exist between ideologues and religious conservatives who prioritize the purity of the Islamic cause and those who are more prepared to work with non-Muslims to achieve larger political objectives.

Along with these issues of opportunities and constraints is the deeper question of the terms of reference that inform engagement toward the end of political cooperation. A fundamental principle on which coalitions involving PAS have been built is consensus. Put simply, this means that parties avoid areas in the agenda where disagreement might arise, and focus on areas where prospects for agreement or consensus are high. One immediate example is the Islamic state, which has become the sine qua non of PAS's political platform while at the same time it is anathema for many of its coalition partners, past and present. It should be noted that this approach differs markedly from a principle of "agreeing to disagree," which implies mutual acceptance of the validity of the other's project. Given how some of these earlier alliances have unraveled, this has certainly not been the case for PAS and its partners in the past, and is likely to remain the party's gravest challenge insofar as political alliances are concerned.

The Effects of Islamist Participation:
Party Unity and Internal Divisions

There are several intersecting planes within PAS where leadership profiles and policy positions differ. These include between ulama and professionals, between Terengganu and Kelantan chapters of PAS, and between PAS-UMNO "Unity Government" (those in the party who are amenable to some form of cooperation with UMNO) and pro-PR camps.[54] Rather than detail the contours of each of these intersections or the issues at stake, which are too numerous to address here, we will confine our discussion to two issues that arguably posed the most severe challenge to party unity in recent time—the issue of dialogue with UMNO on the basis of the Unity Government concept, and the "Allah" issue. In both instances, the fundamental issue revolved around the matter of party identity and commitment to its core ideals.

As alluded to earlier, one of the most significant challenges that confront Islamist parties as they attempt to moderate their agendas is the question of internal unity and coherence. In that respect, PAS has been no different. In fact, internal divisions have intensified along with the party's move to broaden its appeal beyond its core constituency of party cadre. As the party becomes an increasingly normalized actor in the political system, much of the internal tensions arise from concerns emanating from several quarters in the party that in attempting to embrace pluralism, PAS is losing track of its core identity and purpose as an Islamic party. While these internal divisions have always been present in latent form and periodically surface, it is ironically in the wake of the 2008 elections, when PAS is closer than it ever has been to national power, that they have become more persistent and acute.

Unity Government and the Dialogue with UMNO

As implied in the conceptual framework of this volume—a point reinforced throughout this chapter—the normalization of PAS was not unanimously endorsed by all segments of the party. This was certainly so with respect to the core conservative Malay-Muslim constituency, which harbored residual reservations at both the pace of normalization and its costs for the party's core identity and Islamic distinctiveness. These concerns came to a head over the issue of dialogue with UMNO and deliberations on a concept of Unity Government toward the end of Malay-Muslim unity.

Immediately after the success of the 2008 elections, the first signs of internal rifts became evident as the incumbent UMNO attempted to entice PAS to form a coalition on the grounds of Malay-Muslim unity. Very soon after the election results were announced, UMNO under the leadership of Abdullah Badawi moved to extend an olive branch to PAS in the hope of stalling the opposition juggernaut, while attempting to revive its own flagging fortunes. These overtures, couched as Malay unity talks, were received and discussed by the Majlis Shura, the highest decision-making body in PAS. A decision was subsequently made to accept the overtures and proceed with nonbinding dialogue with UMNO. PAS's decision to open channels to UMNO with an eye to cooperation stemmed from three concerns. First, certain segments, especially in the conservative ulama, were at the time concerned that deepening cooperation with opposition allies might force the party to compromise its Islamic agenda. Second, the Selangor branch was apparently displeased that the party's central leadership had allowed coalition partner PKR to fill the post of chief minister rather than press a PAS candidate. Third, many senior PAS leaders were taciturn toward Anwar Ibrahim. While undoubtedly the only person with the standing and persuasive influence to hold the PR together, Anwar's political ambitions and the persistent sodomy allegations against him were a cause of concern for many in the Islamic party. The depths of this reticence were demonstrably evident at the PAS general assembly in 2008, when the party rank and file refused to formally endorse Anwar as the candidate of choice for prime minister should the opposition alliance come to power. In fact, certain assembly delegates had argued the possibility that PAS should endorse party president Abdul Hadi for the position.

When it was publicized, the decision of the PAS leadership to accept UMNO's invitation for talks proved immensely unpopular among the party rank and file, senior members from the progressive camp committed to the opposition coalition, and the so-called Kelantan faction (supporters of spiritual leader Nik Aziz Nik Mat, who was opposed to unity talks). Internal debates intensified when the issue was recast by party president Abdul Hadi Awang as "unity government" talks.[55] Popular opposition in the party rank and file continued, forcing the proponents of Unity Government to stand down.

The "Allah" Issue

Another issue that threatened party unity was PAS's stand on the so-called "Allah" issue.On December 31, 2009, the Malaysian High Court overturned a ban on a Catholic magazine's use of the term "Allah" in its publications for non-Muslims. The decision was met with protests in various segments of the Malay-Muslim community, and was believed to have been the cause of various attacks on houses of worship across Malaysia. The events surrounding the ruling have been treated elsewhere and need not preoccupy us here.[56] What was striking and is pertinent to our discussion is PAS's response to the ruling in the context of its appeal to dual constituencies and strategy toward normalization. The point to stress here is that some in PAS saw this as a political opportunity to capture a large non-Muslim protest vote and address non-Muslim concerns that a PAS government would curtail religious freedoms, whereas others saw it as a threat to the party's diminishing Islamic distinctiveness.

Not surprisingly, the progressives, led by Nik Aziz, were most vocal in their support for the right of non-Muslims to use the word "Allah" on the grounds that the word predated the coming of Islam and hence was already being used by non-Muslims. What caught many by surprise, though, was PAS president Abdul Hadi Awang's support of the court ruling, particularly given his characteristically strong positions on religious issues (e.g., calling UMNO members kafir, and pressing for implementation of *hudud* in Terengganu when he was chief minister there in 1999–2004). In fact, it was Abdul Hadi who in his capacity as party president publicly pronounced PAS's official stand on the issue—that it stood by the court decision on the grounds of constitutionally enshrined religious freedom.[57]

However, not all who are affiliated with PAS agreed with the court, thereby drawing attention to internal divisions on this issue that spoke once again to broader concerns about the party's Islamic distinctiveness. The Timbalan Mursyidul Am (vice spiritual leader) of PAS, Harun Din, warned that supporting use of the term by non-Muslims could indirectly lead to "deviation or polytheism," and voiced disappointment at those who supported the court decision.[58] Other senior PAS leaders who opposed the decision (and by virtue of that, the party's position as well) were Taib Azamuddin, MP for Baling who was also the grand imam of Malaysia's National Mosque, and Harun Taib, the head of the Dewan Ulama (Ulama Wing).[59]

Whether or not PAS's position on the Allah issue was a deliberate act to enhance the party's standing in the eyes of non-Muslims, the fact is that it achieved that effect. It was widely surmised that by openly protesting the court decision and tacitly endorsing public displays of Malay-Muslim opposition, UMNO was testing the resolve of PAS, forcing its hand while attempting to divide the PR alliance.[60] Evidently aware of this, PAS's allies have expressed relief that the UMNO gambit failed.[61] Then again, progressive members of the party have also conceded that PAS's position on the "Allah" issue has cost the party Malay-Muslim votes in subsequent by-elections.[62] Indeed, differences of opinion in PAS over the court ruling speak to the larger issue of the extent to which PAS is prepared to compromise on its distinctiveness and core objectives to achieve political ends.

Clearly, from the above discussion, PAS's normalization in terms of its embrace of a multiethnic, multireligious opposition coalition and corresponding restraint from pressing its Islamist aspirations has not gone unchallenged from within the party, especially when it appears that normalization requires compromise of Islamic principles as defined by certain segments of the party. To that end, party assemblies since 2008 have become more captivating because of the intensity of debates among leaders and rank and file over issues of the party's core identity in the context of political opportunism and alliance politics. While these tensions have not resulted in a split in the party, and are not likely to do so in the near future, they nevertheless are likely to define internal party affairs for the next few years as the Islamist opposition continues to strike this tenuous balance even as it entertains prospects of coming to power as part of a coalition government.

Conclusion

Hitherto, analyses on PAS have frequently focused on its exclusivist Islamist agenda, especially its support of *hudud* and the Islamic state. The brand of politics that PAS has chosen to pursue in recent years, however, belies such caricatures of Malaysia's Islamist opposition. This chapter has drawn attention to the dilemmas that PAS has faced as it sought to moderate and normalize its political agenda in recent years. These efforts have been most evident in how the party is straining to enhance its appeal to non-Muslims. PAS has reined in overtly Islamist discourse and rhetoric, participated in various political coalitions that have included non-Muslim partners, and refrained from pressing its Islamic state agenda with its coalition allies. Rather than overwhelm Malaysians with the distinctively Islamist rhetoric of *hudud*, shari'a, and the Islamic state, PAS has used the themes of political and economic reform as the point of entry of its engagement in mainstream politics, in the process capitalizing on popular misgivings toward the incumbent on a host of issues ranging from corruption to perceived curbs on religious freedoms. Cognizant that its aspirations to be a national political party would not be realized without political allies, PAS has pragmatically partaken in various opposition political alliances. To be sure, these coalitions have served at least two purposes: they have allowed PAS to demonstrate its amenability to embracing non-Muslim constituencies, and have provided PAS effective advocates. All this has translated to a discernible reduction in non-Muslim suspicion and, not to mention new bases of support. Yet notwithstanding its efforts, the perennial problem of winning the trust and support of non-Muslim minorities remains, and ultimately PAS is limited in terms of the concessions it can afford to make without undermining its own core identity as an Islamist party.

On the other hand, PAS is aware that it has to balance dual constituencies as another segment of its support have cast their lots with the Islamists because they are foremost a Malay and Islamic party. These are voters who are sympathetic to issues of Malay and Muslim unity and implementation of shari'a and *hudud*. Recent by-election results indicate that the Malay-Muslim ground is shifting back to UMNO. There is a perception among this constituency that PAS is not doing enough to address the concerns of the Malay-Muslims, and may be placing too much emphasis on endearing itself to non-Muslims. In the wake of this evident erosion of Malay-Muslim support, PAS has attempted to reinforce its Malay and Islamic credentials in recent times. The National Race Empowerment Convention in February 2011 appeared to be aimed at attracting Malay support, with top PAS leaders including Nik Aziz attempting to convince Malays that their interests were the party's top priority.[63] March 2011 saw the PAS state government in Kelantan ban the sale of lottery tickets, sparking a riposte from its DAP coalition partner.[64] This was followed by the aforementioned *hudud* controversy.

Ultimately, though, whether Malay-Muslim or non-Muslim, it appears that the surge in PAS membership owes less to its Islamist agenda than to its reform agenda. Their electoral success, in short, is due to the large protest vote made up mostly of non-Islamist voters. To that effect, even some PAS leaders have acknowledged: "the Malay vote is really the middle ground. In 2008 they came to PAS because of their hatred of UMNO excesses, not because of a love for PAS."[65] Hence, PAS must realize that large segments of its membership support the party because they deem it to be multiracial (at least more so than UMNO, particularly in the view of the members in the Supporters Congress), open to feedback, and just and efficient in its model of Islamic governance that does not (in theory) prejudice against non-Muslims. And if the results of the 2004 election were anything to go by, to read any gains, especially in non-Muslim support, as endorsement of its Islamist agenda would undo all that the party has achieved.

Chapter 5

Searching for Political Normalization: The Party of Justice and Development in Morocco

DRISS MAGHRAOUI

SALOUA ZERHOUNI

While a number of countries in the Middle East have gone through major revolutions and social upheavals since 2011, the Moroccan regime, thanks to well-orchestrated constitutional reforms, has effectively managed to avoid some of the violent outcomes that characterized politics in other authoritarian regimes in the region. An important component of this outcome was ultimately the role the Islamist Party of Justice and Development (Hizb al-Adala wa al-Tanmiyya; PJD) was allowed to play by the regime to achieve what some Moroccan analysts called the "second *alternance.*" The first *alternance* occurred in 1998, when long-excluded political parties were allowed to form a government under leftist prime minister Abderrahman Youssoufi of the Union Socialiste des Forces Populaires (USFP), and were integrated directly into the political system. What made the contemporary integration of the Islamist PJD into government possible is not only the astute political maneuverings of the monarchy and its established strategies of segmentation and co-optation of the opposition, but also the presence of PJD as an alternative to other largely discredited political parties. We argue here that by virtue of its predisposition to further normalize its presence in Moroccan politics, PJD took full advantage of the Arab Spring and the more recent pressures on the regime to engage in constitutional reforms.

The Moroccan case presents a situation in which an Islamist party has become a strategic political actor not by seeking to establish a new political order as in Tunisia or Egypt, but by increasing its power through a process that helps perpetuate a structurally undemocratic political system. PJD has done well in recent elections and has emerged at the forefront of formal politics in Morocco; however, it is not entirely within formal institutions that real political power resides.

This chapter articulates the processes PJD went through to ultimately play a governing role and normalize as a mainstream political party. We first contextualize the nature of political participation in Morocco and then highlight the dynamic interaction between the Moroccan monarchical regime and PJD as it has evolved politically. We subsequently assess the nature of Islamist electoral participation in Morocco by looking first at the 1997 local and legislative elections and then at the 2011 elections, which resulted in a historical success for PJD. We argue that PJD was able to achieve electoral success in part because of the juxtaposition of its Islamist credentials with its "normal" political behavior, which allowed it to both maintain a foothold in the existing system and also capture protest voters. We conclude the chapter by stressing that in the absence of a real democratic system in Morocco, PJD will remain entangled in the institutional constraints of an undemocratic regime that still has full control over the decision-making process, which may undermine its long-term credibility.

PJD in the Moroccan Political Context

Although not the only Islamist group in Morocco, PJD is the most important Islamist actor in the electoral system, and emerged as the dominant political party in Moroccan politics in 2011. It has nonelectoral Islamist challengers, such as the Justice and Charity Movement (Al-Adl wal-Ihsane), as well as non-Islamist party challengers. The PJD emerged out of a broader Islamic movement in the 1990s, and after an initial incarnation when it was known as the Popular Democratic and Constitutional Movement (MPDC), became known as PJD in 1998. Its first foray into the electoral arena was as the MPDC in 1997, a critical political period for the movement, and it subsequently competed in elections throughout the 2000s, enlarging its support over time, most dramatically in 2011. Although it is a major political party in Morocco, the attributes and behavior of PJD cannot be understood without reference to its place in the broader Moroccan political system, in which political parties have traditionally been comparatively weak political actors compared to the monarchy, which dominates the political system and shapes its political culture. In the last several decades, much has remained constant in the Moroccan system, although periods of constitutional reform have increasingly allowed political parties opportunities to participate in the system.

Since independence, the Moroccan regime has been reluctant to expand political competition in a manner that would support meaningful contestation from a wide range of opposition actors. The institution of the monarchy is central to the Moroccan political system and has been the axis around which political mobilization and party politics has revolved. During his tenure, Hassan II (ruled 1961–1999) adapted to changing situations and managed political challenges through a combination of repression, co-optation, and consensus-building. The king was able to ensure the stability and continuity of the regime without completely closing public space to political participation. His successor Mohammed VI (1999–present) has maintained, if not reinforced, the centrality of the monarchy by championing some relatively liberal causes, and has thus far guaranteed the continued predominance of the monarchy in politics.

Moroccan political culture has historically been shaped by the central power of what is known in Morocco as the *makhzan*, that is, the monarchy and its hegemonic state apparatus.[1] French sociologist Éduard Michaux-Bellaire referred to this form of rule as a "despotic authority" that aspires to maintain a certain social disorder to maintain its own power to arbitrate between political interests.[2] Other scholars have highlighted the adaptability of the monarchy to maintain cultural, economic, and political hegemony despite a range of competing forces.[3] To survive, monarchical authority has retained a set of allegiances and has succeeded in converting allegiance into submission by creating a culture of obedience that stigmatizes any form of political dissent or challenge. Even as Morocco underwent a number of constitutional reforms in 2011, the political culture and economy that maintained the monarchical system did not lose its potency, allowing the king to retain meaningful strategies for control over the political field.

The nature of the monarchical system has created a framework for co-opting or repressing any national actors that could propose alternative political agendas beyond the orbit of palace politics. Political culture in Morocco is such that the monarch consistently considers himself the only actor capable of finding solutions for difficult challenges, protecting national interests, and making major strategic decisions. This culture has created a political atmosphere in which critics, dissidents, and potential political challengers have often been controlled, muted, or labeled as subversive if they openly challenge the king's authority. Moreover, the monarchy has played an important role in the perpetuation of existing political elites by creating a clientelist network in which economic self-interest has become part of political parties' shared values. Even the most democratically oriented elite from the left have gradually fallen into a culture of political apathy based on participation in a clientelist political economy. It is this political culture that has hindered the establishment of appropriate rules for political competition, and which PJD still confronts despite its 2011 electoral victory.[4]

Another structural constraint that an Islamist party like PJD is faced with is the reality that the Moroccan regime has historically built its legitimacy, in part, on its Islamic religious authority. While the first constitution in 1962 established a multiparty system and delineated the powers of an elected parliament and a government, the king as *amir al-mu'minin* (commander of the faithful) held disproportionate prerogatives to control both the parliament and the government. As amir al-mu'minin the king appointed the Minister of Islamic Affairs, proclaimed legislative decrees known as *dahirs*, and pushed for new laws to be enacted. Article 23 of the 1996 constitution stated that the "the person of the King shall be sacred and inviolable," and article 28 declared that "the King shall have the right to deliver addresses to the nation and to the parliament and shall not be subject to any debate."[5] These powers came in part through the mantle of religious as well as temporal authority. Islam is thus at the center of the monarch's legitimacy and is central to the definition of the Moroccan state. Hassan II had aspired to keep the image of his father as a "monarch-saint, a fusion of a holy man and strong man."[6] Constitutionally, the monarchy is, therefore, assigned the role of the "guardian" and "protector" of a particular form of Islam that ought not to be challenged by any political actor. While the most liberal and left-wing parties argue for the separation between state and religion and are critical of PJD when it uses religious discourse and symbolism, they are mute when it comes to criticism of the monarchy as a symbol of religious authority.

The political participation of PJD should therefore be seen in light of the constrained political culture based both in respect for the monarchy and in the Islamic legitimacy claimed by the Moroccan king. PJD's religious discourse is open to criticism from a variety of actors because the religious field is constitutionally reserved for the king.[7] On the other hand, PJD is also faced with religious challenges from the popular Islamic movement Al-Adl wal-Ihsane under the leadership of sheikh Abdeslam Yassin, as well as from smaller Islamic movements that question PJD's religious legitimacy. Therefore, despite being the dominant Islamist party in Morocco, PJD has had to navigate a difficult terrain in establishing itself as representative of Islamic interests in the country.

On his ascension to the throne in 1999, Mohammed VI appeared to break from earlier conceptions of monarchical authoritarianism practiced by his father, Hassan II. This created the potential for a more open political environment in which Islamist politics could thrive. In his second address to the nation in August 1999, Mohammed VI affirmed his attachment to the principles of a constitutional monarchy, respect for human rights, and individual liberties. He called for a new conception of authority based on accountability and proclaimed that defining a new status for women and fighting against corruption and poverty were his top priorities. He refrained from interfering in the internal affairs of political parties and urged reform of the electoral law to ensure more representativeness. He also called on Moroccans to take elections seriously and to vote. The first legislative elections under Mohammed VI, in September 2002, orchestrated by interior minister Driss Jettou, occurred under relatively transparent conditions. Many observers perceived them as an important moment for the prospect of democratization in Morocco. But parallel to his declared democratic intentions, the king simultaneously reinforced his powers through creation of royal committees on strategic issues that maintained the monarchy's monopoly on a number of pivotal issues. Important, however, the reform agenda has been more closely associated with the monarch than with any political party.

New constitutional reforms enacted in 2011 have also contributed to the image of a reformist monarchy, and shaped the climate of Moroccan political competition. Though far from democratic, the reforms were guided by the "politics of consensus" with a domesticated political elite that proved unable to propose more democratic alternatives.[8] In the 2011 constitution the king retains major powers that ensure him a dominant role in political life, including executive powers to make royal decrees (*dahirs*), although he notably agreed to choose the leader of the winning political party to head the government and delegated a number of additional powers to the head of the government.[9] It is in this political landscape that Islamist political participation *à la Marocaine* takes place.[10]

The Moroccan political context thus limits the possibilities for effective political participation by actors without a close relationship to the palace. The hegemonic powers of the palace have helped to effectively "depoliticize" much of Moroccan politics over time,[11] leading to a "technocratic turn" in Moroccan policy-making that limits the political influence of even popular political parties like PJD. In this context, even free elections may not see active competition between divergent political and social projects.[12] PJD's behavior and the evolution of its political strategy should thus be seen in the context of limited political agency and a narrow political space dominated by the monarchy. Since its inception, the party has been dependent on the monarchy, and thus saw that it was in its interests to become a "normalized actor" within the Moroccan political system. As its participation has evolved over time, PJD has become more pragmatic and less distinct in its behavior in comparison to non-Islamist political competitors, as hypothesized in Chapter 1, due to both the electoral opportunities and structural constraints of the Moroccan political system.

The fifteen years of interaction between the regime and PJD show how both the members of the party and the palace were capable of adapting their strategies to changing circumstances in order to achieve their specific goals. For the monarchy, the integration of moderate Islamists has been a means of consolidating control over a key challenger and making it play by the rules of the game. For the Islamists of PJD, the main objective behind their participation has been to secure access to established political institutions and the resources (legitimacy, patronage networks) that come as a result. The interaction between the regime and PJD has been characterized by alternating phases of collaboration and conflict. The success of the Islamist party in the 2002 legislative elections as well as the terrorist attacks of May 16, 2003, in Morocco marked a turning point in the relationship. The period from 1996 to 2003 was more collaborative as the regime worked to manage PJD's political behavior by integrating it into the existing system. After 2003, the relationship became more confrontational, as the regime worked to weaken PJD influence in politics.

Islamist Participation: The Development and Integration of PJD

Significant levels of Islamist opposition to the Moroccan monarchy began to develop in the early 1980s, which forced the monarchy to find ways of dealing with its Islamist challengers. The regime initially responded with repression,[13] along with the restructuring of the institutions of "official Islam"[14] in order to ideologically counter the activities of Islamic groups and neutralize the emerging Islamist movement. The movement was both broad and fragmented, composed of small underground groups that operated secretly at the local level. It was fragmented both organizationally and ideologically with respect to the strategies of expressing discontent. To organize their activities and mobilize around their discourse, Islamic activists used the mosque and a large network of cultural and sporting associations, as well as the universities.[15]

In the mid-1980s, one segment of the Islamist movement called the "Islamic Group" (al-Jamaâ al-Islamiyya) opted to participate openly through the established rules and institutions, and this group would evolve to compete in politics as PJD. This segment was led by Abdelilah Benkirane, the current PJD secretary general and head of government. It published a declaration in 1988 in which the principles and objectives of the movement were stated. According to a member of the PJD national bureau, "The logic of reform through the established institutions, moderation and nonviolence constitute the founding principles of this ideological transition, which was a big intellectual development of the Islamists in Morocco."[16] Since then, what would become the PJD Islamists distinguished between the separate roles of religious (da'wa) and political activities.

The Islamists' interest in political normalization through formal participation was further emphasized in the 1990s. Some members of the original al-Jamaâ al-Islamiyya reformed themselves as al-Islah wal-Tajdid and developed the idea of creating their own political party. Their demand was initially rejected by the palace under the pretext that political sensitivities at the time were not conducive to creating an Islamist party. At that time, neighboring Algeria was mired in a civil war between supporters of the Islamic Salvation Front (FIS) and the military junta. By the mid-1990s, however, the monarchy allowed Islamists to find a pathway into partisan politics. What subsequently became PJD was initially established under the leadership of Dr. Abdelkrim Al Khatib, who headed a dormant party known as the MPDC, which had a very cordial relationship with the monarchy.[17] It is important to note that from the onset PJD was established under the auspices of the Ministry of the Interior with the guidance of hardline minister Driss Basri, the late minister of the interior and close ally of King Hassan II. The integration of PJD was thus part of a regime strategy to co-opt and domesticate opposition forces. With their participation in the legislative elections in 1997 and subsequent participation in parliament, the Islamists finally reached their goal of formal political participation. In 1997, they won nine seats in parliament, a number that would grow in subsequent elections. At a party congress in 1998, the MPDC changed its name to PJD.

Beginning with the 1997 elections, the broader Islamic movement, since 1996 known as the Unity and Reform Movement (MUR), was careful to separate its religious and political activities. It competed in elections under the banner of MPDC, and then PJD (from 1998), but not as the Islamic movement itself (MUR). The formal participation of religious movements and associations remained confined to specific arenas in the public sphere, such as education, cultural activities, and charity work. Islamist movements also commonly preached at the universities through the so-called "summer school for Islamic revival, or *sahwa*," an institutional framework that acts as "an orientation" for Islamic education.

Realizing that using direct references to Islam could constitute a strategic threat to the monarchy and thus to the party's longevity, party leaders sought to separate religion from politics in their own activities. PJD made a technical separation between "preaching" and "politics" by arguing that the party was responsible for typically political questions while the MUR would concentrate on more religiously oriented questions. This does not mean that the MUR as the broader movement was totally apolitical, but it was kept as an independent movement with its own institutions and programs that remained much broader than the short-term objectives of PJD. It is in this context that PJD started seeing itself as having an explicitly political rather than religious mission, although this distinction has been difficult to uphold over time.

The Islamists' initial experiment with electoral participation was very cautious and pragmatic. In the 1997 legislative elections, they presented only a limited number of candidates for election. This was done for several reasons. First, they were new to politics and did not have the necessary experience in the field of elections. Second, they were very strict in the choice of candidates who would run under their banner. The main criteria adopted for selecting candidates were professional skills and competence, although high moral standards were compulsory. Their foremost objective was *not* electoral success but rather to normalize their presence in the political scene and introduce themselves to both the people and the institutions of state. As noted by one leader, "our objective is not to gain seats in parliament, but to introduce the party and its program, communicate a new political discourse to the people and also to the administration, so that they know that we are moderate and not radical as some speculate. For the international scene the idea is to show that Islam has an enlightened side."[18]

In the discourse of party leadership, the decision to participate in the legislative elections was motivated by a number of factors. In the words of one party leader, "our willingness to participate is first to practice *da'wa* (preaching) to God inside the parliament, within a category of people (the elected MPs) who are decisive (*faela*). Second, we want to learn because we are illiterate in the field of politics. . . . We want to know more about the 'oven' in which a number of important decisions are cooked. Third, we want to have an influence on issues."[19] Another party member, Ahmed Raissouni, also mentioned in one of his discourses during the electoral campaign, "I ask all sisters and brothers who are going to participate in the electoral campaign in one way or another to consider themselves as people doing "preaching" (*da'wa*), people with a *kadeya* (cause), people who are doing *jihad fi sabil allah* (jihad for God); they should not consider themselves as presenting support or doing a favor for the candidate."[20]

There was a general consensus between political parties and the monarchy that the 1997 elections would be held under more transparent conditions than were previous elections in Morocco.[21] There was a renewal of the electoral lists and a reform of the electoral code,[22] which consisted of the establishment of new mechanisms for control of the electoral process. This helped give the Islamists some measure of confidence that participation in the electoral process could reap some political rewards. From the perspective of the Moroccan regime, the 1997 legislative elections might also be considered a first test of the credibility and intentions of the Islamist movement as far as its moderate political position was concerned. The regime may also have seen integration of Islamists into the elections as an opportunity to apply its classic "divide and rule" policy by deepening the division between the members of the MUR who were for electoral participation and those who supported a boycott of the elections. For the Islamists, it could be considered an experiment to test the plausibility of direct political participation and to gain information about the level of their political support.

Despite the fact that the legislative candidates wanted to differentiate themselves from the broader Islamic movement, it did not mean that reference to religious discourse was absent. Part of the strategy of their electoral campaign in 1997 was a consistent reference to Islam. One could argue that a principal Islamist objective in this election was the "moralization" of electoral discourse. The electoral campaign was based on support for good morals, which informed the choice of candidates to present, as well as the party platform. However, in their electoral campaign, the Islamists were very careful about when to use or not use religious references. The general framework of the discourse included universal themes such as "dialogue and communication," "agreement and conviction," "equity and objectivity," "truth and science," "consolidation of a state of consultation," and "democracy and human rights." The themes also included principles to reassure the palace of their intentions. Here the reference to fundamental principles (*dawabit*) of Moroccan politics generally means supremacy of the monarchy, Sunni Islam, and support for Morocco on the contentious issue of Western Sahara. Other broad notions such as "support of security and stability," "support of the state's national and independent choices," and "dealing with the economic and social crisis" were also part of their election discourse. The overall slogan of their program was "for a complete renaissance: authenticity, justice and development" (*min ajli nahda chamila: asala, a'dl wa tanmiya*). In comparison to political parties that had lost some political stamina, this kind of discourse was rather progressive in the overall 1997 uninspiring political scene.

One of the target audiences of the legislative candidates was Islamists who were against political participation in the Moroccan political scene as orchestrated by the state, which led them to make religious arguments about why participation in the election was important. These included people with *salafi* aspirations inside the MUR, the popular Justice and Charity movement, and the Movement for the Islamic Community (*umma*), among others. In addition to demonstrating their pragmatism to the regime, a main objective of the party was to convince these social categories to vote and to present it as part of a religious duty to do so.

During the 1997–2002 legislative session, PJD participation was shaped by both its religious values and the desire to normalize its presence in parliament. The PJD representatives adopted "nuanced" strategies, which have allowed them a certain degree of flexibility. When they were part of the parliamentary majority, they did not want to be associated with the weaknesses of the government of alternance led by the leftist USFP. Hence, during the first thirty months of the legislature, PJD members declared they would support the leftist government of alternance and its policies only if those policies did not contradict the ethical principles and values of PJD. They referred to this position as a "critical endorsement" (*moussanada nak-diyya*). They explained their decision to cooperate with the government in this cautious manner, drawing on the following points. First, from a religious perspective, they argued that Islam compelled them to cooperate and communicate with all political parties for the sake of public interest. Second, they believed economic development in Morocco could not succeed in a context characterized by conflict among political parties. In hindsight this was a signal that they were willing to accept the rules of the game as established by the monarchy and should be trusted and considered like any other "normal" party in Morocco.

In an effort to adapt to the rules of the Moroccan political game and gain the trust of its key stakeholders, the Islamists voted for the leftist USFP candidate for the presidency of the House of Representatives. They also voted for a majority of the draft bills presented by the government, including those on education reform and economic planning, criticizing a few points they considered incompatible with Islamic values. They also cooperated on a number of issues regarding establishment of fact-finding committees.[23] Later in the legislative session, however, PJD changed its strategy from "critical endorsement" to "advisory opposition" (*al-mouarada an-nassiha*). It justified the change by citing the inability of the government to implements parts of its program. More important, the PJD representatives were concerned with the fact that religion was still not taken into consideration in most draft bills presented by the government. They objected to what they saw as a tendency to secularize political life in Morocco. The introduction of a system of financial loans and the plan for social integration of women were examples of such tendencies viewed as potentially incompatible with Islamic values. At the local level the moral component of their political action was often present as well.[24]

While pragmatic in their overall orientation, the PJD parliamentarians made clear that they would not make concessions on issues that contradicted Islamic principles or were in conflict with the "cultural identity" of the country as they conceptualized it: "Sunni Muslim, Arab and monarchical." In addition, they opposed policies seen as inspired by external "Western pressures," for example, those that could normalize relations with Israel. In general, the PJD parliamentary activities were often shaped by religious concerns. Their representatives presented a bill to forbid production, sale, export, and consumption of alcoholic beverages in Morocco.

They voted against the draft bill on loans and called for a change in the banking system due to concerns over usury (al-riba). However, the official position of the party would not preclude occasional and informal statements by party leaders that were more flexible on issues like the sale of alcohol.

New Regime Strategies and the Growth of PJD (2002–2010)

In the first legislative elections under Mohammed VI[25] in 2002, PJD widely expanded its seats in parliament and became the third-ranked party after the USFP (center-left) and the Party of Istiqlal (PI) (center-right).[26] Five years later, in 2007, the party increased its seats again from forty-two to forty-six, but without achieving many of the objectives identified by the leadership. During both the 2002–2006 and the 2007–2011 legislative periods, PJD experimented with the balance between its ideology and political pragmatism, and faced a number of political and policy challenges from the regime designed to weaken the party's political impact.

By 2002, PJD legislators were not applying ideological considerations in a consistent manner to all draft bills. As PJD became more and more integrated into the system, its emphasis on religious issues decreased, consistent with the arguments of this volume. This could, in part, be interpreted as part of the goal of normalizing its presence in Moroccan politics, but it was also a response to the political environment following the May 16, 2003, terrorist attacks in Casablanca, which put additional public constraints on the behavior of PJD. Under pressure to compromise on several bills, most notably the reform of the family code and the anti-terror law, the PJD Islamists demonstrated their ability to adapt their strategies to new political circumstances.

Normalization and the Reform of the Family Code

Beginning in the early 1990s, the reform of the legal system became the most important issue for the Moroccan women's movement. By 1993, women had gained several victories in the reform of the family code (moudawana). For example, a marriage contract now required the consent and signature of the bride. However, reform was still quite limited. When

Mohammed VI took the throne in 1999, debates about women's issues and the reform of the moudawana became increasingly public.[27] The new king showed a greater interest in addressing human rights issues and improving the status of women. In the same spirit, the government of alternance led by the USFP presented a plan for integration of women in social and economic development. This plan addressed most of the issues raised by the nation's women's associations. The reforms introduced in this plan were subject to heated political discussions, which triggered a national debate because they touched on issues of Islamic law. In reaction to the government action plan on the family code, PJD, in collaboration with other factions such as al-Adl wal-Ihsane, organized mass rallies against the reforms. Simultaneously, liberal women's NGOs organized smaller demonstrations in favor of the reforms.

After this initial reform attempt proved unsuccessful as a result of conservative opposition from the traditional ulama and the Islamists, Mohammed VI and then prime minister Abderrahman Youssoufi met with representatives of women's organizations in March 2001. The king announced the creation of a royal committee to consider reform of the family law. After two and a half years, the committee submitted a report to the king. In October 2003, in a speech before the nation, the king announced the reforms aimed at improving the status of women and redressing their unequal status in marital laws.[28] The changes were presented via a religious discourse to lend them more legitimacy. The PJD reaction was very different compared to its earlier reaction in response to the plan of action under Hassan II. Vice general secretary Dr. Saad Eddine Othmani declared to the Moroccan newspaper *Al-Ayyam*, "the general outline of the royal speech is positive and will have a positive effect on some of the problems that families confront. The reforms combined the concern of giving equal rights to women with giving the family its due role."[29] In the same way, Ahmed Raissouni, one of the MUR leaders, declared in a public conference that the reforms announced by the king were not in contradiction with Islamic norms.

The PJD reaction to the king's discourse was similar to that adopted by other political parties with different ideological backgrounds. The ideological disagreements that characterized the discussion of this issue were bypassed when the monarchy took direct control of the issue. This reveals the capacity of the regime to make different political players obey the rules of the game. The change in the position of the Islamists should also be understood in the context of the 2003 Casablanca terrorist attacks, which put PJD and its supporters under suspicion for any sympathies with the bombers. The Islamists who initially opposed reform of the family code were not able to voice much opposition because of their vulnerable political situation. In addition, the king's role as Commander of the Faithful[30] was responsible for giving these reforms more strength and religious legitimacy.

Despite the political constraints that the Islamists faced in the discussion of the proposed family code, they presented fifty-three amendments, of which twenty-six were ultimately adopted. Most of the amendments touched on the "formulation" of the text, not its actual content. The proposed family code contained 400 articles, of which 116 had been discussed and amended or changed. Despite the fact that PJD accepted the code because it came down from the monarchy, their representatives still introduced a few amendments. This highlights the PJD ability to adapt without appearing to give up on its core values. The party sought to find a measure of space to maneuver in order to provide input into the decision-making process.

The Anti-Terror Law: Concessions for Survival

Morocco had been known as a safe and peaceful place and its people for their tolerance. This image was shattered with the suicide bombings that rocked Casablanca on May 16, 2003 and took more than forty lives. These bombings were the first and most violent terrorist attacks in its history. On May 21, 2003, the government pushed for adoption of an anti-terror law including prerogatives that arguably constitute a threat to the civil rights of Moroccans.[31] PJD Islamists chose to cooperate with the law, despite reservations.

The debate about the anti-terror law actually started before the attacks took place. The parliament convened an extraordinary session in February 2003 and the government presented a draft bill, discussed in the Justice and Human Rights legislative committee. Before May 16, the Islamists were in a position of strength with their forty-two elected MPs. They criticized the law as presented by the minister of justice and were ready to oppose it. However, the terrorist attacks constrained their action. The attacks had led to a new environment of fear and contempt for any form of radicalism. The regime and other political actors took this opportunity to use discourse that created fear of Islamists and to revive sentiments of skepticism toward political Islam in general.

Quickly, the position of the PJD Islamists changed from rejection to acceptance of the anti-terror law. In their discussion of the law, they decided not to present amendments. The leader of the parliamentary group, Abdallah Baha, explained in a speech before the plenary session that their position regarding the anti-terror law was the result of three considerations. First, PJD wanted to send a clear message to the terrorists that Moroccans held a unified front in their fight against terrorism, and they did so under the guidance of the monarch, Mohammed VI. Second, PJD wanted to show that it had nothing to do with terrorist groups. Third, PJD voted for the anti-terror law with some reservations, particularly those that it viewed as contradicting human rights.

The different strategies adopted by PJD members in parliament during this legislature show their ability to adapt to changing political circumstances while obeying the rules established by the regime. In their reaction to the reform of the family code, they confirmed, as other political actors in the system do, the supremacy of the monarchical institution and its role as arbiter. Their reaction to the anti-terror law demonstrates that Islamists as much as any political actors must make concessions to be part of the political game. Despite the fact that the May 16 attacks constrained the Islamists, their pragmatism and flexibility enabled them to survive politically.

Regime Attempts to Marginalize PJD: Creation of PAM

The survival of PJD and its capacity to maintain its constituency despite its evolving positions appeared as a challenge to the regime. Indeed, by 2006 the regime was concerned with another, potentially more dramatic PJD electoral success in the 2007 legislative elections. A survey conducted by the International Republican Institute (IRI) in Morocco in 2006 that predicted PJD could win 47 percent of the votes helped reinforce regime feelings of insecurity.[32] Thus, according to some observers, the regime opted for the creation of its own political party, the Party of Authenticity and Modernity (Hizb al-Asaleh wa al-Hadatheh; PAM), to compete directly with PJD in the electoral field and thus limit its influence.

There are a number of explanations regarding the emergence of PAM in Moroccan politics.[33] Some analysts contend that PAM was created to counter the rise of the Islamists in Moroccan politics. In effect, since the election of Fouad Ali El Himma of PAM (a close friend of the monarch and more recently his political advisor) in the 2007 legislative elections, he has not hesitated to declare PJD as his principal political adversary. PAM's political program denounced the instrumentalization of Islam in politics, contending it was a "threat against Moroccan national unity and spiritual peace of its people." This position as an "adversary of the PJD"[34] was followed by personal attacks, defamations, and serious accusations by the leaders of both political parties. Abdelilah Benkirane declared in June 2010 that only four parties should contest elections in Morocco: Istiqlal, USFP, the Independent Party, and PJD—clearly excluding PAM, which it considered a "newborn" or "intruder."[35] This expression in reference to PAM was, in fact, also used by most established parties such the USFP and the Istiqlal.

The main objective of the creation of PAM was to maintain an institutional configuration in which PJD remains only one player among a divided political field, a fragmented field that has little chance of altering the status quo without the express consent of the monarchy.[36] The entrance of the PAM's Fouad Ali El Himma to the parliament influenced political alliances, and allowed PAM to pull together a large parliamentary caucus that negated the perceived PJD threat. El Himma initiated different actions through PAM to confront any real or perceived "threats" against the stability and continuity of the regime. The project of PAM was, however, soon going to be confronted by the Arab Spring and its manifestation in Morocco via the February 20 movement. The constitutional reforms that emerged in response to the movement helped pave the way for the largest PJD electoral success to date.

The February 20 Movement, Constitutional Reforms, and the 2011 Elections

Beginning in the late 1990s, Moroccan parties began to include a predominantly domesticated elite that gradually developed into consistent supporters of the monarchy's political agenda. It is in this context of discredited political parties that the February 20 (2011) movement emerged to call for nationwide protests demanding major political changes, including reform of the constitution. It is referred to as the February 20 movement because on that day between 150,000 and 200,000 Moroccans in fifty-three cities across Morocco took to the streets to call for democracy and change symbolized by the slogan "the people want a new constitution" (*al-shai'b uridu dusturan jadid*). Inspired by the Arab Spring and making use of Internet and social media such as Facebook, thousands of young Moroccans supported the movement and became active in the protests. The movement can be seen also as a reaction to the persistent problems in Moroccan politics, and was successful in mobilizing so many in part due to the active role civil society has played for at least two decades.[37] The demonstration effect of other uprisings associated with the Arab Spring added more weight to the movement and subsequently energized a dormant Moroccan political field.

The February 20 movement was made up of people from different ideological orientations who oppose the authoritarian nature of the palace, including many youth and elderly people who did not associate themselves with political parties or associations. The movement was also not well organized and lacked a clearly identifiable leadership. The protesters called for more social equality and improvement to social welfare services, health, education, and housing, but also for major political reforms. Some of the major demands included a more democratic constitution that makes popular sovereignty the basis of rule in Morocco, an independent judiciary, and separation of powers.[38] According to the movement, the "king should reign but not rule." The protesters also called for freedom of the press and independent media. More immediate and specific concerns include the end of nepotism and the dismissal of corrupt government or security officials responsible for human rights abuses.

As the February 20 movement increased demands for political reform, PJD benefited due to its long-standing reputation as interested in pushing for greater reform, but in conjunction with the palace. PJD found the new context of popular mobilization an opportunity to convince the regime it could be trusted to support the regime's interests in an uncertain political environment. As the palace led plans for limited constitutional reforms, few parties could credibly challenge the monarchy's approach, demonstrating their acquiescence to palace leadership on this issue. Among others, PJD called on Moroccans to vote "yes" on the constitution submitted to referendum on July 1, 2011. Secretary general Abdelilah Benkirane declared repetitively, in both newspapers and press interviews, that he supports a monarchy that both reigns and governs. For him, a monarchy following the Spanish or British model is not a convenient alternative for Morocco because of the role of the monarch as arbiter and as *amir al mu'minin*. The unconditional support of many PJD leaders for the initiatives of the monarchy resulted initially in some internal conflicts and divisions. Moustapha Ramid, one of the most respected PJD leaders, did not support the decision of his party to avoid the marches of the February 20 movement.[39] Some PJD members decided to take part in the protests as individuals, though not with the sanction of the party.

It appears that within the regime there are those who supported Islamists' increased participation in the formal institutional framework, while there were others who sought to block their participation. As one interviewee from the leadership of PJD put it, "we were not successful in establishing channels of communication to voice our concerns and ideas directly to the monarch."[40] For this member of PJD, "there was a lack of communication between the palace and the Islamists of the PJD and this is creating confusion and sometimes tensions."[41] After the results of the November 2011 elections it appeared that this confusion had ceased to exist and that the palace was now strategically more ready to open the space of government for the Islamists as they represented the plurality vote.

On November 25, 2011, PJD won a historic election by obtaining 107 of 395 legislative seats, a position that gave the party the right to lead the Moroccan government. As a result of the new constitutional reforms, Mohamed VI had to appoint the head of government from the party that held the majority seats in the parliament. The PJD success in these elections was in fact good news for both the party and the makhzan. For PJD, this was what it had been looking for since integration into the political system. The PJD has progressively increased its support from 9 seats in 1997, to 42 seats in 2002, 47 seats in 2007, and ultimately 107 seats in 2011. This electoral success also epitomizes its long evolution toward political integration and normalization. According to official state records, voter turnout was 45.4 percent in what was widely regarded as a free and fair election, a meaningful increase from 37 percent in 2007.

Why did PJD perform so well in 2011? It was not simply because of the voters' religious identification with the party. Rather, a large number of Moroccans are searching for an alternative given the failure of previous parties. In support of one argument of this volume, the PJD 2011 electoral success is in large part a protest vote at the lack of meaningful alternatives and the slow pace of change. The fact that PJD was in the "opposition" to the existing government facilitated its reputation as a protest party. The positive reputation of the PJD leadership has also allowed it to become a more trusted party, which is less associated with the problems of mainstream parties. As Abdelilah Benkirane, head of PJD and current head of government, put it after the election, voters "are clearly rejecting the past policies by picking a former opposition party."[42] While PJD supported constitutional reforms, some members, including the newly nominated minister of justice, were marching with the February 20 movement. The symbolic association of PJD with the movement ultimately played in its favor.

In addition, the party focused in its campaign on social issues with broad voter appeal that relate to the fight against both corruption and high unemployment. During the 2011 campaign, the party said that it would create about 240,000 jobs, cut poverty in half, and raise the minimum wage by 50 percent. On December 3, 2011, ten PJD members took up the functions of ministers as a result of a coalition government that included the conservative PI, as well as the Popular Party and a leftist party known as Hizb al-Takadum wa al-Ishtirakia (Party of Progress and Socialism). The fact that Morocco ended up with a government comprised of Islamists as well as nationalists, center-right, and leftists is not only revealing about the process of normalization that has gradually characterized PJD but also reflects the reality that much Moroccan political power remains outside the control of parliament. Following the decision by the nationalist party to drop out of the government coalition in September 2013, the new government now included the Hizb al-Ahrar (Party of Independents), initially a close ally to PAM, and a group of technocrat ministers clearly parachuted into government through palace pressures. PJD put its members into positions at the heads of key ministries including the Ministry of Justice and the Foreign Ministry, although the Foreign Ministry was retaken in October 2013 by the head of the Party of Independents.

PJD success in Moroccan politics will depend largely on how the party does on two fronts. First is how well it provides meaningful social and economic change for ordinary Moroccans, including tackling corruption. This is a major task the party so far not only has been incapable of dealing with, but has started to manage expectations around, arguing that reforms will take a substantial period of time. Second, success also depends on the party's ability to carve out an independent political space vis-à-vis the palace, where much of the power and decision-making remains today. On this front, as well, PJD will find it hard to demonstrate that it is not subservient to palace politics and is genuinely responsive to the will of the people who voted for the party.

Conclusion

The case of the Moroccan PJD supports a large number of the arguments introduced in this volume, including those articulated in Chapter 1. First, participation over time has led PJD to gradually deprioritize the religious content of its platform. Although that content has not disappeared, it has become less front-and-center over time as the party has focused increasingly on more universal and centrist political concerns. Second, PJD appears to have a dual constituency, those that vote for it for religious reasons, and those that vote for it within the broader context of its political positions vis-à-vis other parties and the regime. This is most prominent in the 2011 elections, when PJD more than doubled its number of seats, drawing largely on protest voters, including many supporters of the February 20 movement that has led demonstrations against the existing regime. Third, PJD has become less distinct from other Moroccan political parties over time, particularly as it has been increasingly co-opted into the regime and is required to support such policies as the revised family code and anti-terror law. Fourth, the Moroccan regime has shown its increasing willingness to accommodate PJD, particularly in 2011, as the party has sought to demonstrate its loyalty to the premises of the monarchical regime. PJD's full integration into the Moroccan political system makes the party's exit from the system highly improbable, although there is the clear potential for more ideological Islamic challengers to emerge, either from PJD or in opposition to PJD from other Islamic movements such as Al-Adl wal-Ihsane.

The popularity and success of PJD in Morocco cannot be explained by voters' affinity for an Islamic identity, religious interests, or concerns over moral values alone. While PJD has never done away with Islamic symbolism, and while it has included in its program Islam-specific issues such as a call to promote Islamic finance, the source of its popularity lies elsewhere. It is intimately connected to its participation within a constrained monarchical political system, and its history of moderate opposition. PJD has often sought to cater to the interests of mainstream Moroccan voters, and

to appear moderate in its ideological preferences. Soon after the 2011 electoral results, one of the key figures and current minister of foreign affairs
reassured Moroccans in an interview that "as far as alcohol is concerned, I
need to remind you that it is PJD that had forced the government to raise
taxes on its sale. Some people have told me that it is *haram* (forbidden
by Islam) to do it and I responded that I am not a *faqih* (cleric). I am here
to increase the revenues of the state. Morocco is a country that is historically open to the world. We are ready to apply the Canadian law about
alcohol in Morocco. Banning alcohol will not resolve the problem because
the Moroccans who like to drink will anyways get it or even make it
themselves."[43]

As we have tried to show here, while there are objective factors for the
PJD success, it also became politically important for the regime to allow
PJD to take part in the government to help manage potentially more serious
political challenges (such as from the February 20 movement). In fact,
allowing PJD to take power is consistent with the classic makhzan logic of
recycling the Moroccan political elite. In this sense, one of the very reasons
PJD became successful (co-opted into a constrained system) might ultimately contribute to its failure in the long term. We need to keep in mind
that its survival and mainstream political success was in significant ways
determined by its strategy of making concessions to the regime, a reality
that did not change with the 2011 elections. As members of the government, PJD has already been perceived as submissive to the palace, and critics in different Moroccan newspapers have started to raise issues about this
submissive relationship, a reality that applies to all other parties as well, but
will contribute this time to the gradual waning of PJD popularity. In the
long term, it is possible that government participation by PJD could
encourage more radical currents.

Indeed, the political behavior of PJD and its acceptance of a government
that is not completely drawn from the electoral process shows its political
vulnerability and illustrates that in the constrained and politically fragmented context of Morocco, political parties of all ideologies gradually turn
into instruments of the regime and ultimately lose their credibility. Ironically, even though the party seeks to play by the rules of the game, it might
not sufficiently reassure a regime that has a long history of maintaining its
control by manipulating and co-opting its opposition. Regardless of the
willingness of PJD to normalize its political participation, from the perspective of palace politics, it remains potentially threatening especially because

it relies in competing ways on parallel religious "symbolic capital" that has served the monarchy for ages and that has become its "special domain" (*domaine reservé*) since the start of its modern political history.

In the absence of a real democratic constitution and popular sovereignty, PJD, like the PI, USFP, or Independent Party before it, is more likely to remain an instrument in the hands of an authoritarian makhzan in constant quest to maintain its own survival. In the words of Ahmed Snoussi, the most popular Moroccan political humorist, who is informally banned from public shows because of his political views, "Morocco has turned out to have a political system that is more like a *democtature*." Constitutionally, the monarch remains the country's most powerful figure with political, military, judiciary, and religious powers and neither PJD nor any other major political party is at this point willing to seriously challenge that power. Whether the first PJD foray into government leadership will increase or decrease the party's power over time is an open question.

Chapter 6

Mapping the Terrain of Reform in Yemen:
Islah over Two Decades

STACEY PHILBRICK YADAV

In words that captured well the Yemeni Islah party's trajectory over more than two decades, a member of the party's consultative council once explained that the typical Islamist in Yemen "does not come in any one color, but is always open to change."[1] The notion that Yemeni Islamists affiliated with Islah vary widely in their ideologies and methods has been borne out by twenty-three years of vibrant political practice, against a backdrop of authoritarian regime encroachment and, ultimately, regime transition. This variation was made evident from the outset, in an intra-Islamist debate over whether to participate in Yemen's post-unification political institutions, in differences over how to relate to the regime once elected, and most recently in deep cleavages related to the formation of a cross-ideological alliance of opposition parties. Islah also played a role in Yemen's 2011 "Change Revolution," and is now a member of the transitional unity government and a dominant figure in the National Dialogue Conference. Whether serving as junior partner in alliance with the ruling party in the 1990s, leading the formal opposition in the 2000s, or contributing to post-conflict conciliation today, Islah's flexibility has enabled it to remain at the center of Yemeni political life for more than two decades.

This flexibility is owed in part to the role of internal cleavages in the Islamist movement, particularly in its most visible institutional expression, the Yemeni Congregation for Reform (Islah, or the Islah party). While internal factionalism makes it difficult to identify unitary Islahi "party positions," the lessons derived from Islah's practice from Yemen's unification in 1990 to the present sheds light on some core assumptions about the dynamic effects of Islamist parliamentary participation, for Islamists themselves and for the broader political field. In particular, Islah's experience highlights the dual direction of change brought about through Islamist participation in formal political institutions, and poses a challenge to linear expectations of Islamist "moderation." Party discourse has had a powerful effect on Yemen's political vocabulary and has contributed to major shifts in what Yemenis view as politically desirable and pragmatically possible. At the same time, internal balance among factions and external alliances with other partisan and extrapartisan actors and organizations have been transformed along the way.

As this chapter will demonstrate, over the last two decades of parliamentary participation, factions in Islah have gained and lost political power, within the party itself and in the broader political field. Indeed, Islah's experience suggests that the nature of the political interlocutors with whom Islamists compete has mattered considerably for the content of Islamist party activism. Factions have negotiated their internal positions in the party by investing in important extrapartisan institutions and cross-ideological alliances. This practice became even more pronounced in the mid-2000s, once the triangular balance of power that characterized the party's internal dynamics throughout the 1990s gave way to a more bipolar distribution of power (and ideology) within the party. This has begun to reverse itself again in the wake of the momentous events of 2011, further illustrating the fluid and nonlinear nature of the party's ideological composition and the impact of its practical choices, which together make the case of Islamism in Yemen so interesting and potentially elucidatory.

While it is difficult to write about Islah, or Yemen more generally, during a period of substantial transition and political restructuring, what can be said today is that the process of participation and competition with ideological others has undeniably shaped the content and practice of the Islah party. Alliance-formation and cross-ideological networks have strengthened factions, but also exacerbated existing tensions between them. Relationships with actors and organizations outside the party have shaped the balance of power within it, leaving a clear mark on its discourse and practice. Thus, to say that "the party" has been responsive to the structural constraints it has confronted in the face of declining pluralism at the national level is undoubtedly true, but also obscures the elemental characteristic of Islah—its internal factionalism—in determining what "the party" stands for or pursues at any given moment.

This chapter will trace the transformation of the Islah party through three distinctive periods in its development. First, it will examine the period at the point of unification between North and South Yemen, when the existing Islamist movement in the North debated and ultimately decided to participate in newly unified Yemen's electoral system, even while expressing considerable skepticism about the concept of *hizbiyya*, or partisanship. This section will also discuss the implications of Islah's strong showing in the 1993 polls, and its role in the brief 1994 civil war. Second, the chapter will detail Islah's decision to work in partnership with the ruling General People's Congress in the latter half of the decade. The chapter will then trace the decline of that relationship and discuss Islah's role in both the growth and limitations of the opposition alliance known as the Joint Meeting Parties (JMP). This last section includes a brief discussion of Islah's role during and after the 2011 Change Revolution and the party's return to government through the transitional agreement brokered by the Gulf Cooperation Council (GCC). The chapter concludes with an evaluation of some of this volume's central organizing questions.

The periodization of Islah's history in this chapter is designed to be both descriptive and explanatory. It allows for in-case comparison of an Islamist party in government and in opposition, requiring an account of the discursive and practical shifts party members have undertaken to justify these different roles. The chapter illustrates how Islamists in Yemen serve multiple constituencies, mobilizing support on the basis of ideological appeal and as a form of protest against the prevailing political order. This is made particularly evident in the discussion of the JMP and the Change Revolution. At the same time, the chapter explores the ways speaking to multiple constituencies can create important tensions within the party and among its allies. As Islahi centrists have downplayed ideological considerations to cement an alliance with different kinds of Islamists, secularists, and Leftists, they have been met with a strong backlash by a Salafi faction within the party. While this tension has most often been expressed at the margins of the partisan system (and thus should remind scholars to attend to the important role of the informal, even in analysis of formal institutions), it has not prevented Islah from sustaining (and even expanding) its role in Yemen's formal political system. This suggests that one of the most marked effects of Islamist party activism is the durable investment in the state and its institutions that sustained participation helps to generate. As a representative of the political opposition in the transitional process and a well-represented party at the National Dialogue Conference that aims to restructure Yemen's formal political system, Islah is today more heavily invested in the formal political process than ever before.

Mapping the Islamist Terrain in Contemporary Yemen

Locating Islamism in contemporary Yemen entails navigating distinctions based on ideology but also based on sectarian and regional identities, and a history of class politics among Yemen's Muslim majority.[2] All this is laid against the backdrop of differing institutional histories in the Yemen Arab Republic (YAR), or North Yemen, and the People's Democratic Republic of Yemen (PDRY), or South Yemen. Yemen's Muslim population has historically been divided between Zaydi Shi'a and adherents to the Sunni legal school of Imam al-Shafa'i, with Zaydis concentrated most heavily in the far North. In the 1970s and 1980s, Yemen witnessed the expansion of a Salafi form of Islam, promoting a kind of "generic Sunnism which claimed to be non-sectarian."[3] This new ideology has competed for and won loyalties in more established Shafi'i and Zaydi communities through grassroots activism, educational outreach, and the offer of a kind of emancipatory equality in a highly stratified society.[4]

In the context of the formal political system, however, Islamists have been represented largely (though not exclusively) by the Yemeni Congregation for Reform. As a political party, Islah has brought together Salafis, Shafi'i Sunnis, and even some Zaydis who are mobilized less by Zaydi concerns than by social conservatism associated with the tribal system. The relative weight and meaning of each of these groups has shifted over time in response to a number of considerations, outlined in the sections that follow.

Islamism Prior to Yemeni Unification

Organized Islamism in Yemen was historically interwoven with an explicitly nationalist politics, tracing at least to 1939, with the foundation of Muhammed al-Zubayri's "First Batallion," and expanding through cooperation with and participation in the nationalist "Free Yemeni" movement in 1944.[5] The ecumenical idioms of nationalism were able to partially bridge the sectarian divisions in Yemen, a fusion enabled in part by a 1946 meeting of Yemeni figures brokered by the Egyptian founder of the Muslim Brotherhood, Hassan al-Banna, who had been able to achieve much the same Islamo-nationalist synthesis in his local context.[6] At the same time, nationalism never fully masked distinctions among Muslims over the nature of the ideal political order. As Sheila Carapico has noted, organizations like Hay'at al-Amr bi-l-Ma'ruf wa l-Nahi 'An al-Munkar or Hay'at al-Nidal were "also about competing visions of Islam—Zaydi and Shafi'i, old-guard and modernist, elitist and popular."[7]

Amid the political upheavals of revolution and civil war, particularly in the North, conflicts over Islamic doctrine and practice unfolded between and within communities. Between Zaydi and Shafi'i Muslims, the distinction related to different beliefs over the right to rule, and was tied to the dissolution of the Zaydi imamate following the 1967 revolution. The emergence of the Salafi trend in recent decades has complicated the simple Zaydi/Shafi'i distinction by perpetuating a kind of nondenominational Sunnism that has attracted adherents from both Zaydi and Shafi'i families, not only because of its substantive ideological appeal, but also because it has offered new adherents a means of escaping certain hierarchies of power and privilege in existing communities.[8] In particular, in the Zaydi community, which affords political legitimacy and communal authority to a narrow set of descendants of the Prophet Muhammed, the *sada* (sing. *sayyid*, descendent of the Prophet) have historically enjoyed considerable social privilege and practiced an exclusive form of endogamy that has alienated many in and outside the community.[9] This has been used to explain what might otherwise seem to be a counterintuitive Zaydi "defection" to Salafi communities of believers.

As an institutional accompaniment to this process, resources from the Saudi government, particularly during the 1970s and 1980s, allowed for the proliferation of Salafi "scientific institutes" and other organizations throughout the Northern part of the country (the former YAR), which helped the Salafi movement to expand.[10] Salafi irregulars were essential allies of the Northern regime in its battle against the leftist National Democratic Front (NDF), and while Saudi financial support for Yemeni Salafis began in this context, it extended well after the decline of the NDF.[11]

In the South, the Marxist government of the PDRY offered no parallel support for and deliberately enacted barriers against the proliferation of such institutes or related organizations. However, Islamist idiom—albeit in an anticolonial Islamo-nationalist form—was never entirely erased in the South, though it faced severe challenges under both British and Marxist rule. Exiled leaders of the Free Yemeni movement established a Southern branch of their organization as the Greater Yemeni Association (GYA), and the comparative press freedom of the British period (as compared with the Zaydi imamate in the North) allowed them to publish a newspaper, *Sawt al-Yaman* (The Voice of Yemen). Its "Islamism" was strikingly nationalist, as with the Free Yemeni movement more generally, combining anticolonial and constitutionalist critiques with a call for fraternity among Muslims "guided by the Book of God and His greatest Prophet."[12] Eventually, this kind of oblique reference to the mobilizational potential of Islam was deemed too threatening to British interests and the GYA was dissolved.[13]

Following the rise of the Marxist government in the South in 1967, the climate for Islamist activism declined farther, with the PDRY government taking steps to limit use of Islamic idiom and references in public life. As historian Paul Dresch notes, "religion was treated by the Party as something that would one day disappear and Islam viewed as at best a primitive form of socialism."[14] As a consequence of this attitude, new legal codes were introduced to diminish or erase the imprint of Islamic law, which had been protected (if modified) by British rule.[15] As one Adeni human rights activist recalls, Islamist activists were suppressed under Marxist rule. "There were individual *shaykhs*, but no organizational frameworks. To even think of [Islamist organizing] was impossible."[16]

Prior to the unification of the PDRY and the YAR in 1990, therefore, Islamists in general and Salafis in particular lacked formal institutional expression within the organs of either state, though there were more opportunities to pursue Islamist objectives in the North through informal ties to regime figures and via the education system. While both states were governed as single-party revolutionary regimes, the YAR General People's Congress (GPC) functioned as a big tent, in which multiple "trends" eventually competed in internal elections. It is out of the experience of intraparty elections that post-unification Islamist politics emerged. One of the major political trends in the GPC in North Yemen was clearly identifiable as Islamist, with a Muslim Brotherhood-influenced orientation, and prominent Salafi figures like Shaykh ʿAbd al-Majid al-Zindani were also active figures.[17] It was from this foundation that Islah ultimately developed.

Islamists in the Republic of Yemen

With the legalization of multiparty competition following unification of North and South in 1990, Islamists debated the desirability of forming political parties to compete in the scheduled elections for Yemen's parliament. Three Islamist parties ultimately won seats in the first parliamentary election in 1993: Hizb al-Haqq (Party of Truth), the Union of Popular Forces (UPF), and the Yemeni Congregation for Reform.

The first of these, Hizb al-Haqq, is a Zaydi Islamist party with a constituency drawn mainly from provinces to the north of Sanaa, in the Zaydi highlands. Al-Haqq secured two seats in the 1993 election, but has failed to win seats since then, as the political dynamics of party competition have shifted and explicit Zaydi identification has become complicated by the Zaydi-led (and infused) al-Huthi uprising in the Northern province of Saada beginning in 2004. That said, in recognition of the significance of the Zaydi community, al-Haqq members have on occasion held ministerial appointments, even when they have lacked representation in parliament. As a small but symbolically significant party, al-Haqq is included in the JMP opposition alliance, bringing it into close contact with Islah.

The UPF is not widely considered an "Islamist" party in the conventional sense, but is rather seen as a party vehicle for the advancement of a particular Yemeni family, that of Ibrahim al-Wazir. Dresch notes of the UPF in the period immediately following unification, "they were not a plausible electoral power, but the al-Wazirs produce admirable books and pamphlets and they gained positions on committees of several kind."[18] One of the principal UPF leaders, Dr. Muhammed 'Abd al-Malik al-Mutawakkil, is a leading public intellectual and professor with a progressive Zaydi Islamist orientation. He has played an essential role in the JMP since its inception, helping to narrow the gap between Islah and its rival, the Yemeni Socialist Party, by emphasizing notions of good governance common to the member parties.[19] While Al-Mutawakkil's prominence has declined as Yemen's sectarian politics have become more polarized, he is still held in high regard by many of the Muslim Brotherhood faction within Islah in particular, and helps retain UPF significance, despite its minimal electoral impact.

In comparison to al-Haqq and the UPF, Islah is unquestionably the most significant Islamist party in Yemen. For two decades, its changing relationship to the regime of President 'Ali 'Abdullah Saleh served as a metric of the broader openness of the political system and a means of measuring the decline in pluralism from unification to the present. As the only party in the JMP alliance with a genuinely national constituency and the ability to mobilize large crowds of supporters, Islah has also exerted a considerable influence on the internal dynamics of the political opposition, up to and during the transitional period.

Islah's formal name, the Yemeni Congregation for Reform, itself reveals a great deal about the internal dynamics of the party (and, later, the alliance), revealing party leaders' preference for avoiding, rather than resolving, contentious issues of ideology. The name itself can be attributed to a debate among Islamists at the point of unification regarding the acceptability and desirability of *hizbiyya*. Acceptance of *hizbiyya* signals the fundamental legitimacy of organizing and participating in the kind of formal, competitive (and thereby potentially divisive) politics that produces winners and losers. Among those who reject *hizbiyya*, it is also tied to the concept of *tahazub* (bigotry), insofar as partisan affiliation may constitute an unfounded favoritism toward some members of the *umma* over others. Those opposed to *hizbiyya* do not necessarily reject political activism per se, but have favored more explicitly social and religious channels. In the context of the debate among Yemeni Islamists at the point of unification, some Salafis were reconciled to the concept, others rejected *hizbiyya* and retreated from political life altogether, and others have continued to engage in what we might call "lobbying" through a variety of more or less influential organizations of ulama peripheral to the formal political system.[20]

This debate over *hizbiyya* became the first issue onto which Islah's emerging internal divisions were grafted.[21] The Muslim Brotherhood trend in the movement was already politically active under the GPC umbrella, and embraced the opportunity to compete in free elections. Some tribal shaykhs and Salafi clerics, however, worried about the limiting effects and potential divisiveness of a system that produced clear winners and losers. As Islah's general secretary 'Abd al-Wahhab al-'Ainsi explained, the decision to name the organization a "congregation" (*tagammu'*) was driven by this conflict. "We had a long internal discussion, especially over the name of the party. We wanted to avoid any negative or divisive terms," particularly those that would invoke the Manichean distinction between *hizb Allah* and *hizb al-Shaytan*, the Party of God and the Party of Satan, a distinction rooted in the Qur'an.[22] Instead, the language of congregation, of gathering together, was designed to emphasize what the members of the organization had in common, as opposed to what divided them from each other and from other Yemenis. This has been reinforced by careful discipline among most of the party's leadership, who are careful to avoid the more colloquial phrase *hizb al-Islah* in official statements, though the term is used by many Islahis in casual conversation.

The ambiguous relationship toward pluralism reflected in the *hizbiyya* debate has also found expression in the JMP alliance, driven in large part by Islahi preferences and the relative weaknesses of the smaller parties that are at odds with Islah on substantive political issues. The dynamics of this alliance are detailed more thoroughly below, but it is worth noting that the general emphasis on what is common or shared—at the expense of engagement with points of substantive disagreement—is a practical approach Islahi leaders adopted from the outset and carried into the opposition politics of the 2000s, as well.

Islah as Regime Ally: 1993–2000

The 1990s were years during which Islah functioned largely as a partner to the ruling GPC and aided in the consolidation of Saleh's regime, though the nature of this partnership changed considerably over the course of the decade. This partnership should be viewed as tactical, not strategic, insofar as it reflected a logic of cooperation driven by a shared desire by the GPC and Islah to limit the influence of the Yemeni Socialist Party, but was not rooted in any shared ideology uniting the two parties. At most, it reflected a convergence of regional power. Though the social base of Islah has changed somewhat over time, in the early 1990s, it was unquestionably a "Northern" party, though one with evangelical ambitions throughout the new country.[23]

The unity accord signed between the leaders of the PDRY and the YAR distributed power relatively equally between the leaders of the two former states. The parliaments were fused into one, pending new elections in 1993, and a five-member Presidential Council including both former presidents assumed the functions of the executive branch.[24] This agreement, while not proportional to the share of the population living in each part of the new country (which tilted roughly 3:1 in favor of the North), was designed to hold together leaders who were deeply skeptical of one another, each of whom hoped to expand his control at the expense of the other.[25] Despite this mutual suspicion, or perhaps because of it, unification was accompanied by adoption of laws governing the formation of parties, civic organizations, and media outlets that encouraged flourishing political activity by groups outside established frameworks, leading to the registration of more than twenty new political parties and hundreds of civic associations in the time between unification and the first election in 1993.[26]

It was on this exciting but uncertain terrain that Islah emerged as a viable third way, in contradistinction to the GPC and YSP. As the two former ruling parties vied for control over the institutions of the state, Islah contested unified Yemen's moral future, articulating an ideology that was more coherent than anything on offer from the GPC and could appeal to voters uncomfortable with (or hostile to) the YSP's secular Marxism. Even before unification was formalized on May 20, 1990, the man who would soon become the leader of Islah's Salafi wing, Shaykh 'Abd al-Majid al-Zindani, had begun his campaign against the godless YSP, calling on Yemenis to resist "the tiny group of pagans within the communist party of South Yemen, who have been influenced by an imported culture and stand disgraced before the Yemeni people."[27] Such allegations of "foreignness" were a powerful currency in Yemeni political discourse at the time, and Zindani himself was accused of owing "allegience to foreign parties," most notably Saudi Arabia. The fight to define the normative boundaries of legitimate national belonging was particularly acute around the time of unification, and it was a fight in which Islah quickly became a significant contender.

Having settled the internal issue of *hizbiyya*, Islahis now sought to frame their participation in the scheduled elections in ways that were both practical and ideologically consistent with the party's critique of the foreign/ imported, which meant avoiding wholesale adoption of the rhetoric of democracy. Like Islamist parties elsewhere, Islah's leaders did so by adopting and modifying a number of well-established Islamic concepts, the most important of which was the concept of *shura* (consultation), whereby the ruler is obliged to seek the council of his community. According to Islah's statement of principles, the party viewed parliament as "the practical instrument for representing the will of the people and concretizing the principle of *shura*."[28] The intellectual impetus behind the party came from the Muslim Brotherhood, which was more overtly comfortable with the language of democracy, but which lacked secure enough social foundations in or outside the party to proceed alone against the established power of the GPC or YSP in these early years. As a result, the Brotherhood built and

Table 6: Post-Unification Parliamentary Elections

Seats won/year	1993	1997	2003
GPC	123	188	238
YSP	56	—	8
Islah	62	53	46
Other	12	5	5
Independent	48	55	4

Source: 1993 and 1997 figures from Sheila Carapico, *The Political Economy of Activism in Modern Arabia* (Cambridge: Cambridge University Press, 1998): 149); 2003 figures from International Foundation for Electoral Systems (IFES) Election Guide, http://www.electionguide.org/.

maintained what had often been a strained and sometimes costly relationship with tribal traditionalists, preventing Salafi dominance within the party, but at some cost to its own prerogatives.[29]

Following the 1993 election, there was a marked shift in North-South representation in parliament, shaped by Islah's popularity at the polls. While the provisional parliament following unification included 159 MPs from the North and 111 from the South,[30] the 1993 elections produced a parliament in which nearly 80 percent of the MPs were drawn from constituencies of the former North.[31] The strategic withdrawal of candidates in the weeks leading to the elections helped confirm the suspicions of Southern political leaders that the GPC and Islah were coordinating in ways designed to produce Northern hegemony.[32] While YSP leaders attributed their comparatively poor performance to outright collusion between the two parties, some scholars have suggested that the electoral outcome highlights differences in the political cultures of North and South, with fluid alliance formation a more consistent and long-standing feature of Northern politicking.[33]

Whether collusion or realpolitik, Islah's success in the 1993 elections was a bitter disappointment to the YSP, which was displaced by the new party. Islah's showing offered the GPC an enticing opportunity to further marginalize its Southern rival. While the terms of the power-sharing agreement between the GPC and YSP continued to be honored at the presidential level, the parliamentary elections illustrated that the Presidential Council was overrepresenting the YSP.[34] The elections were thus a step toward dismantling the foundations of the unity agreement and consolidating Northern—and ultimately Saleh's—power. While Islah was brought

onto the council as a junior partner, the obvious disconnect between electoral outcomes and the composition of the council continued to elicit critical responses from Islahi leaders more than a decade later, prompting one
to characterize Islah's underrepresentation as a "sacrifice" the party was
willing to bear for the sake of national unity.[35] This sacrifice was viewed
quite differently among members of the YSP, who viewed Islah and the
GPC as two coordinated fronts in an effort to suppress the South.[36]

The Civil War and Its Aftermath

In addition to its formal integration into a power-sharing government,
there were informal ways in which Islahis worked with the GPC to curb
any substantial socialist influence in policymaking during the short interval
between the elections and the 1994 civil war. While this was by no means
the singular cause of the war, Islah's participation in government undoubtedly contributed to the decline in cooperation that resulted in the months-
long violence. Islahi clerics contributed directly, by issuing *fatwas* that justified vigilante violence against socialist apostates, and Islah's weekly paper,
as-Sahwa, contributed to the polarization of the political climate. During
the three months of the war, Islamist irregulars associated with Islah participated in looting and vigilante violence, primarily in the South.[37] This continued in the aftermath of the war. One ranking socialist party leader
recalls: "We lost all of our dreams after the war. I stayed at home for a full
year after that. We feared discrimination. People were scared, they barri-
caded themselves in their homes. People were informing on their neighbors, saying 'that's a socialist's house.' People think it's *hizb kafir,* and if you
marry one of your daughters to a socialist, then the whole family becomes a
family of *kufa*" (apostates).[38]

Immediately following the civil war, Islah was able to achieve its greatest
policy-related gains. With the YSP leadership in exile and its assets seized,
Islah's main ideological opponent was effectively neutralized. Islah's voice
in government expanded considerably, when Islahi 'Abd al-Wahhab al-
'Anisi was appointed deputy prime minister and the party's ministerial
portfolios increased from six to nine. But in the face of the YSP obsoles-
cence, Islah no longer had much to offer the GPC, and the Islamists saw
their influence decline at precisely the moment they had expected to be
ascendant.[39] From 1994 to 1997, Islah participated as a partner in a ruling

coalition with the GPC, and so had a front row seat from which to observe its own diminution of influence over and, ultimately, relevance to an increasingly authoritarian regime.

While the overall picture was one of declining pluralism, Islah nonetheless enjoyed two broad victories as a coalition partner, pressing for policy changes that had been strenuously resisted by the YSP before the war. The first was the final resolution of an ongoing debate regarding the place of shari'a in the constitution and in judicial practice. Following the war, the parliament quickly passed an amendment to the constitution that made shari'a the sole source of legislation, bringing it back in line with the Northern constitution of 1970, which itself had been shaped by some of the same Islamist figures now active in Islah.

This victory came at a cost, though at the time it appeared to be a cost Islah was willing to pay: the 1994 amendment to the constitution also abolished the five-member Presidential Council and reduced the executive to the person of the president, significantly extending his powers relative to the parliament and making provision for direct presidential elections.[40] Thus the parliament was doubly weakened by the amendment (in both substantive powers to legislate and procedural ability to influence the executive), but it may have increased somewhat in legitimacy among Islamist conservatives both North and South who favored redefinition of its legislative scope in keeping with shari'a.

This weakening of parliamentary capacity did not mean that parliament became irrelevant altogether. On the contrary, it provided a means of visibility for core Islah objectives. Parliament "provided a platform from which members of the Islah attacked the president on what they saw as his lack of commitment to an Islamization of Yemeni society."[41] Islah was able to block the president's effort to make Aden a free zone after the war as a means to attract foreign investment, and succeeded in passing legislation that would require nationwide Islamic banking practices, though the latter was eventually vetoed.[42] During this same period, parliament also served as site of budgetary oversight for members of all parties, and Islah was active in these debates. While later critics would complain that MPs needed to see that "oversight is much more than finding fault," it was a major first step,[43] and Islah's increasingly vocal articulation of an anticorruption position was the beginning of the alliance-building that found full expression in the JMP.

The second Islahi victory during this period was seen in its strengthened control over the Education Ministry. While Islah was awarded this ministry (and the Ministry of Awqaf, or religious endowments) before the war, the YSP had effectively checked the party's ability to enact some of its more conservative prerogatives. As Franck Mermier notes, "during the first phase of Unity (1990–1994), the Socialist party, which at that point was [still] capable of participating, had made the scientific institutes [tertiary religious schools] one of their principal themes in mobilization against the Islamists."[44] The marginalization of the YSP after 1994 enabled the party to more fully pursue the curricular independence of these institutes, as well as the increased Islamization of the curriculum in government schools. Both were viewed by party leaders as key components of Islah's evangelical ambitions.

For Socialists, secularists, and Southerners more generally, Islah's control of the Education Ministry meant the end of coeducation, the introduction of mandated veiling at all levels, and an increased role for traditional religious subjects in the curriculum, prompting some critics to claim that Islah's education plans "declared war on women's rights," and human rights more broadly. By immediately moving in 1994 to ban coeducation at all primary and secondary schools, Islah was seen by rights activists as creating a system whereby boys and girls were "unnaturally segregated" at a very early age.[45] By mandating the veil before puberty, another activist poignantly complained that "girls are losing their innocence and their childhood. When you tell them that they're a temptation in the eyes of boys, you sexualize them even at that early age. You turn them into animals."[46] These changes in the educational framework have not been reversed, despite substantial changes in Islah's priorities and the remarkable and visible role of several Islahi women activists.[47]

At the level of higher education, the ministry first suspended and then permanently closed the Philosophy and Social Science departments in 1996.[48] Islah's interest in comprehensive education was called into question, and these and other examples contributed to the climate of distrust and antagonism between members of Islah and the remnant of the YSP, in particular, and Leftists more generally. This was exacerbated by Islah's control over the scientific institutes, which focused on the teaching of Salafi-oriented *fiqh* (Islamic jurisprudence) and *usul al-din* (the fundamentals of the faith). Because of the declared importance of these institutes to Islah, the regime was able to manipulate the issue through its deputies in parliament, appearing to concede to Islahi demands, but nevertheless strengthening its own position. At the internal party congress for the GPC, members openly debated whether to support further development of the scientific institutes, a move interpreted by Islahi leaders as an effort to pressure Islah to abandon other objectives in exchange for GPC support. In particular, it was seen as an effort to blunt Islahis' increasingly vocal critique of government corruption. In this context, "the GPC threat was issued in order to pressure Islah and bring to a close the problem of the fraudulent acts that took place during the voter registration period [in the 1997 elections]."[49] Islahi leaders took heed of the warning. Schwedler notes that "a consensus emerged among former ministers and leaders of Islah that their biggest mistake had been trying to implement reforms too quickly, particularly in challenging corruption."[50]

In looking the other way on the registration issue to maintain support for the institutes, Islah at least temporarily abandoned its concern for political accountability in favor of a substantive gain in curricular autonomy. That said, this conflict and others were clear indications to Islah's leadership that their bargaining position within the governing coalition had decreased considerably with the departure of the YSP, and that they should begin looking for other means to ensure their survival and achieve their objectives. Islah ministers resigned one by one between 1995 and 1997, conceding that threatening the prerogatives of the ruling party was fruitless. Former ministers complained that "they were being prevented from taking steps to reduce corruption within their ministries" and this was partially confirmed when each resigning minister was replaced by a GPC loyalist.[51]

Regime Encroachment and Islah's Realignment

In many ways, Islah was doomed by its own success in driving the YSP out of the formal political system in the 1990s. The YSP leadership decision to boycott the 1997 parliamentary elections transformed a competition between three parties into a race between the GPC and Islah, in which one player had access (legitimate or not) to the resources of the state. Under conditions in which GPC candidates were able to make use of state funding, security protection, and media access, the 1997 election was a discernibly less fair fight than the 1993 elections had been, establishing a pattern of electoral manipulation that continued to intensify through subsequent elections, giving Yemen many of the characteristics of "competitive authoritarian" or "dominant power" systems.[52] Despite maintaining its position as the second-largest political party (and, given the nonideological nature of GPC, perhaps also the most ideologically salient), Islah has seen a decline in its share of votes in every election. While at least some of the reasons behind this decline have to do with the politics of Islah itself, structural considerations—most notably the decline of the YSP and the shift from trilateral to bilateral electoral competition—had a decisive impact on Islah's ability to pursue its policy objectives effectively.[53] This ineffectiveness, in turn, helped to make internal debates about the future of the party and its potential allies more pressing.

Following its electoral decline in 1997, Islah was therefore in a difficult position. Some within the party—particularly those associated with the Brotherhood circle—were already thinking about the need to work more closely with other parties to check the growing power of the GPC and the Saleh regime. Others, most notably the tribal cadre led by Shaykh 'Abdullah bin Hussein al-Ahmar, were concerned about alienating the country's power brokers by distancing themselves from the GPC more aggressively. This particular tension played out most evidently in the 1999 presidential election, in which Islah opted not to field an independent candidate, but rather to endorse Saleh's bid for reelection. Some alleged that this was a "trade"—that the regime allowed Islah to continue its influence in the educational sector, especially with the government's agreement to close a controversial university research center devoted to women's studies, but it is difficult to verify such claims with certainty.[54]

What *is* clear is that 1999 stands today as a turning point in the minds of many Islahis, and that the decision to endorse Saleh had ramifications for Islah's relationship to other parties and among its own members. In terms of its relationship to other parties, the endorsement of Saleh's reelection bid further undermined what little trust had developed between Islah and members of the Supreme Committee for the Coordination of Opposition, to which Islah had been intermittently (and unconvincingly) committed. Internally, it meant the marginalization of the Brothers who had been working to cement that relationship. But two factors worked in concert to shift this tide again beginning in 2001: first, the initiation of the U.S. Global War on Terror, and second, the assassination of YSP leader and human rights activist, Jarallah 'Omar. Both events shaped the internal politics of Islah, and its relationship to both ruling and opposition parties as the party's second decade unfolded, leaving this former regime partner the ablest source of opposition.

Islah as Opposition Leader: 2000–2013

As the Saleh regime continued to consolidate its power, a younger generation of leaders came up in Islah, beginning a process of internal reorientation that culminated in Islah's eventual participation in (and leadership of)
the JMP, a cross-ideological opposition coalition. Enabling this shift was
the Saleh regime's cooperation with the United States in combating militancy and extremism—a cooperation that was instrumentally manipulated
by the Saleh regime, to be sure, but nonetheless offered an opportunity for
party moderates to more effectively press their demands within Islah and
marginalize their own hardline. The Saleh regime's tactic of excoriating
Islah as an extremist organization was countered by the party's elevation of
moderates to key decision-making positions within the party and its related
institutions. Among the most notable of these was Muhammed Qahtan at
the head of the party's Political Directorate, the organ that sets party policy
and is most active in day-to-day political practice, and the appointment of
Nabil al-Sofee as the editor of the weekly *al-Sahwa,* which took a notably
more moderate turn under his leadership, a turn that it largely retained
after his resignation. Party leaders stressed in interviews the significance of
these shifts to the articulation of a nonextremist countenance following not
only the attacks of September 11, 2001, in the United States, but also the
earlier attack on the U.S.S. *Cole* off the port of Aden in 2000, which placed
Yemen's broader Islamist movement under particular scrutiny in the context of the Global War on Terror.

A domestic tragedy shortly after these two events also had considerable
consequence for the rise of younger moderates within Islah and their eventual alliance with Leftist parties in the JMP. The assassination of human
rights activist and YSP deputy secretary-general Jar'allah 'Omar on December 23, 2002, as he addressed an Islah party conference, sent a shock wave
through Yemen and opened the door to a nationwide debate about political
extremism and the role of *takfir* in public discourse.[55] Because the assailant
was a disaffected former Islah member, the party was eager to distance itself
from the act of violence, though its efforts to do so were unevenly received.
Members of the YSP recalled vividly the role that Islah publications and
Islah-affiliated clerics played in the 1990s, particularly at the time of the
civil war, in portraying Socialists as apostates and, in the view of many,
inciting violence against them. Members of Islah, for their part, were
divided: members of the party's Salafi wing published clear apologia

defending the killing of apostates (if not 'Omar explicitly), and other members and party-sympathizers spoke and wrote publicly in criticism of this position, calling for internal housecleaning to sweep away what they saw as the remnants of the party's 1990s encouragement of such violence. For its part, the regime endeavored to exploit this cleavage by publicizing in its own official media statements by Islah's most extreme members, most notably Shaykh 'Abd al-Majid al-Zindani.

Aided by the growth of an independent press and its vocal critiques of encroachment on political pluralism since the 1999 election, and inspired by efforts initiated by 'Omar and Qahtan before the former's death, a younger cohort of Islahi leaders began to establish links with members of other opposition parties.[56] What began as an informal series of relationships strengthened through a variety of civil society fora (ranging from symposia and conferences to *qat* chews) eventually developed into a shared commitment to procedural reform and the JMP alliance was formed.[57]

It is important to note that significant ideological cleavages existed from the outset among JMP members and have grown deeper in the face of several national crises. The durability of the alliance required that JMP members essentially agree to set aside substantive questions regarding Yemen's political future in favor of procedural reforms that could curtail the Saleh regime and offer opposition parties a change to compete. Thus, in the years immediately preceding the 2011 popular uprising in Yemen, the member parties of the JMP focused almost exclusively on electoral law reform, transparency in the Supreme Council for Elections and Referenda, and other oversight mechanisms, often at the expense of pressing issues that most resonate with voters, eroding grassroots support.[58] Within the JMP, Islah has played the preeminent role. This makes sense in terms of the voter share Islah enjoys relative to the other parties (which include the YSP, Ba'ath, Nasserists, al-Haq, and UPF, together accounting for only a handful of parliamentary seats), but it is also a consequence of the party's earlier discursive and institutional practices in the 1990s and its work to Islamize a wide range of social and educational institutions.[59] YSP members, however much they may resent Islah's role in fomenting violence in the 1990s, have often curtailed their demands within the JMP out of deference to their senior partner, engaging in what one party leader called "discursive capitulation" to Islah. Through such concessions, the opposition has taken on a rhetoric that is only mildly Islamist, but Islah's more substantive influence has been expressed as a *silence* on essential and divisive issues, such as creedal freedom, the rights and roles of women, and freedom of expression in the press.[60] This has had a dampening effect on partisan politics in general, but particularly among women, many of who have found opposition parties as unresponsive to them as the regime itself, or more so.[61]

As important as Islah has been to shaping the priorities of the JMP, the opposition alliance has clearly influenced internal Islahi politics as well, heightening existing cleavages in the party. In part, this is owed to the death of Shaykh 'Abdullah bin Hussein al-Ahmar in 2007. As speaker of parliament and a close associate of the president, 'Ali 'Abdullah Saleh, al-Ahmar was instrumental to Islah's relationship to the GPC in the 1990s. As Islah realigned in the 2000s, his role became increasingly one of mediation and counterbalance between the pro-JMP Brothers and their Salafi critics. Following his death, what was once a triangular relationship between Brothers, Salafis, and tribal constituencies has become a far more contentious competition between two ideological camps for the future of the party. According to one party leader, there has been considerable debate within the party about its role in the JMP looking forward, but it has endeavored to conduct this debate behind closed doors.

While the JMP fielded a joint candidate for the presidential election in 2006, internal divisions in the alliance teamed with a series of political crises across the country meant that it was able to do little else to challenge the narrowing of Yemen's political field during the final years of the Saleh regime.[62] The procedural focus of the JMP, however necessary it may have been to cementing such a broad coalition of parties, led observers to note the relatively weak appeal of the alliance at the grassroots level well before the 2011 Change Revolution.[63] When the JMP demands for electoral reform failed in 2008, they consented to the postponement of the 2009 parliamentary election, further distancing themselves from their grassroots constituents. As the Saleh regime expanded the use and scope of extrajudicial courts and tribunals and used resources designated for combating international terrorism to surveil and suppress its domestic critics, the JMP—and Islah, as its most significant member—had little means of recourse. While some younger members of Islah and other JMP member parties have provided critical linkages between "the opposition" and "the youth," the 2011 Change Revolution was, generally speaking, not the product of the JMP, though one could argue that its cross-ideological antecedents lay in JMP organizing.[64] Youth activists' slogans during the revolution nonetheless reflected a comprehensive critique of the status quo, including the JMP and Islah. Most prominent among them was the refrain, "la qabilah la ahzab—thawratna thawrat shabab," no tribe, no parties—our revolution is a youth revolution.

The international community, however, was ill-equipped (or perhaps ill-inclined) to work with youth activists outside the formal partisan opposition, including those who constituted the Supreme Coordination Committee for the Yemeni Youth Revolution. Instead, the GCC, working with U.S. and European support, brokered an agreement between JMP representatives and the Saleh government to bring about Saleh's orderly departure from power and lay the groundwork for a new political regime. This was met with tremendous opposition by youth activists and non-JMP figures, especially in provincial capitals like Taiz, Hodeidah, and Mukalla. Hundreds of thousands of Yemenis marched on foot to the capital in coordinated events in December and January, now in protest not only against the provision in the GCC agreement guaranteeing Saleh legal immunity for the thousands of deaths during the 2011 uprising, but against the opposition politicians who signed the agreement.

Islah has rallied firmly around the transitional agreement and stands to benefit more than any other political party from its terms. As the leading opposition party in a power-sharing national unity government, the party helped to secure the (uncontested) election of president 'Adb Rabbuh Mansour Hadi, and has supported the National Dialogue Conference where Yemenis are currently debating the shape of their future institutions. At the "end" of what many view as an unfinished revolution, it is difficult to say with any certainty what the shape these new institutions will take, whether the JMP will survive the transition intact, or what Islah's fortunes will be. What is clear is that Islah is more deeply invested in Yemen's political system today than it has been at any point over the last two decades.

Conclusion: What Islah Can Teach Us About Islamism

Islah is an instructive case for evaluating several of the central questions introduced in the theoretical chapter that frames this volume. In particular, it helps to highlight the ways in which Islamists respond to various constituencies (within and outside Islamist parties), and to structural changes in the political field. Islah's story also strongly supports the contention advanced more broadly in this volume that participation makes exit from the formal political system less likely in the long term, even when participation no longer yields many clear benefits, or when those benefits must be shared with others. While the shape of Islah's participation has changed considerably over time, it is more heavily invested in Yemen's political system today than ever before.

Less clear is the role or importance of religious ideology in the party's discourse and practice. On the one hand, by building and sustaining the JMP alliance, one could argue that Islahis have "downplayed" religious priorities in pursuit of a pragmatic politics of opposition. But this would be too convenient an interpretation. In fact, the silences on certain ideologically divisive issues speak to their power, and to party leaders' decisions to honor the religious sensibilities of party hardliners against their own preferences. Many progressive members of the Brotherhood wing of the party would happily advance women candidates, for example, and did so in Islah's internal 2007 election. Yet the party would not endorse women (and the JMP will not commit on the issue) out of deference to what one leader described as al-Zindani's ability to "deliver the street" and mobilize Salafi Islahis in opposition to such a policy. The power to produce and enforce policy silences is felt in Islah, and among its allies, who have also succumbed to this pressure, at the cost of alienating constituents, evidenced by the disavowal of partisan politics that accompanied the 2011 uprising and has continued, in more muted form, since then.

Islah's story also suggests that participation in alliances and in governing coalitions shapes the relative weight enjoyed by different factions within the party, whereby the balance of power may be tipped in favor of one internal faction over another by opportunities afforded by the formal political system and processes of alliance-formation. The rise of younger and much more liberal Muslim Brothers to leadership positions in the party was facilitated by the institutionalization of their alliance with likeminded (and similarly educated) leaders from other political parties and their networks among a range of civil society organizations and the media. At the same time, this rise has not been unlimited, as evidenced by the emergence in 2007 of the Fadilah Group, a group of Salafi clerics that bridges Islah and the ruling GPC, as a counterweight to the liberal Brothers, raising the specter of Islah's earlier cooperation with the ruling regime. In the cases of both Fadilah and the JMP-oriented Brothers, the bid for power within Islah was negotiated through networks outside the partisan framework as it is most strictly understood. This also serves as a realistic reminder that "party politics" is enacted in spaces and through discourses that are not limited by the formal rules of the partisan game.

Another lesson about Islamist participation that can be derived from Islah's experience relates to its powerful ability to set the discursive agenda. Participating in cross-ideological alliances may say less about ideological convergence or forging consensus than forms of "discursive capitulation" to more powerful alliance "partners." The formal equality between JMP members is broadly acknowledged as a practical fiction by Islahis and non-Islahis alike. Islah's weight in decision-making and discursive framing is seen as deriving from the party's electoral success relative to its alliance partners, but is unquestionably also rooted in years of institutional Islamization and extralegal violence (both discursive and physical) that Islahis used to intimidate Socialists, other Leftists, and Zaydis in the 1990s.

This relates to a final lesson. While it can be tempting to analyze Islamist participation largely through the lens of electoral gains and losses, power can be and often is expressed by political parties much more broadly. If we are mainly concerned with counting votes, Islah has seen a consistent decline in power in every election since its first in 1993. The existing parliament was elected in 2003, but will not face reelection before 2014. It is an imperfect proxy for party support, at best. At the same time, if we consider Islah's *relative* electoral power under conditions of constrained competition, Islah has fared substantially better than any other political party, even after repositioning itself as a chief adversary of the Saleh regime. Its electoral power—coupled with its discursive power—has conditioned the internal dynamics and public positions of the opposition as a whole. And beyond this, concerns about the electoral significance of one of its members, Shaykh al-Zindani, has determined, in part, choices made by centrists within the party who consider him an extremist, but fear for the viability of the party without his mobilizational power.[65]

In sum, the effects of Islahi participation in Yemeni political life have been nonlinear, but profound, for Islamists and their non-Islamist interlocutors. Participation and alliance formation have led to the rise and empowerment of genuine and committed progressives, but have also enabled an Islamization of institutions and discourses that Leftists, in particular, see as disadvantaging their ability to compete. As Yemenis of all political orientation endeavor to shape the new, post-Saleh political order, this ambiguity is unlikely to be far from anyone's mind.

Chapter 7

Islamist Parties, Elections, and Democracy in Bangladesh

ALI RIAZ

This chapter examines the performance of Islamist parties in elections over the past three decades and its implications for the future of democracy in Bangladesh, the world's third most populous Muslim majority country. The chapter argues that the behavior of the Islamists in Bangladesh is different from the pattern suggested by the "inclusion-moderation" hypothesis, which asserts that "as Islamist parties participate in their political systems, their Islamist behaviour begins to moderate."[1] It demonstrates that the behavior of Bangladeshi Islamists is different from experiences in other Muslim majority countries discussed in this volume. In most cases, Islamists have been or are "normalizing" ("behav[ing] more like mainstream political actors within their given contexts over time, and less like distinctive, anti-establishment, religious actors"[2]). Bangladeshi Islamists, on the contrary, despite more than two decades in the legislature, have remained focused on their own agenda because they have realized they can shape the political agenda through functioning in parliamentary coalitions as a kingmaker.

Islamist parties in Bangladesh, particularly their electoral performance, warrant closer examination because over the last three decades Islamists have been gaining in strength. Once consigned to oblivion due to proscription by the constitution, Islamist parties reemerged in the mid-1970s and have positioned themselves as a formidable political force in Bangladeshi politics. Political parties and organizations with an Islamist agenda have grown significantly since 1991, and Islamist parties and groups have carved out a significant space in the political landscape of Bangladesh. Five characteristics make the role of Islamist parties in electoral politics in Bangladesh worth studying: (a) elections played a key role in the reemergence of Islamists who were proscribed in the early days after independence; (b) the number of Islamist parties with popular appeal has remained small; (c) popular support for the Islamist parties has not increased significantly in the past two decades; (d) despite these weaknesses Islamists have emerged as a kingmaker; and (e) Islamists have influenced important policies and the direction of the country. In the discussions that follow, I elaborate on these features. In the final section, I make some concluding remarks on the possible trajectories of Islamist parties in Bangladesh.

Throughout the chapter, the political parties that "draw on Islamic referents—terms, symbols, and events taken from Islamic tradition—in order to articulate a distinct political agenda"[3] are referred to as Islamist parties. Although other political parties in Bangladesh may occasionally use Islamic symbols and icons to attain immediate objectives or demonstrate Islamic values, I have excluded them from this discussion as their overall political agenda does not include Islamization of society or transformation of the Bangladeshi state into an Islamic state. The scope of this volume precludes us from discussing the parties or organizations that have not participated in the elections. In a similar vein I have excluded political parties that have not been able to establish a distinct identity as an Islamist party in the eyes of the electorate despite bearing Islam in their name.

Although Bangladesh became independent in 1971, elections between 1973 and 1991 are generally considered highly flawed and severely rigged in favor of the ruling parties.[4] Most of these elections were held under military rule or pseudo-civilian regimes. The country moved from a parliamentary system to a presidential system in 1975 and did not revert to the parliamentary system until 1991. Between 1991 and 2008, five elections were held (1991, February 1996, June 1996, 2001, 2008). However, the February 1996 election was boycotted by all opposition parties and the parliament lasted for less than two months. The chapter, therefore, focuses on the four parliamentary elections that are considered free and fair in the parliamentary system of governance. There is one exception, the 1979 parliamentary election, which enabled Islamists to participate in politics. The Bangladeshi political landscape is dominated by two political parties—the center-left Awami League (AL) and the center-right Bangladesh Nationalist Party (BNP). State power has alternated between these two parties since 1991. In the past four elections 80 percent of popular votes went to these two parties, which can be described as an endorsement of a two-party system. In any two-party polity, third parties struggle to play any meaningful role and are often consigned to the role of spectator. Conversely, Bangladeshi politics has given leverage to some smaller parties to play significant roles. These include the Jatiya Party (JP), led by former military ruler H. M. Ershad, and the Jamaat-e-Islami (JI), the most prominent Islamist party and a member of the 2001–2006 ruling coalition led by the BNP. Similarly the Islami Oikya Jote (IOJ)—the United Islamic Front, an alliance of small Islamist political parties—enjoyed the status of a ruling coalition between 2001 and 2006, though they did not form part of the cabinet. The rise of other Islamist parties has been less spectacular but definitely no less significant.

Election as a Gateway

Following Bangladesh's independence, all religious parties were banned, due to the commitment of the independence movement to the separation of religion from politics and also the collaboration of Islamist parties, particularly the JI during the independence war with Pakistan. However, following the military coup led by Ziaur Rahman in 1975, Islamist parties were permitted to form, register, and mobilize. The two key developments that allowed the Islamist parties to become visible were the repeal of the constitutional proviso (Article 38) banning religion-based political parties and the decision to permit Islamist parties to register for political activities in 1976 under the Political Parties Regulation (PPR) Act. However, these parties did not appear in public until the 1979 parliamentary election. Two prominent Islamist platforms, the Muslim League (ML) and the Islamic Democratic League (IDL), formed an alliance to participate in the election. While the ML was an established party before independence, the IDL was entirely a new entity. In fact, the IDL was a conglomerate of seven Islamist parties that had existed in pre-independence Bangladesh, the most prominent of these being the JI and the Nezam-i-Islami party (NI). Despite internal schisms within the IDL (between the JI and the non-JI supporters) and between the IDL and the ML, the alliance remained intact through the election, which its members viewed as the means to reenter politics. The IDL-ML secured 8 percent of the popular vote and netted twenty seats in the legislature. Of these twenty, six were known JI members. The result was remarkable considering that these parties had been absent from the political scene for almost five years. By late 1979, the IDL faced a formal split and JI supporters and leaders revived the JI. The revival was precipitated by the return of Ghulam Azam, the supreme leader of the then East Pakistan Jamaat-e-Islami, who left the country immediately before independence, but by then the need for a political cover for the JI was over. The election had provided them a way back into mainstream politics. In the next election, in 1986, JI ran openly without cover of an alliance and highlighted its Islamist credentials. A total of 76 persons were nominated by the JI and 10 candidates won, with a total of 4.61 percent of popular vote.

Although the 1979 election was severely rigged, it played two key roles: providing constitutional legitimacy to the military regime and, most important for the purpose of our study, bringing the Islamists back into mainstream politics.

Election as the Means of Selection

It is a cliché to say that elections serve as a means to choose representatives. But insofar as Islamist politics is concerned, the elections since 1979 have also served as a means to identify which parties have been successful in establishing their credentials as Islamist in the eyes of the electorate. In other words, supporters of Islamist ideology have registered their party preferences through these elections. Election Commission (EC) records show that at least 35 political parties bearing names suggestive of an Islamist agenda participated in elections between 1979 and 2001. In 1979 and 1986, only two Islamist parties participated, but the number increased to 17 in 1991 and 18 in 1996. The number declined slightly in 2001, to 11.[5] In 2008, as the new law requiring registration with the EC for participating in elections was enacted, 10 Islamist parties were registered, including Jamaat-e-Islami (JI), Islami Andolon Bangladesh (Bangladesh Islamic Movement, BIM), IOJ, Bangladesh Khelafat Majlish (MKM), Bangladesh Khelafat Andolan (MKA), Zaker Party (ZP), Bangladesh Muslim League (ML), Bangladesh Tariqat Federation (TF), Jamiat-e-Ulama-e-Islam Bangladesh (JUIB), and Islamic Front of Bangladesh (IFB).[6] But a closer look, particularly at the results, reveals that only a few have received recognition from the electorate. These include two parties and an alliance: the JI, BIM, previously Islamic Constitution Movement), and IOJ.

Jamaat-e-Islami is the most prominent and largest among these parties. Founded in 1941 in undivided India, the party maintained its presence in the politics of Pakistan after independence. The eastern chapter of the party was proscribed in 1972 and reemerged in 1979 (see previous section). It has since participated in nearly all national elections (except 1988 and February 1996, both boycotted by all opposition political parties). It played a key role in the ruling coalition between 2001 and 2006.

Founded in 1990, IOJ is not a single political party but a confederation of seven smaller relatively radical organizations, some of which have previously expressed solidarity with the Taliban regime. These include Khilafat Majlis, Nezam-e-Islam, Faraizi Jamaat, Islami Morcha, Ulama Committee, a splinter group of NAP (Bhasani), and the Islami Shashantantra Andolon (Islamic Constitution Movement). The alliance underwent several splits in past decades and thus, four factions actually claim to carry the mantle of the original IOJ. However, only Fazlul Huq Amini's faction is registered with the EC and was a member of the ruling coalition between 2001 and 2006. The alliance first participated in the election in 1991, filing 59 candidates. In 1996, a total of 166 candidates were nominated by the IOJ.

The BIM was a member of the IOJ at the inception of the alliance, but founded a separate alliance in 2001 with the JP of General Ershad, former military ruler. The alliance filed 281 candidates and secured 14 seats. All of the victorious candidates were members of the JP who soon left the alliance and acted alone. The election demonstrated that the party has a better grassroots organization to mobilize its supporters than any other parties save the JI and the IOJ. The party is led by Syed Fazul Karim, commonly known as the Pir[7] (saint) of Chormonai. The BIM wooed eleven smaller parties and launched a new alliance in early 2006, but the alliance was short-lived.

The platforms of the JI, IOJ, and BIM share the goal of establishing an Islamic state in Bangladesh through an "Islamic revolution," even though they have differences on many issues, including the ideal disposition of an Islamic state. Despite participation in the liberal democratic process, their ultimate goal is to transform the Bangladeshi state into an Islamic state and introduce Islamic law. In their view, pluralist liberal democracy cannot provide a solution to the "moral crisis" of the nation and its citizens. These parties do not openly subscribe to the ideology that violence is the *only* means to achieve their goals, but they are not totally averse to using violence if needed. The defining feature of the IOJ and the BIM, however, is their opposition to the JI. Although some of them are not averse to the idea of working with the JI they prefer to maintain some distance. The IOJ is a case in point. Both the JI and IOJ were partners in the four-party coalition government (2001–2006) led by the BNP. It is worth noting that the differences between IOJ and BIM are more personal than ideological, although the leaders frequently couch their differences in ideological terms.

There is a marked difference in the constituency base of the JI versus the other two parties. Both the IOJ and the BIM rely on the same support base: students, teachers and management personnel (such as the head cleric) involved with the privately operated Islamic seminaries called qwami madrassahs[8] and led by a *pir*. The support base of the JI, on the other hand, is more diverse, both in terms of geographical and social strata. It has supporters in both urban and rural areas. Election results of 2001 illustrate the extent of the JI's support. JI candidates succeeded in capturing seats in five out of the six administrative divisions.[9] They did well in the midwestern and southwestern parts of the country where they secured 13 seats. Although JI candidates were not nominated in the major metropolitan cities, the number of votes garnered by candidates in other smaller cities was reasonably significant. By contrast, the IOJ filed 7 candidates, all of which were in the rural areas. Altogether the IOJ candidates secured 376,343 votes, of which 210,639 votes were secured by two winning candidates. Although the BIM filed 166 candidates in 2009 election, it did not file candidates in major metropolitan areas. Moreover, there are also differences in the leadership of the parties. Since the 1980s the JI leadership has undergone a major shift toward Western-educated individuals from middle-class backgrounds, while leaders of other Islamist parties, for example the IOJ, are mostly educated in traditional Islamic educational institutions and come from modest backgrounds.[10]

Electoral Support of the Islamists: Small But Steady

The full extent of the role of the Islamist parties within the electoral system cannot be comprehended without an incisive analysis of the election results since 1991. Drawing on these results I argue that electoral support for the Islamists has remained low, although their number of seats in Parliament has varied. However, contrary to the apparent interpretations, the core base of support for Islamist parties in Bangladesh has remained relatively constant.

Table 7: Election Results 1991–2001

Party	1991		1996		2001	
	Seats	% of votes	Seats	% of votes	Seats	% of votes
Bangladesh Awami League (AL)	88	30.08	146	37.46	62	40.13
Awami League's alliance partners	12	3.59	n/a	n/a	n/a	n/a
Bangladesh Nationalist Party(BNP)	140	30.81	116	33.61	193	40.97
Jamaat-e-Islami, Bangladesh	18	12.13	3	8.60	17	4.28
*Jatiya Party (N-F)	n/a	n/a	n/a	n/a	4	1.12
Islami Oikya Jote (IOJ)	1	0.79	1	1.09	2	0.68
BNP-led 4-party Alliance		n/a		n/a	216	47.04
Jatiya Party (Ershad)	35	11.92	32	16.40	14	7.25
Jatiya Party (Manju)	n/a	n/a	n/a	n/a	1	0.33
KSJL	n/a	n/a	n/a	n/a	1	n/a
Independents	3	4.39	1	1.06	6	4.06
JSD	1	.33	1	0.33	0	0
Other parties	2	6.29	0	1.79	0	1.52
Total	**300**	**100.00**	**300**	**100.00**	**300**	**100.00**

Source: compiled from information from Bangladesh Election Commission.
*In 2001, the Jatiya Party (Ershad) contested as a partner of a two-party alliance with the Islamic Constitution Movement.

Between 1991 and 2001, three elections were held that were deemed free and fair. The results of these elections are presented in Table 7.

The results of these three elections show that support for JI dwindled over time from 12 percent in 1991 to 4 percent in 2001. The IOJ won one seat in both 1991 and 1996, but the percentage of votes it received in the two elections was 0.79 and 1.09 percent—a negligible rise of 0.33 percent. Statistics compiled from the documents of the EC reveal that the total share of the vote won by Islamist parties declined by 4 percent between the 1991 and 1996 elections. In the 1991 election 17 Islamist parties secured 14.87 percent of the votes, compared to 10 percent in 1996. This took place against a 20 percent rise in voter turnout.[11]

The shares of the major Islamist parties in these three elections are shown in Table 8. Although the number of seats won by the Islamists in general and particularly the JI has fluctuated, their share shows a particular trend: a progressive decline. In 2001 the JI share of popular votes was 4.29 percent, and the IOJ share was 0.68 percent. Cognizant of the trend, one might conclude that the support base of the Islamists has been eroding.

Table 8: Islamists' Share of Votes, 1991–2001

Party	1991			1996			2001		
	Seats won	Votes (million)	%	Seats won	Votes (million)	%	Seats won	Votes (million)	%
Jamaat	18	4.13	12.13	3	3.64	8.61	17	2.38	4.29
IOJ	1	0.26	0.79	1	0.46	1.09	2	0.37	0.68
Khelafat Andolan	0	93,049	0.27	—	—		—	—	
Zaker	0	417,737	1.22	—	—		—	—	

However, this would be mistaken. An examination of the 2008 elections illustrates the reasons behind the seeming dichotomy. The election produced a landslide victory for the AL-led alliance, which secured an unprecedented three-fourths majority in the parliament (Table 9).

The first reading of the results of the 2008 elections reveals that the Islamists did very poorly. The popular press in Bangladesh heralded the demise of the JI as a formidable political force in Bangladeshi politics. The number of seats secured by the JI seemingly gave credence to the argument that JI was on the decline, for the party secured only 2 seats as opposed to 17 seats in 2001. The key senior leaders, including party chief Motiur Rahman Nizami, secretary general Ali Ahsan Mohammad Mojahid, and central leader Delwar Hossain Saydee—lawmakers in the last parliament—were defeated. Moreover, no other Islamist party has succeeded in coming close to winning any seats where they fielded their candidates. The two IOJ leaders who were previously elected also lost, including Fazlul Huq Amini, the firebrand Islamist, who attracted international media attention because of his radical views and alleged connection with militants.

However, these poor results do not indicate that Islamists are losing ground; a careful comparison of the 2001 and 2008 election results indicates that the Islamists' base support has remained steady.

In 2008, the JI, a partner of the BNP-led alliance, fielded 40 candidates, compared to 31 in 2001. Moreover, JI received 3.16 million votes in 2008, compared to 2.38 million in 2001. Thus, JI received slightly more votes in 2008 compared to 2001. However, approximately 15 million more Bangladeshis voted in 2008 than in 2001; it is this fact that accounts for JI's decline. Despite an increase of about 15 percent in cast votes, the JI vote remained almost static, growing by only 0.2 percent. In short, it is not that

Table 9: Election Results, 2008

Alliance	Party	Votes	Percent	Seats
Grand Alliance	Bangladesh Awami League	33,887,451	49.0	230
	Jatiya Party	4,867,377	7.0	27
	Jatiya Samajtantrik Dal	429,773	0.6	3
	Workers Party of Bangladesh	214,440	0.3	2
Four Party Alliance	Bangladesh Nationalist Party	22,963,836	33.2	30
	Jamaat-e-Islami Bangladesh	3,186,384	4.6	2
	Bangladesh Jatiya Party-BJP	95,158	0.1	1
Liberal Democratic Party		161,372	0.2	1
Independents and others		3,366,858	4.9	4
Total		69,172,649	99.99	300

Source: data from Bangladesh Election Commission, computation by author. For one account of popular votes secured by the AL and BNP in the December 29 election, see "Popular Votes: AL 25pc up, BNP 20pc Down," *Daily Star*, January 1, 2009, 1. For constituency-wide results, see Bangladesh Election Commission website: http://www.ecs.gov.bd/English/.

Elections for 299 seats were held December 29, 2008. The election for one seat, canceled due to the death of a candidate, was held January 12, 2009. The BNP candidate won the seat. Numbers represent complete results including share of popular votes. Among the seats won by the AL, BNP, and JP, Sheikh Hasina, Khaleda Zia, and General Ershad won three seats each. According to election law they vacated two seats each. One of the MPs from the AL, Zillur Rahman, was later elected president. By-elections were held in these seven seats. Coalition members who did not secure any seats are not included in the table. The fourth partner of the 4-party coalition, Islami Oikya Jote, secured 0.16 percent of the vote.

the party is losing the votes of its core constituency; instead, the party is failing to make inroads into new segments of the voting public.

These trends continue when we examine other Islamist parties. The best known, the IOJ, a member of the four-party alliance), suffered badly, but like the JI managed to hold on to its support base. For example, Fazlul Huq Amini secured 94,273 votes in Brahmanbaria district, at the east-central region of Bangladesh, with 246,892 total registered voters. This represents 30 percent of total votes cast, not sufficient to carry him through as his opponent gained 143,672 votes (59 percent). Yet, the total number is almost equal to his 99,804 votes in 2001. The BIM fielded the largest number of candidates. The BIM registered 166 candidates. It is one of the twenty-five small political parties that together fielded 716 candidates but did not win any seats. However, it is the only such party that succeeded in securing more than 1 percent of the popular vote. These parties together won 2.38

Table 10: Islamists' Share of Popular Votes, 2008

Party	Candidates	Votes	Cast votes (%)
Bangladesh Jamaat-i-Islam	40	3,160,000	4.48
Islami Andolan Bangladesh (Bangladesh Islamic Movement Bangladesh, BIM)	166	733,969	1.05
Jamiat-e-Ulama-e-Islam Bangladesh	6	173,633	0.25
Zaker Party	36	129,289	0.19
Islami Oikyo Jote	4	108,415	0.16
Bangladesh Islami Front	17	31,450	0.05
Bangladesh Khelafat Majlish	9	28,546	0.04
Bangladesh Tarikat Federation	31	19,750	0.03
Bangladesh Khelafat Andolan	30	13,759	0.02
Total			**6.27**

Source: "25 Small Parties Get 2pc Votes in Total," *Daily Star*, January 2, 2009, 1.

percent—1.65 million—of which the BIM share was 1.05 percent (733,969). The share of the other Islamist parties was far lower (Table 10).

Taken together, Islamist parties garnered 6.27 percent of the total votes cast on December 29, 2008. This number is very important in understanding the political landscape in Bangladesh, for it is almost equal to the number of respondents who chose the Islamic form of government in a preelection survey conducted by the *Daily Star* and Nielsen in November 2008.[12] In response to a question as to which form of government she or he likes, 7 percent of the respondents favored Islamic, versus 81 percent who chose [parliamentary] democratic. The concurrence of these two numbers reveals that the Islamists have an unwavering base of 7 percent in the population of Bangladesh. The number is also consistent with the results of the 2005 World Values Survey (WVS), which recorded 9 percent support for an Islamist government in Bangladesh.[13] This small number is also indicative of the popular attitude toward the role of religion in public life: personal religiosity aside, Bangladeshis are not comfortable with the mix of politics and Islam. It is also clear that the dual constituency hypothesis is not applicable to Bangladesh. Islamist parties are prioritizing the concerns of their core base and defining their agenda in clearly religious terms, not attempting to make inroads into new segments of society.

The relationships between the Islamist parties, which I have alluded to in the previous section, warrant further explorations. The foregoing discussion clearly demonstrates that the Bangladeshi party system is what

Mecham has described as a "fragmented system."[14] In a fragmented system "'multiple Islamist parties . . . compete for the 'Islamist' label, a label that is important if the party is to carry an identity-based constituency, Islamist parties have to work harder to convince voters that they are 'the Islamist choice.' This . . . led to a pattern of competitive 'outflanking,' in which Islamist parties move increasingly toward Islamist rhetoric to demonstrate that they are the best representatives of their identity group." In Bangladesh, the presence of the large number of Islamist parties makes the competition an imperative. Therefore, as more Islamist parties emerged in the past years, Islamist parties have emphasized "the Islamic parts of their platform in order to highlight their distinctiveness vs. their competitors." This is one of the driving forces behind the continuous fragmentation of the IOJ. The other dimension of this "outflanking" effort is the contestation between the JI and the other Islamists, particularly the IOJ and the BIM. The latter organizations insist that the JI have moderated its position and can no longer represent the Islamic constituency.[15]

Islamists as Kingmaker[s]

Despite such a small support base, the Islamists have succeeded in playing the role of kingmakers over the past twenty-two years by successfully shaping electoral alliances and postelection coalitions. Thus, they do not need to increase their share of the vote to affect the political agenda; instead they play their political cards astutely, switch sides at opportune moments, and use that influence to push their goals. Such behavior has become increasingly commonplace over the past two decades, with the Islamist parties becoming bolder over time. The 1991 elections brought the BNP to power with the tacit support of the JI. By 1994, the JI shifted allegiance to the opposition AL and participated in demonstrations on its behalf, which ultimately led to the demise of the Fifth Parliament. The opposition parties, especially the AL, demanded an amendment to the constitution to make permanent the role of an interim government to oversee the elections.[16] The government finally agreed to the demand. The Sixth Parliament, brought in via elections boycotted by the opposition and blatantly manipulated in favour of the BNP, amended the constitution and made the caretaker government (CTG) a part of the constitution.[17] In June 1996, fresh elections were held under the CTG headed by the immediate past chief justice. The

AL emerged as the largest single party in the Seventh Parliament, although it was short of the majority required to form the government. The unconditional support of the JP of General Ershad ensured the return of the AL to power after twenty-one years. This displaced the JI as kingmaker.

In the October 2001 elections for the Eighth Parliament, the JI had regained its position as kingmaker. The BNP, JI, and IOJ formed an alliance against the ruling AL, which secured a landslide victory with a two-thirds majority in the subsequent elections. In the run-up to the elections former military ruler H. M. Ershad was forced to leave the four-party alliance. The JP did not contest the election on its own, but formed an alliance called the Islami Jatiya Oikya Front (IJOF, Islamic National United Front). The coalition partner was then the Islamic Constitution Movement (later BIM, in 2008) led by a pir, Syed Fazlul Karim. These developments between 1991 and 2001 demonstrate that although two parties (the AL and the BNP) occupied preeminent positions in Bangladeshi politics, neither of them had enough electoral support to form a government on its own. This is true not only in terms of the share of popular votes and the seats they won, but also because they wanted to be seen as a party that values the Islamic sentiment of the voters. This is what made Islamists the principal contender of being the kingmaker. It is well to bear in mind that the JP, headed by General Ershad, has always underscored that Islam was declared state religion under their reign in 1988, and, therefore, they too should be considered as the guardian of Islam in Bangladesh. In late 2006, leading up to the scheduled elections in January 2007, these parties engaged in a race to bring Islamists to their side to achieve the immediate goal of securing victory. The AL, in its bid to form a broad alliance against the BNP-led four-party combine, created "the Grand Alliance" comprised of the JP, various breakaway factions of the BNP, and its usual allies such as the Jatiya Samajtantrik Dal (JSD). Leading up to the nomination, many other smaller political parties joined the Grand Alliance. The alliance leaders did not hesitate to embrace any political party willing to oppose the BNP.

While a number of political parties joined the alliance, the Islamists in general, particularly the militant Islamists, took advantage of the situation. The most conspicuous example was the Memorandum of Understanding (MOU) signed between the AL and the Bangladesh Khelafat Majlish (BKM) on December 23, 2006. Although the BKM was well-known for its radical views and the involvement of its leaders with militant groups such as the Jamaat-ul Mujahideen Bangladesh (JMB),[18] the AL had no reservations about sharing a platform with them. The five-point MOU stipulated that if the Grand Alliance came to power, the government would allow certified ulama the right to issue *fatwas*, impose a ban on enacting any law that goes against Quranic values, initiate steps for proper implementation of the initiative for government recognition of the degrees awarded by Qwami madrasahs, and ban criticism of the Prophet Muhammad, or in other words introduce a blasphemy law.[19] As part of the deal the AL, on behalf of the Grand Alliance, nominated six Islamists in the elections. These included Mufti Shahidul Islam and Muhammad Habibur Rahman—two veterans of the Afghan war[20]—and another, Habibur Rahman, who had issued a *fatwa* against voting for the AL in the 2001 elections because of its secularist credentials. Despite severe criticisms by allies and members of the civil society, the AL leaders insisted that the MOU and the nomination of the Islamists were consistent with the spirit of secularism.[21]

The BNP, on the other hand, insisted that the only way to save Islam was to vote for the four-party alliance.[22] Pointing to this race among the two alliances to cajole the Islamists, IOJ leader Fazlul Huq Amini gleefully declared that "no one can attain power without the support of the Islamic forces."[23]

Islamists' Influence on Policy and Directions

In spite of the fact that the major Islamist parties operate within the constitutional framework of the country and regularly participate in elections, they are not deemphasizing the Islamic aspects of their platform,changing their political behavior,or moderating their religious agenda. Their adherence to democratic norms remains suspect as they often express their disdain for democracy and declare their intent to use elections as a means to power. It is yet to be determined whether the Bangladeshi Islamists, under favorable conditions, would seek to institute legal and constitutional changes so sweeping as to practically unmake democracy.

There are certain characteristics of the Islamists, particularly their opposition to the idea of pluralism, political or otherwise, and their rejection of democracy as non-Islamic, which give cause for concern. The leader of the Jamaat-e-Islami Bangladesh, Ghulam Azam, has made it amply clear that sovereignty of the people and parliament, a basic tenet of liberal democracy, is a completely unacceptable precept for the party and its followers. Ghulam

Azam writes, "the people or parliament does not have legitimate right to take any decision contrary to the laws and regulations imposed by God."[24] Clause 2.5 of the party's revised constitution reaffirmed that principle. The preamble of the party constitution states that Allah has vested mankind with the responsibility to establish Khilafat (Islamic rule) and made mankind responsible for following and practicing an Allah-directed lifestyle without following and practicing a manmade ideology. Similarly, clause 3.1 states that the party's objective is to defend the country from both internal and external threats and anarchy through the revival of Islamic values; clause 6.4 states that the party will work to bring expected changes in the state system to establish "complete Islam" through constitutional means and establish "honest and God-fearing" leadership in all walks of life. Clause 7 states that the JI members cannot keep any relationship with an organization opposed to *aqidah* (Islamic theology). These provisions became sources of contention between the JI and the EC as the party submitted the constitution for registration in 2008. In response to the objection of the EC the party agreed to remove clause 2.5 before the election of 2008. However, the party reneged on its commitment after the election and restored it in the revised version submitted to the EC. The JI leaders claimed it was a "printing mistake." These issues largely remained unresolved to date.

Interestingly, militant Islamists in Bangladesh share the same ethos. The JMB, for example, in a leaflet distributed after the bomb attacks on August 17, 2005, called the present democratic system a creation of kafir (infidels). "Those who want to give institutional shape to democracy are the enemies of Islam," says the leaflet, adding that if they want "hedayet (blessings) of Allah," both the government and the opposition should introduce Islamic law immediately by burying party differences. They called for rejection of the "evil" constitution and removing all "shirks" (Setting up partners in worship with Allah/ polytheism), and "bida't" (innovations contrary to Islamic teachings), and for allowing the people to perform Islam the "correct" way. In a similar vein the IOJ has repeatedly called for secular civil laws to be scrapped and the issuing of *fatwas* to be allowed. Between 2001 and 2006 they threatened to withdraw their support from the government if the anti-*fatwa* verdict issued by the High Court on January 1, 2001, was not annulled.

Tolerance is one of the fundamental principles of democracy. To many, it is the litmus test of the democratic credentials of any group or political party. Over the past decade, as they have garnered power, the JI and IOJ have not only championed radical legislation but also acts of violence. Two examples are instructive in this regard; first, the JI's attempt to use state power to silence its ideological opponents, and second its support for virulent attacks on minorities.

In 2002, as a supporter of the ruling BNP, the JI had some say in setting the agenda of the Parliament. Taking advantage of their position, the JI tried to pass a blasphemy law. On July 2, 1992, Motiur Rahman Nizami, secretary general of the Jaamat-e-Islami and member of the Parliament, introduced a private members bill at the Parliament. Apparently an amendment to the Penal Code of 1860, the bill was in essence a proposal to enact a "Blasphemy Law" similar to the one introduced in Pakistan under the Ziaul Huq regime at the insistence of the Jaamat-e-Islami Pakistan. In his statement of reasons for introducing the bill, Motiur Rahman Nizami suggested it was intended to "halt the trend of causing disrespect to the Holy Koran, defiling the Holy Prophet Mohammad (SM)," which has "caused great hurt (sic) to the Muslim people of Bangladesh, and thereby given rise to the possibility of a disruption of law and order." The bill sought to establish two criminal offenses of "defiling the Koran" and "defiling the sacred name of the Prophet," punishable by a maximum sentence of life imprisonment and death respectively. An almost verbatim copy of the amendments introduced in the Pakistan Penal Code under the authoritarian regime of General Ziaul Huq, the proposed bill envisaged the addition of the following two new clauses:

> *295B. Defile (sic) etc of the Holy Koran.*—Whoever willfully defiles, damages, or desecrates the Holy Koran or any extract thereof or uses the Holy Koran or any extract thereof in any derogatory manner shall be punished with imprisonment for life.

> *295C. Defile (sic) of the sacred name of the Holy Prophet (SM)*— Whoever by words either spoken or written, or by signs or visible representations, or by any imputation, immuendeso (sic) or insinuation, defiles, directly or indirectly, the sacred name of the Holy Prophet Muhammad (peace be upon him) shall be punished with death, or imprisonment for life and shall also be liable to a fine.

It should be noted that the proposed clauses were in fact,superfluous as the existing clause 295A of the Penal Code is explicit enough to handle circumstances where any statement or act of an individual hurts the religious sentiments of others. The aim of the proposed bill, however, was not to meet the needs of society but to use legal measures and a legal mechanism to put an end to the critical secular discourse that the Jamaat perceives as opposed to their activities. The bill failed to pass, primarily because of opposition from the civil society, but also because the relationship between the BNP and the JI had soured and the JI began to move toward the opposition AL. The BNP was therefore less inclined to support the bill. Although the bill did not pass, the issue of blasphemy, an issue with no precedence in Bangladeshi social discourse, was introduced with success. It reappeared on other occasions and was included in the MOU signed between the AL and the BKM in late 2006. The acceptance of the clause and the effort of the AL to justify it showed how Islamists shape the public discourse and try to shape the policies of government.

The second example of the Islamists' lack of tolerance is demonstrated in their behavior toward the Ahamadiyyas, a small Muslim community of less than 150,000 who have been living in Bangladesh since the 1900s.[25] Beginning in 2002, the Ahmadiyyas have come under virulent attack from the Khatme Nabuwat (KN), an umbrella organization of Islamist groups dedicated to the preservation of the "finality of the prophethood" of Muhammad. They have begun a campaign to declare Ahamadiyyas "non-Muslims." Both the JI and the IOJ have lent their support to the campaign against Ahmadiyyas.

Although JI leaders have insisted that they are not a part of the KN, the Bangladeshi media have shown that local-level JI activists are at the forefront of the KN movement.[26] Additionally, in February 2004 JI leader Delwar Hossain Sayedee inflamed the situation with publication of his book *Why Qadianis Are Not Muslims*. The book is full of venomous statements against the Ahamadiyya community. IOJ leaders not only support the measures, but also participate in and organize various KN programs. In a public gathering on March 11, 2005, the leader of a faction of the IOJ, Shaikhul Hadith Azizul Hoque, said, "It (the government) lacks courage to declare Ahmadiyyas Kafir (non-Muslim). Those who do not consider Qadianis as Kafir are themselves Kafir."[27] Consistent with their contempt for the "other"—religious or secular—Islamists have been trying vigorously to marginalize the Ahmadiyyas. Islamists see the Ahmadiyyas as a serious challenge to their narrow interpretation of Islam, because unlike the secularists,

Ahmadiyyas can offer an alternative Islamic interpretation and thus undermine their opponents' legitimacy and subvert the claim that they are the
true interpreters of Islam.[28]

The demise of the government's effort to frame a women's development
policy in 2008 is testimony to the influence and power of the Islamists over
policymakers and Islamists' lack of commitment to gender equality. On the
eve of International Women's Day on March 7, the military-backed caretaker government announced the National Women Development Policy
2008. The proposed policy had the government set aside one-third of parliamentary seats for women and suggested arrangements for direct election
to the reserved seats. It also recommended appointment of an adequate
number of women, if necessary, under the related section of the constitution to the highest level of the Cabinet Division and the policy-making level
of the administration. The policy provided for equal property inheritance
rights to women.[29] Islamists immediately launched violent protests against
the policy and forced the government to set up a review committee dominated by clerics and Islamic scholars. Despite a state of emergency, which
prohibited demonstrations, the activists were allowed to congregate at the
national mosque at the capital, conduct processions, and even attack the
police.[30] JI leader Matiur Rahman Nizami described the proposed policy
as "a contentious national issue" and insisted that "the government has
incorporated some sections of law contrary to Quran and Sunnah to the
. . . national women development policy."[31] Finally the government back-
tracked and decided not to implement the policy. The success of the Islamists in forestalling the changes to the women's development policy by the
caretaker regime (2007–2008) is indicative not only of their influence on
policy-making but of their outlook toward women's role in society. Their
unwillingness to accord equal rights to women in the name of religion has
greater implications for the country and speaks volumes to their commitment to democratic principles of equality, capacity to mobilize, and procliv-
ity toward street agitation.

Conclusions: The Road Ahead

The foregoing discussion shows that the Islamist parties in Bangladesh have
remained a part of the political landscape and have participated in the elections. One can easily argue that the Islamist parties have made a strategic

choice to participate in the democratic process. However, whether this participation comes from a principled commitment or is a product of self-interested calculation is an open question and probably varies from party to party. Their ideological positions on some of the fundamental tenets of democracy such as tolerance and equality are causes for concern.

The results of four elections since 1991 indicate that the Islamist parties have a small but unwavering support base and it is neither possible nor democratic to wish them away. The number of seats won by the Islamists has fluctuated, thanks to the "first past the post system," but their base has not experienced major erosion, although some decline has occurred since 1991. Equally important, they are having difficulties in appealing to new voters. The Islamists, aware of their smaller support base, have been engaged in alliance-building with major parties such the AL, BNP, and JP. Their calculated maneuvering has allowed them to exert disproportionate influence over state power. Despite their criticisms of the nation-state, they have made use of it, especially by cultivating sympathizers at various levels of the state, particularly the local level. While in power, these parties have been in charge of key government ministries (e.g., agriculture, industry, and social welfare) allowing them to dispense resources to their supporters.

Our discussion shows that there are variations among Islamists who participate in the electoral process. There are internal contestations among these forces, particularly in securing support for their disposition of Islamization of state and society. Since Islamists are not a single, monolithic, homogeneous group, there cannot be a single trajectory for them. The variations open a variety of options for the future; there can, perhaps will be many trajectories. This calls for a more nuanced and evidence-based discussion on Islamist forces and an understanding of their internal struggles.

The future trajectories of Islamist politics will take place in the broader global political milieu and political and social dynamics of Bangladeshi society. The role of the Islamists in the democratic process depends in part on respect for democratic principles, commitment to the rule of law by all political parties, and strengthening of democratic institutions—a key requirement for deepening the democratic process. In short, unless a qualitative transformation of the democratic process—from formal to substantive democracy—takes place, the Islamists will find ways to evade the question of their commitment (or the lack of) to the fundamentals of democracy. The global political milieu, that is, the role of the Western powers and Islamists elsewhere, will have an important impact on the future role of the Islamists in Bangladesh. If global politics encourages the strengthening of the sense of Muslim victimhood, due to the role of Western countries, particularly the United States, their appeal to the masses in Bangladesh is likely to be stronger.

Islamist groups discussed in this chapter, in large measure, have a circumscribed nationalist agenda and seldom overtly use the universalistic message of political Islam (i.e., to be a member of global umma and act as the champion of the causes of Muslims elsewhere). This does not mean that they are opposed to the universalistic message of Islam. Instead, despite being preoccupied with a national agenda, these parties also subscribe to the universalistic message and thus connect their agenda with global political developments. The JI is a case in point. Its organizational links and its positions on domestic political issues are both shaped by acknowledgment of and adherence to the global dimension of the Islamic movement.

The important question is whether adherence to the universalistic message will bring these Islamist parties close to the transnational organizations that view the struggle as global and have few reservations about using violence. In simple terms the question to be addressed is whether a relationship exists (and if not, whether it will be established in the future) between these two kinds of organizations. The likelihood of such an alliance is not far-fetched; rather, the Bangladeshi press has documented that leaders of clandestine militant groups have had linkages to the JI at various stages of their political careers. Therefore, participation in mainstream politics by itself is not a proof of a long-term commitment to democratic politics.

Conclusion

The New Dynamism of Islamist Parties

JULIE CHERNOV HWANG
QUINN MECHAM

In the aftermath of newly democratic elections in both Egypt and Tunisia in 2011, which resulted in dramatic showings for the Egyptian Muslim Brotherhood's Freedom and Justice Party (Al-Hurriya wa al-'Adala), Egypt's Salafi Light (Al-Nour) Party, and the Tunisian Renaissance Party (Al-Nahda), interest in the behavior of Islamist parties has increased. Scholars and policy-makers have sought to analyze the election results in Egypt and Tunisia and address potential implications of the Islamist victories. However, electoral success by Islamist parties is not particularly new, as Islamists have regularly competed in elections for decades around the world. What is new is that these electoral victories took place in the context of founding elections in transitional regimes emerging from authoritarian Arab states, which to that point had held only highly managed elections to lend a veneer of democracy to longstanding dictatorships.

This volume has sought to assess the strategic behavior of Islamist parties throughout the Muslim world, centering not only on the Middle East but also on Muslim Asia, which contains both two-thirds of the world's Muslims and some of its most open and democratic political systems. Through examining the identity and actions of Islamist parties across issues of platform, constituency, normalization and moderation, coalition building, and movement-party dynamics, the authors of this volume have collectively highlighted both areas of striking commonality in Islamist party behavior and sharp divergences in strategic decision-making.

A central message of this book is that Islamist parties are not monolithic, but represent a diverse set of interests and political behaviors that are intrinsically tied to the conditions they face in their given domestic contexts. A second key message is that Islamist parties differ little in their strategic behavior from other types of political parties. Specifically, these parties respond to strategic constraints and opportunities; they attempt to balance assuaging the concerns of their base with expanding their network of potential supporters; they debate the extent to which certain strategies and policy programs can yield the desired results; and they pursue electoral success as they choose to define it. As shown in this volume, Islamist parties have been active players in polities from Morocco to Yemen to Indonesia for decades. Where political liberalization and democratization have enabled the potential for securing political access through the popular vote, Islamist parties are responding to the strategic incentives in their respective political systems and participating in elections in a variety of democratic, semidemocratic, and semi-authoritarian contexts. In this process, they are also assessing the extent to which both the normalization of their political behavior and the moderation of their ideological positions is strategically beneficial, given the reality of their current political base and possibility of future electoral gains. Moreover, as Islamist parties participate regularly in elections, they have varied degrees of success depending on their strategic choices and the political context in their polities. Some parties win elections outright or become major political players through elections, while others seem content with a loyal base of supporters and small share of the vote.

As the opportunities for participation have increased and Islamist parties have gained more experience with legislative and electoral politics, many of these parties have adjusted their platforms, vision, and goals accordingly. They have implicitly postponed some of their goals to the distant future, reassessed the viability of others, and even abandoned certain preferences that are dramatically out of step with tthose of the majority of Muslims in their polities. Other Islamist parties, by contrast, choose to hold fast to their original raison d'être. Now more than ever, there is a dynamic range of Islamist parties to assess, given the opportunities and constraints available in a wider variety of political systems throughout the Muslim world. Thus, the very term Islamist party has a broader meaning than it did two decades ago, when the Islamic Salvation Front (FIS) in Algeria, the Egyptian Muslim Brotherhood and affiliates, and the clerical establishment that consolidated the Iranian revolution were primary reference points. Today, Islamist parties the world over cannot afford to ignore the fantastic political success of the AKP in Turkey, which has won a majority of seats in the Turkish government in three successive elections (2002, 2007, 2011), increasing its share of the popular vote over time, and demonstrating its continued ability to govern without the aid of coalition partners. Islamist parties the world over have looked to the lessons of the Turkish experience, even as Islamists at home recognize that such sustained victory has come at the cost of maintaining a cohesive Islamic agenda.

The sheer range of Islamist parties operating in the Muslim world today indicates that identity as Islamist parties can have multiple meanings. There are relatively few similarities between the small IOJ in Bangladesh and the recently victorious PJD in Morocco, if one examines their priorities, strategies, and degree of electoral success. It is difficult to imagine a circumstance in which a party like the IOJ would support the progressive Moroccan Family Code, which passed with PJD support. Yet, both self-identify as Islamist parties and are treated as Islamist parties in their systems and by their constituents. This raises the question of what is meant by an Islamist party as it exists today.

The parties examined in this volume exhibit several commonalities of note. First, all are inspired by Islamic values and religious, symbol-laden narratives. Those values shape the agenda and influence the political priorities of the party, while symbolic Islamic narratives shape the party's worldview and its appeal to constituents. These parties seek to varying degrees to institutionalize these values by passing legislation to make society more reflective of Islamist values. Most notably, all parties examined in this volume prioritize expanding access to and funding for Islamic education, a relatively uncontroversial and popular issue whether one contests elections in Turkey, Yemen, or Indonesia. They all also make claims on what is appropriate in public space, including perspectives on the public dress code for women or fasting during Ramadan. However, they diverge in their emphasis on other points of the agenda. Islah in Yemen, the OIJ and JI in Bangladesh, PKS and PPP in Indonesia, and PAS in Malaysia have all focused to some extent on expanding the application of Islamic law, seeking to pass shari'a-inspired legislation nationally, as well as at local levels, where the opportunity and constituency exist. By contrast, the PJD in Morocco and the AKP in Turkey have steered away from introducing a platform of Islamic law, given the realities of the political contexts in which they compete.

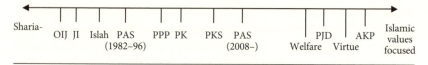

Figure 2. Comparative identities of Islamist parties.

Second, identity as an Islamist party is often defined as much by a party's relationships and political context as by platforms and policy positioning. Party leaders often rise up through allied Islamic movements with broader religious and social goals, a background that have an impact on their public identity. The party's founding ideology may reflect that of a particular movement. For example, the Prosperous Justice Party in Indonesia and the Jamaat e-Islami in Bangladesh have their roots in the Muslim Brotherhood-inspired Tarbiyah movement during the New Order dictatorship and the JI of Pakistan respectively. In Turkey, the National Salvation Party (MSP), the Welfare Party (RP), and the Virtue Party (FP) arose initially from the National Outlook (Millî Görüş) movement. Likewise, historical context can influence party identity. What is today Turkey's AKP is the product of over forty years of conflict-ridden challenges and negotiations between the Kemalist state and prior Islamist parties over the lines of religious permissibility. It is undeniable that the unique aspects of a secular Kemalist ideology and state have shaped how Turkish Islamist parties view themselves and what they can reasonably expect to accomplish within the constraints provided by the state. Likewise, Malaysia's PAS has evolved over the course of more than sixty years of trial and error experimentation regarding how to best compete with UMNO and also claim the public mantle as the one true Islamist party, two goals that have often been at cross purposes.

Finally, members of Islamist parties usually seek to portray themselves as personally devout, often highlighting their (and their families') adherence to Islamic norms of behavior. They use Islamic terminology and reference points in their general and political discourse, wives and female members of party and parliament cover their *aurat* (modest dress, including covering hair, bosom, arms to the wrist, and legs to the ankles), and public displays of obedience to Islamic precepts are commonplace. Based on these three indicators, we have sought to depict the range of Islamist party identities in the parties discussed in this volume in Figure 2. Parties are comparatively positioned on a spectrum ranging from those that focus primarily on the implementation of Islamic law and the creation of an Islamic state, to those that seek inspiration from Islamic values and narratives, rather than trying to create formal Islamic institutions of state. Note that individual parties may change over time, and that parties like the Malaysian PAS and Indonesian PKS have adopted a wide range of positions as these parties have evolved.

As political systems have grown more open and opportunities for legislative gains become more feasible, Islamist parties have struggled over how to maintain and project a coherent Islamist identity. On the one hand, Islamist parties often aim to portray themselves as thoroughly imbued with religious values and clear religious objectives. On the other hand, the lure of competitive party politics often leads them to expand their potential constituency by placing emphasis on universal themes (social justice, economic opportunity) rather than conservative religious values. As noted in this volume, particularly in the chapters on Malaysia, Turkey, and Indonesia, Islamist parties have suffered from internal factionalization, driven in part over personality conflicts, but more important, over the extent to which a party should moderate its rhetoric, policy platform, and goals in order to appeal to a wider array of voters. As Islamist parties struggle to discern the extent to which they are willing to compromise their founding mission in pursuit of electoral success and political power, the push and pull of strategic adjustment can often lead to charges of inconsistency that has the potential to alienate core supporters and undecided voters alike. One hypothesis from Chapter 2 argued that Islamist parties were most likely to split over disagreements about party identity. While we do not see a great deal of support for this being the acute cause of splits (and it is hard to disentangle from personal rivalries), we do see this tension coming up across many times and contexts in internal party disputes.

This volume has found considerable support for two hypotheses regarding Islamist platforms also introduced in Chapter 2, which on the surface appear to be in tension. On the one hand, as Islamist parties increasingly participate in their political systems, they tend to deprioritize religious elements of their platforms in favor of more universal themes. This is clearly the case as Islamist parties have evolved in Turkey, Morocco, Indonesia, and Malaysia, but is much less so in Yemen and Bangladesh. On the other hand, Mecham hypothesizes that parties in competition with other Islamist parties may also choose to distinguish themselves from the competition by emphasizing the Islamist portions of their platforms. We see support for this in Bangladesh, Yemen, Malaysia, and Indonesia among major Islamist actors, less in Turkey and Morocco. Both dynamics, deprioritizing religious content to gain mass support, as well as highlighting Islamic distinctiveness to outflank competitors, are at work at some point in the majority of our cases. The puzzle can be resolved in part by understanding that the largest parties tend to deprioritize religious content over time (as the potential for success becomes clear), while the smallest parties tend to emphasize their religious identity (as a way of remaining relevant and maintaining a core constituency). These dynamics may therefore apply to different parties simultaneously within a given party system (as in Indonesia), leading to divergent political behaviors across Islamist parties.

Participation and Normalization

As observed in the Introduction, Islamist political parties are participating in elections in greater numbers than at any other point in history. Electoral competition is dramatically shaping these parties, just as these parties are influencing the political systems in which they play a part. A key finding of this volume is that Islamist parties are becoming increasingly normalized participants in their political systems (that is, they are moving from contentious politics into the realm of normal politics). Their political behavior has often become normalized (to look more like other political actors) in parallel with the shift in emphasis regarding their party platforms. Islamist parties have participated in Indonesian and Malaysian elections since independence; in Turkish elections since the 1970s; in Bangladesh since Islamist parties were first permitted in 1979, and in Yemen following reunification in 1993. Islamist parties have become a constant fixture in elections from Morocco to Yemen to Bangladesh to Indonesia. This continued participation in iterated election cycles over decades makes the likelihood of exit from normal political processes exceedingly slim.

Most Islamist parties in this study are indeed normalizing as hypothesized in Chapter 2. The majority of parties discussed in this volume have changed their political behavior over time to act more like other parties in their systems, and to increasingly play by the existing rules of those political systems. A number of Islamist parties discussed here have even joined governing coalitions, which often include parties that advocate very different policies than those aligned with Islamists' ideological preferences. As they have evolved and collaborated with non-Islamist parties, Islamists are becoming less and less distinct from their non-Islamist competitors. This is demonstrably the case in Morocco, Turkey, Malaysia, and Indonesia, although less so in Yemen and Bangladesh.

In Morocco, the PJD has moved over time from prioritizing issues of Islamic identity and religious authenticity, to a sustained focus on economic development, investment, democratic reform, and human rights. Likewise, in Turkey, the AKP differs from previous incarnations of Islamist parties by eschewing many religious policy demands in favor of economic development, liberalizing reforms, establishing civilian control over the state, and building positive relationships with neighbors (including Europe). In Malaysia, the PAS 2008 electoral platform included calls for environmental reform, strengthening of the welfare state, and parental leave for both men and women. In its 2009 campaign, the Indonesian PKS ran on slogans of "the Party for Us All," ran ads showing women without headscarves, and focused primarily on the issue of clean government. Although the Indonesian political system is the most open of the countries of this study, lacking the ideological boundaries of the Turkish and Moroccan systems, the PKS and the PPP have chosen to go quiet on shari'a. Though central to its original objectives, the PPP has not taken up the issue of formalizing shari'a in the constitution in more than a decade. In most cases, the strategic objectives that inform this shift in behavior appear to be a desire for greater electoral success; this requires parties to secure the support of protest voters, without whom they can never hope to win an electoral majority.

The process of coalition-building also leads to many political compromises. As the PJD came to power in Morocco beginning in 2012, it formed a governing coalition including three non-Islamist parties close to the palace, which maintains the king's upper hand in policy-making and resource distribution. In Turkey, prior to the AKP's outright electoral victory in 2002, Islamist parties regularly participated in coalitions that constrained their behavior, most notably during the brief RP tenure in office during the 1990s. In Indonesia, the PKS and PPP have both partnered with governing coalitions, giving them some access to political power but restricting their range of political choice. In Yemen, Islah's collaboration with the ruling GPC brought Islah front and center into the political system, where it was required to make compromises that made it look more and more like an establishment party over time.

Subsequently in Yemen, Islah fell out with the ruling GPC and formed a coalition with opposition parties under the umbrella of the Joint Meeting Parties (JMP). This opposition coalition also created incentives for cooperation with non-Islamist groups. Likewise, in Malaysia, where the National Front (BN) coalition has dominated politics since independence, Islamist parties are partnering not with the governing coalition but the multiethnic, multireligious PKR and the secular Democratic Action Party (DAP), neither of which shares PAS's long-term ideological agenda of Islamization of society. Regardless of whether Islamists partner with non-Islamist governing parties or opposition parties, they face a similar set of incentives that lead them to stress universal themes and highlight their receptivity to non-Islamists (or non-Muslims) and their interests. In both instances, ideological preferences must be downplayed for the coalition to endure. Moreover, the goal remains the same—parties that build coalitions have the ability to effect more change by tapping into a dual constituency, both those of their core base and those who support them for what the broader coalition can provide.

However, it is important to note this is a balancing act, especially in states where there is more than one Islamist party competing. As this volume has shown, parties must weigh the incentive to win protest votes against the incentive to outflank Islamist competitors and consolidate the Islamist vote. This is most notable in Bangladesh, where small anti-pluralist Islamist parties participate in elections and join governing coalitions where they can act as "kingmakers" and leverage their minority influence in a proportional system; this helps them pass legislation that is far too conservative for the ordinary BNP or AL parliamentarian. In Malaysia, PAS and UMNO have often engaged in outflanking behavior to claim the mantle of the true Islamist party to represent the interests of Malay Muslims, often racing each other over who could adopt the more hard-line position on a variety of Islamist issues.

Islamist parties affiliated with a broader Islamic religious or social movement are further constrained in strategic flexibility by the need to retain the support and loyalty of their core religious base. This base matters to them for both social and political reasons; the party is undergirded by a devout core movement; this is its base. That core constituency also assists them during the campaign period by lending their time, effort, and financial assistance. If

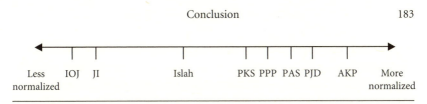

Figure 3. Comparative normalization of Islamist parties.

a movement-affiliated party moderates its positions too quickly or engages in behavior that is controversial to its base, it risks alienating the movement and losing the primary source of party support. Movement-affiliated parties often see their mission as a dual one: the movement seeks to Islamize society beginning with the individual and family through proselytizing (*da'wa* or *dakwah*) and educational (*tarbiyah*) activities, while the party seeks to enact legislation incrementally at the national and local levels in support of that goal. Movement incentives and objectives may occasionally be at odds with party incentives, leading the movement to "rein in" the party. In these cases, deprioritization of religious goals and strategic normalization are rarely linear processes. This has been a particular issue for the PKS, which is both a movement and a party. While the party exerts a moderating influence on the movement, the movement, as the core base of the party, constrains its ability to commit to a sustained ideological shift toward the center, even if doing so will lead to greater electoral success.

Figure 3 represents the extent of the evolution of the parties (and their former incarnations) in this volume over time. Parties to the right of the spectrum have normalized their behavior by evolving closer to other parties in their respective political systems. Parties to the left of the spectrum have remained comparatively aloof from "normal politics" and maintained more distinctive behavior compared with other parties in their systems. Note the significant overlap of a party's behavioral evolution with party identity as depicted in Figure 2.

Factors That Affect Electoral Success

This volume has found three major patterns of competitive behavior among the Islamist parties examined in the study. First, some Islamist parties have credibly committed to a shift to the political center, most prominently the Turkish AKP, and to a significant extent the Moroccan PJD. A central goal of these parties is to win elections and they understand that to do so requires acceptance of the political rules of the game (being Kemalist or monarchical), as well as understanding the range of their potential constituents and the preferences of those potential constituents. A credible shift to the center often involves organizational change (bringing in non-Islamists), public professions of loyalty to non-Islamist principles, or agreement to accept specific boundaries on permissible political discourse. The parties that have made the credible shift to the center have had the greatest success in elections.

Emerging from previous incarnations of Islamist parties but using a more centrist discourse, the AKP won a dominant victory in the 2002 elections. In doing so, they realigned Turkish politics and were able to govern without coalition partners, an outcome not seen in Turkish politics since the 1980s. They achieved and later maintained this level of success in large part because they broke with earlier Islamist leaders, diversified their agenda to emphasize universal themes, and portrayed themselves as a populist party with conservative values, rather than an Islamist party. In so doing, they were able to harness the support of protest voters in addition to their preexisting base that had backed them for their religious motives. The success of the PJD in Morocco, as the party has risen to become the dominant party in a highly fragmented system, illustrates some similar patterns. Its support remained relatively steady in its first two elections in 2002 and 2007, but jumped to 23 percent in 2011, receiving almost double the votes of any other competing party. Over time, it has shifted its language and priorities away from a narrative of preserving Islamic authenticity, focusing much more on universal values, which may help explain part of its political appeal. The jump in support in 2011 is also likely due to the PJD ability to attract a large number of protest voters, who became politicized in the context of uprisings against existing regimes throughout much of the Arab world. By appealing to the widespread desire for political reform and economic justice in Morocco, rather than focusing on religious priorities, the PJD was able to establish itself as the dominant party in Moroccan politics.

Second, there are Islamist parties who have held fast to their Islamic raison d'être and prioritized outflanking Islamist competitors over making gains outside their core base. This group, most notably for the purposes of this volume, the OIJ and JI in Bangladesh and, to a lesser extent, the Islah Party in Yemen, is content with a small yet predictable share of the vote coming from core supporters. Their goals lie in securing passage of key pieces of desired shari'a-inspired legislation and, over time, transforming society through the cumulative effects of such policies. They employ strategies such as joining coalitions to leverage their power as swing voters or negotiating entry into coalitions premised on certain ideological preconditions. Neither the OIJ nor JI in Bangladesh have substantively changed their religious priorities over time in an effort to cater to the political center. As noted in Philbrick Yadav's chapter, Islah in Yemen has a number of competing objectives (particularly tribal) alongside its religious goals, which make it a complex organization. However, it has secured a relatively consistent percentage of the vote in each of the three elections (1993, 1997, 2003) in which it has competed, and did not substantively alter its core religious objectives (though its strategic positioning changed) during that period.

A third group occupies the middle space between those who have credibly committed to a centrist shift and those who have rejected such a strategy in favor of outflanking exercises. These parties, namely, PAS in Malaysia and PKS in Indonesia, have at various points in their history swung moderate and conservative, depending on the strategic incentives at that time. While PAS notably engaged in outflanking vis-à-vis UMNO in the 1986, 1990, 1995, and 2004 elections, it shifted to the center and emphasized a more universalist agenda in both 1999 and 2008. In 2005, it agreed to the establishment of the PAS Supporters Club, comprised of non-Muslims who supported the party's longstanding commitment to nonracial and nonsectarian politics. In 2010, the PAS Supporters Club became an official non-Muslim wing of PAS. Yet there are factions within PAS that have engaged in discussions with UMNO over creating a Malay-Muslim partnership alliance as well as those who are disgruntled with the party's decision to stop talking about shari'a law, *hudud* (the strict Islamic criminal code), and other controversial issues. While the PKS is quite diligent in deemphasizing overt appeals to Islamic themes in its campaigns, focusing instead on universalist ideas like a clean and caring government, and while the party has joined coalitions with non-Islamist parties at the national, state, and local levels, it most often makes news for its support of often controversial Islamic legislation such as the 2006 and 2008 Anti-Pornography Bills. These parties can be classified as parties that pursue a mixed strategy of catering to both their core base on some issues and reaching out to expand their base to non-Islamists on others. As a result, they generally obtain moderate levels of electoral support, when compared to party competitors.

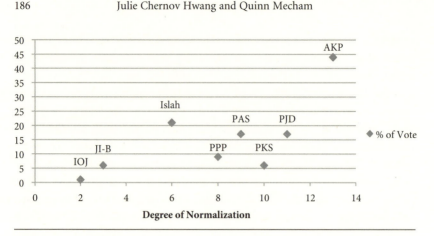

Figure 4. Political normalization and comparative electoral performance.

There is an observable, if imprecise correlation between party normalization and electoral success. Although we are careful to define and measure normalization independently of electoral success, there is a logic to why these two outcomes are correlated. In systems with iterated elections, political learning takes place in which parties learn what behaviors lead to electoral support and tend to coalesce around that collection of behaviors. Therefore, "normal" party behavior should look more and more like winning strategies over time. Of course, not all parties can win elections and they also face difficulties implementing their chosen strategies. Electoral success is much more than simply seeking the political center, although that is often a prerequisite for securing a majority of the electorate. Figure 4 highlights the general relationship between normalization and electoral success across country, which shows mixed results across different countries due to the different size of parties in different kinds of party systems. Degree of normalization (from Figure 3) is plotted on the *x*-axis, with electoral outcomes plotted on the *y*-axis. Electoral results are averaged for the three most recent legislative elections in which the party has competed.[1] Note that because of extensive fractionalization of the Indonesian party system, individual Islamist parties (PPP, PKS) receive a comparatively low percentage of the vote, when contrasted with Yemen or Malaysia.

More telling, however, are jumps in electoral success after a period of normalization in a given party or party system. For example, the Indonesian PKS jumped from less than 2 percent of the vote in 1999 to almost 8 percent in 2004, a shift that coincided with a normalization of its platform and

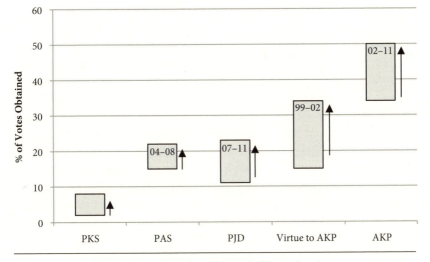

Figure 5. Normalization and electoral gains.

campaign behavior. The Malaysian PAS likewise jumped from 15 percent of the vote in 2004 to 22 percent in 2008, a gain that coincided with a period of moderation in that party's political agenda and approach to both women and non-Muslims. The PJD doubled its percentage of the electorate from 11 percent in 2007 to 23 percent in 2011 after a period of further normalization. Protest votes captured in the wake of enthusiasm around the Arab Spring likely contributed to their success in 2011 as well. Most striking of all is the Turkish case, in which the normalizing AKP doubled the percentage of the vote obtained by its predecessors (Welfare and Virtue), reaching 34 percent.[2] The party gradually increased its support over time, receiving 47 percent in 2007 and 50 percent in 2011. These gains, coinciding with periods of party normalization, are depicted in Figure 5. Note that the Indonesian PPP and Yemeni Islah parties do not have clear electoral results that can be tied to patterns of normalization and are not included. The x-axis indicates the political party, the y-axis indicates the total percentage of votes obtained by the party. The shaded box indicates the electoral gains during the period, and the period between which the gains took place is indicated at the top of each box. We have included the period of transition from the Turkish Virtue Party to the AKP, as well as gains made by the AKP, in separate columns.

New Opportunities for Islamist Parties

Renewed political dynamism throughout much of the Arab world has created new opportunities for Islamist parties, as indicated by Islamist electoral successes during 2011–2012 in Tunisia, Egypt, Morocco, and Kuwait. In the Arab world, Islamist movements and affiliated parties have been considered the primary loci for opposition to authoritarian regimes since the 1970s, and have been both carefully managed and systematically repressed. One of the principal arguments that Arab leaders have used against substantively opening their system through political reform is the disruptive and sometimes violent challenge that Islamist groups may provide to state and society. This has led many Arab regimes to either fully repress or artificially deflate the electoral prospects of Islamist organizations within their reach.

Since the popular overthrow of both presidents Zine Al-Abidine Ben Ali in Tunisia and Hosni Mubarak in Egypt, these political systems opened to newly free and fair elections, in which Islamist parties were able to compete unfettered for the first time in their history. These dramatic political openings led to remarkable success rates, with the Freedom and Justice Party and Al-Nour parties capturing the large majority of the Egyptian electorate, and Tunisia's Al-Nahda capturing a dominant plurality (37 percent) of Tunisia's electorate. Likewise, the removal of long-standing presidents in Libya (Muammar Qaddafi) and in Yemen (Ali Abdullah Saleh) has created the potential for new elections and Islamist party successes in these countries. Lower-level political reforms in the wake of the Arab Spring in countries like Morocco, Jordan, and Kuwait have the effect of upgrading political opportunities for the Islamist opposition in these countries as well. Cumulatively, a new window of political opportunity has opened for Islamists in many parts of the Arab world.

The hypotheses and cases in this volume provide insight into some of the patterns that are currently unfolding among Islamist parties in the Arab world. As Islamist parties take advantage of these new opportunities, their strategic behavior has begun to shift in some of the ways predicted by the evidence in this volume. We have already seen significant evidence for what we have described as moderation and normalization, as groups like Al-Nahda and the Egyptian Muslim Brotherhood have come to realize the very real prospects of capturing the center of their countries' electorates and winning power in new governments.

Al-Nahda's message, as championed by long-time leader Rachid el-Ghannouchi, has changed in the wake of new opportunities—focusing less on the religious components of its platform to articulate a vision of tolerance for pluralistic perspectives, democracy, and economic freedom. In so doing, shari'a has been deprioritized. The Egyptian Muslim Brotherhood's FJP has also moved from more traditional Muslim Brotherhood views to a platform that could attract a wide range of voters not traditionally thought to be Brotherhood supporters. The FJP has articulated a political strategy that in many respects is designed to avoid provoking the military transitional council hovering over Egypt's political transition, or alienating those that were integral to the popular revolution. Interestingly, even the more shari'a-focused Salafi groups have shifted their priorities toward mainstream political positions as they entered the electoral arena. This does not mean that they have suddenly abandoned religiously conservative positions. However, they have found that it is more difficult to speak out openly against women's political participation, against Egypt's treaty with Israel, or against the Egyptian banking system when they are competing in a national election than in their traditional comfort zone of small likeminded groups of men. Egyptian Salafis are newly weighing "the harm against the benefit" of their political positions, which are now more public than ever.[3]

One of the most interesting developments in Egypt, and to a lesser extent in Tunisia, is the emergent competition between Islamist parties. The Egyptian Muslim Brotherhood has been deeply divided on strategy throughout the revolutionary process, and divergent perspectives regarding its religious versus nonreligious priorities have led to very public splits with some key members going so far as to leave the organization. These divisions echo earlier divisions within the Brotherhood, which led to the creation of the more centrist Al-Wasat party in 1996, for example. Political clashes between the Brotherhood's FJP party and the Salafi Al-Nour party have been commonplace, and the collection of Egyptian presidential candidates running for office in 2012 represented a diverse cross-section of Islamist perspectives, ranging from moderate Brotherhood dissident Abdul Moneim Aboul Foutouh to popular religious conservative Hazem Abu Ismail. Salafis have also offered new public challenges in Tunisia, including large protests, one of which was intended to burn down the Nessma TV station broadcasting a controversial film.[4]

These public challenges highlight a clear divergence between different Islamist groups that compete over who frames the Islamist narratives; it has led to some degree of strategic outflanking as rival Islamists seek to shore up their religious credentials against one another. As the historically broad Islamist opposition begins to splinter, Islamist parties begin to compete against other Islamist parties (as they have long done in places like Indonesia) and find ways of distinguishing themselves from their competitors. We have found that the larger of the Islamist parties in a competitive system tend to moderate toward the center, while the smaller tend to distinguish themselves vis-à-vis their Islamist competitors by stricter adherence to conservative Islamic positions. This appears to be the case in Egypt, and a similar pattern may yet emerge in other countries in transition.

One theme of the volume has been that Islamist parties may depend on "protest votes" to succeed electorally, a recognition that may pull them to the center to pick up voters outside their core Islamist constituency. Protest voting may be particularly relevant to voting patterns during the first election in the course of a transition to a free electoral regime. In these "founding" elections, such as those in Egypt and Tunisia in 2011, voters situate their choices by juxtaposing them against the previous (often hated) regime, signaling that a vote for Islamist parties is foremost a vote for change over continuity. The capture of these protest or "revolutionary" voters is a key to understanding the widespread success of Islamist parties in Egypt, Tunisia, Morocco, and Kuwait during 2011. The challenge with basing an electoral strategy on capturing protest votes is that these voters dissipate over time, particularly if the party succeeds in gaining power. To the extent that some of those who recently voted for Islamist parties did so for reasons other than their Islamist preferences, they are unlikely to be loyal constituents of Islamist parties over time. Some evidence suggests that Egyptians who voted for the Brotherhood's FJP party in late 2011 began to rethink their support as the FJP reneged on previous commitments, such as their pledge not to run a presidential candidate.[5] Few parties have managed to consolidate the support of protest voters over time as has the Turkish AKP, making that case a rare exception.

As Islamists in the Arab world discover new political opportunities, they also have a wider set of reference points than ever before. Islamist parties are learning from the strategies and experiences of one another, collecting their own "cases" and drawing their own implications about what kind of political platforms, campaigns, coalitions, and governing principles they want to adopt. This does not mean that they are all becoming uniform over time, or that individual parties are making the same strategic choices as one another. Indeed, their domestic competitive context remains the most important determinate of party behavior. However, the rise of Islamist parties, coupled with the increasing ease of global communication over the last decade, has provided new opportunities for these parties to observe other Islamist parties' choices and learn from their examples. Islamists in the Middle East have the opportunity to learn from the long experience of Islamist parties in Asia, and Asian Islamists are looking to places like Turkey as they frame their identities and design political strategies.

This volume has sought to frame these cross-country comparative lessons in a systematic way, highlighting both the diversity across Islamist parties, and also the patterns of behavior that many hold in common. New political dynamism in much of the Middle East, coupled with the increased political learning across countries and parties that globalization provides, will make the behavior and collaboration of Islamist parties worldwide a very vibrant subject for political inquiry for years to come.

Notes

Introduction: The Emergence and Development of Islamist Political Parties

1. Jillian Schwedler, "A Paradox of Democracy? Islamist Participation in Elections," *Middle East Report* 209 (1998): 25–29; Jillian Schwedler, "Yemen's Aborted Opening," *Journal of Democracy* 13, 4 (October 2002): 48–55; Vickie Langohr, "Of Islamists and Ballot Boxes: Rethinking the Relationship Between Islamists and Electoral Politics," *International Journal of Middle East Studies* 33 (2001): 591–610; Daniel Brumberg, "Islamists and the Politics of Consensus," *Journal of Democracy* 13, 3 (July 2002): 109–15; Syed Vali Reza Nasr, "The Rise of Muslim Democracy," *Journal of Democracy* 16, 2 (April 2005): 13–27; William Case and Chin Tong Liew, "How Committed Is PAS to Democracy and How Do We Know It?" *Contemporary Southeast Asia* 23, 3 (December 2006): 385–406; Nathan Brown and Amr Hamzawy, "Islamist Parties: A Boon or a Bane for Democracy?" *Journal of Democracy* 19, 3 (2008): 49–54; Malika Zeghal, *Islamism in Morocco* (Princeton, N.J.: Markus Wiener, 2008); Ihsan Dagi, "Turkey's AKP in Power," *Journal of Democracy* 19, 3 (2008): 25–30.

2. Carrie Rosefsky Wickham, *Mobilizing Islam: Religion, Activism, and Political Change in Egypt* (New York: Columbia University Press, 2002); Janine Clarke, "The Conditions of Islamist Moderation: Unpacking Cross-Ideological Cooperation in Jordan," *International Journal of Middle East Studies* 38 (2006): 539–60; Jillian Schwedler. *Faith in Moderation: Islamist Parties in Jordan and Yemen* (Cambridge: Cambridge University Press, 2006); R. Quinn Mecham, "From the Ashes of Virtue, a Promise of Light: The Transformation of Political Islam in Turkey," *Third World Quarterly* 25, 2 (2004): 339–58; Murat Somer, "Moderate Islam and Secularist Opposition in Turkey: Implications for the World, Muslims and Secular Democracy," *Third World Quarterly* 28, 7 (November 2007): 1271–89; Gazme Cavdar, "Islamist *New Thinking* in Turkey: A Model for Political Learning?" *Political Science Quarterly* 121, 3 (Fall 2006): 477–97; Mona El-Ghobashy, "The Metamorphosis of the Egyptian Muslim Brotherhood," *International Journal of Middle East Studies* 37 (2005): 373–95; Ihsan Yilmaz, "Muslim Democrats in Turkey and Egypt: Participatory Politics as a Catalyst," *Insight Turkey* 11, 2 (April 2009): 93–112; Julie Chernov Hwang, "When Parties Swing: Islamist Parties and Institutional Moderation in Malaysia and Indonesia," *South East Asia Research* 18, 4 (December 2010): 635–74.

3. Brown and Hamzawy, "Islamist Parties"; Schwedler, "A Paradox of Democracy?"; Schwedler, "Yemen's Aborted Opening"; Langohr, "Of Islamists and Ballot Boxes."

4. Case and Liew, "How Committed Is PAS to Democracy and How Do We Know It?"; Joseph Chin Yong Liow, "Exigency or Expediency? Contextualizing Political Islam and the PAS Challenge in Malaysian Politics. *Third World Quarterly* 25, 2 (2004): 359–72; Anthony Bubalo, Greg Fealy, and Whit Mason, "Zealous Democrats: Islamism and Democracy in Egypt, Indonesia and Turkey," Lowy Institute Paper 25, Lowy Institute for International Policy, 2008.

5. Stathis Kalyvas, "Commitment Problems in Emerging Democracies: The Case of Religious Parties," *Comparative Politics* 32, 4 (July 2000): 379–99; Schwedler, *Faith in Moderation*; Clarke, "The Conditions of Islamist Moderation"; Carrie Rosefsky Wickham, "The Path to Moderation: Strategy and Learning in the Formation of Egypt's Al Wasat Party," *Comparative Politics* 36, 2 (January 2004): 205–28.

6. Wickham, "The Path to Moderation"; Clarke, "The Conditions of Islamist Moderation"; Somer, "Moderate Islam and Secularist Opposition in Turkey"; Schwedler, *Faith in Moderation*.

7. El-Ghobashy, "The Metamorphosis of the Egyptian Muslim Brotherhood"; Julie Chernov Hwang, *Peaceful Islamist Mobilization in the Muslim World: What Went Right* (London: Palgrave, 2009); Mecham "From the Ashes of Virtue, a Promise of Light"; Farish Ahmad Noor, "Blood, Sweat and Jihad: The Radicalization of the Discourse of the Pan-Malaysian Islamic Party (PAS) from the 1980s to the Present," *Journal of the Center of Southeast Asian Studies* 25, 2 (August 2003): 200–232; J. A. Stacher, "Post-Islamist Rumblings in Egypt: The Emergence of the Al Wasat Party," *Middle East Journal* 56, 3 (Summer 2002): 415–32; Yilmaz, "Muslim Democrats in Turkey and Egypt."

8. Wickham, "The Path to Moderation," 206.

9. Nasr, "The Rise of Muslim Democracy."

10. Wickham, "The Path to Moderation."

11. Mecham "From the Ashes of Virtue, a Promise of Light"; Cavdar, "Islamist New Thinking in Turkey."

12. Somer, "Moderate Islam and Secularist Opposition in Turkey"; Mecham "From the Ashes of Virtue, a Promise of Light."

13. Somer, "Moderate Islam and Secularist Opposition in Turkey," 1273.

14. Bubalo et al., "Zealous Democrats"; Hwang *Peaceful Islamist Mobilization in the Muslim World*; Liow "Exigency or Expediency?"; Joseph Chinyong Liow, *Piety and Politics: Islamism in Contemporary Malaysia* (Oxford: Oxford University Press, 2009); Clarke, "The Conditions of Islamist Moderation"; Schwedler, *Faith in Moderation*.

15. Clarke, "The Conditions of Islamist Moderation."

16. Jillian Schwedler and Janine Clarke, "Islamist-Leftist Cooperation in the Arab World," *ISIM Review* 1, 18 (2006).

17. Schwedler, *Faith in Moderation*.

18. Shadi Hamid, "The Islamist Response to Repression: Are Mainstream Islamist Groups Radicalizing?" Brookings Doha Center Publications (online), August 9, 2010.

19. Noor, "Blood, Sweat and Jihad"; Joseph Chinyong Liow, "Political Islam in Malaysia: Problematizing Discourse and Practice in the UMNO-PAS 'Islamisation Race," *Commonwealth and Comparative Politics* 42, 2 (2004): 184–205.

20. Noor, "Blood, Sweat and Jihad," 202–5.

21. Egypt: Wickham, *Mobilizing Islam*; Bruce K. Rutherford, *Egypt After Mubarak: Liberalism, Islam, and Democracy in the Arab World* (Princeton, N.J.: Princeton University Press, 2008); Malaysia: Liow, *Piety and Politics*; Turkey: Jenny White, *Islamist Mobilization in Turkey* (Seattle: University of Washington Press, 2002); Algeria: Michael Willis, *The Islamist Challenge in Algeria: A Political History* (New York: New York University Press, 1999); Morocco: Zeghal, *Islamism in Morocco*; Jordan: Schwedler, *Faith in Moderation*; Palestine: Saul Mishal and Avraham Sela, *The Palestinian Hamas* (New York: Columbia University Press, 2000).

22. Pakistan: Vali Nasr, "Military Rule, Islamism and Democracy in Pakistan," *Middle East Journal* 58, 2 (2004): 195–209; Indonesia: Hwang, *Peaceful Islamist Mobilization in the Muslim World*; Tunisia: Mohamed Elhachmi Hamdi, *The Politicisation of Islam: A Case Study of Tunisia* (Boulder, Colo.: Westview Press, 2000); Jordan: Quintan Wiktorowicz, *The Management of Islamic Activism: Salafis, the Muslim Brotherhood, and State Power in Jordan* (Albany: State University of New York Press, 2000); Lebanon: Judith Palmer Harik, *Hezbollah: The Changing Face of Terrorism* (London: Tauris, 2004); Senegal: Leonardo A. Villalon, *Islamic Society and State Power in Senegal: Disciples and Citizens in Fatick* (Cambridge: Cambridge University Press, 1995); and Iran: Olivier Roy, *The Failure of Political Islam* (Cambridge, Mass.: Harvard University Press, 1996).

23. Western Europe: Stathis Kalyvas, *The Rise of Christian Democracy in Europe* (Ithaca, N.Y.: Cornell University Press, 1996); Communist: Michael Waller and Meindert Fennema, eds., *Communist Parties in Western Europe: Decline or Adaptation?* (New York: Blackwell, 1988); radical right: Hans-Georg Betz, *Radical Right-Wing Populism in Western Europe* (London: Palgrave Macmillan, 1994); Herbert Kitschelt, *The Radical Right in Western Europe: A Comparative Analysis* (Ann Arbor: University of Michigan Press, 1997); Pippa Norris, *Radical Right: Voters and Parties in the Electoral Market* (Cambridge: Cambridge University Press, 2005).

Chapter 1. Islamist Parties as Strategic Actors:
Electoral Participation and Its Consequences

1. Including provision of a religious council to review legislation, and ineligibility of women or Christians for the Egyptian presidency.

2. Freedom House 2010 political rights scores for the six countries in this study are Indonesia 2, Turkey 3, Malaysia 4, Pakistan 4, Morocco 5, Yemen 6. Scores range from 1 to 7, with 7 the most authoritarian.

3. Donald L. Horowitz, *Ethnic Groups in Conflict* (Berkeley: University of California Press, 1985).

Chapter 2. When Is Normalization Also Democratization? Islamist
Political Parties, the Turkish Case, and the Future of Muslim Politics

1. Among others, Stathis N. Kalyvas, "Unsecular Politics and Religious Mobilization," in *European Christian Democracy*, ed. Thomas Kselman and Joseph A. Buttigietg (Notre Dame, Ind.: University of Notre Dame Press, 2003); Jeffrey Haynes, "Religion and Democratization: An Introduction," *Democratization* 16, 6 (2009): 1041–57; Jillian Schwedler, "Can Islamists Become Moderates? Rethinking the Inclusion-Moderation Hypothesis," *World Politics* 63, 2 (2011): 347–76.

2. Murat Somer, "Moderation of Religious and Secular Politics, a Country's 'Center' and Democratization," *Democratization* (November 2012): 1–24.

3. Şerif Mardin, "Center-Periphery Relations: A Key to Turkish Politics?" *Daedalus* 102, 1 (1973): 169–90; Şerif Mardin, *Religion, Society, and Modernity in Turkey* (Syracuse, N.Y.: Syracuse University Press, 2006); Niyazi Berkes, *The Development of Secularism in Turkey* (New York: Routledge 1998); Kemal H. Karpat, *Ottoman Past and Today's Turkey* (Leiden: Brill, 2000); Jenny B. White, "Islam and Politics in Contemporary Turkey," in *The Cambridge History of Turkey*, ed. Reşat Kasaba, vol. 4, *Turkey in the Modern World* (Cambridge: Cambridge University Press, 2008), 357–80; Carter V. Findley, *Turkey, Islam, Nationalism, and Modernity: A History, 1789–2007* (New Haven, Conn.: Yale University Press, 2010).

4. Umit Cizre Sakallioğlu, "Parameters and Strategies of Islam-State Interaction in Republican Turkey," *International Journal of Middle East Studies* 28 (1996): 231–51.

5. Scott Mainwaring and Timothy R. Scully, *Christian Democracy in Latin America: Electoral Competition and Regime Conflicts* (Stanford, Calif.: Stanford University Press, 2003).

6. Haldun Gülalp, "Political Islam in Turkey: The Rise and Fall of the Refah Party," *Muslim World* 89, 1 (1999): 22–41.

7. Sultan Tepe, "Turkey's AKP: A Model 'Muslim-Democratic' Party?" *Journal of Democracy* 16, 3 (2005): 69–85; Gamze Çavdar, "Islamist New Thinking in Turkey: A Model for Political Learning?" *Political Science Quarterly* 121, 3 (2006): 477–500; Murat Somer, "Media Values and Democratization: What Unites and What Divides Religious-Conservative and Pro-Secular Elites," *Turkish Studies* 11, 4 (December 2010): 555–77.

8. Güneş M. Tezcür, "Judicial Activism Activism in Perilous Times: The Turkish Case," *Law & Society Review* 43, 2 (2009): 305–36; Meltem Müftüler-Baç and Fuat Keyman, "Turkey Under the AKP: The Era of Dominant Party Politics," *Journal of Democracy* 23, 1 (2012): 85–99; Berna Turam, "Turkey Under the AKP: Are Rights and Liberties Safe?" *Journal of Democracy* 23, 1 (2012): 109–18; Somer, "Moderation of Religious and Secular Politics."

9. Akin Ünver, "Turkey, Past and Future: The Forgotten Secular Turkish Model," *Middle East Quarterly* 43 (2013): 57–64.

10. Somer, "Moderation of Religious and Secular Politics."

11. Mardin, "Center-Periphery Relations"; Somer, "Moderation of Religious and Secular Politics."

12. Cizre Sakallioğlu, "Parameters and Strategies of Islam-State Interaction."

13. Ergun Özbudun, "Established Revolution Versus Unfinished Revolution: Patterns of Democratization in Mexico and Turkey," in *Authoritarian Politics in Modern Society: The Dynamics of Established One-Party Systems*, ed. Samuel P. Huntington and Clement H. Moore (New York: Basic Books, 1970), 380–405; *Otoiter rejimler, seçimsel demokrasiler ve Türkiye* (Authoritarian Regimes, Electoral Democracies, and Turkey) (Istanbul: Bilgi Üniversitesi Yayinlari, 2011).

14. Michele P. Angrist, "Party Systems and Regime Formation in the Modern Middle East: Explaining Turkish Exceptionalism," *Comparative Politics* 36, 2 (2004): 229–49; William Hale and Ergun Özbudun, *Islamism, Democracy and Liberalism in Turkey* (London: Routledge, 2010); Somer, "Moderation of Religious and Secular Politics."

15. Murat Somer, "Is Turkish Secularism Anti-Religious, Reformist, Separationist, Integrationist, or Simply Undemocratic?" Review Essay on Berna Turam, ed., *Secular State and Religious Society: Two Forces in Play in Turkey* (New York: Palgrave, 2012), *Journal of Church and State* 55, 3 (2013): 585–97.

16. Mehmet Ali Soydan, *Türkiye'nin refah gerçeği* (Turkey's "Welfare" Reality) (Erzurum: Birey Yayincilik, 1994); Serdar Şen, *AKP milli görüşçü mü?* (Is the AKP Pro-National Outlook?) (Istanbul: Nokta Kitap, 2004).

17. Hakan M. Yavuz, *Islamic Political Identity in Turkey* (New York: Oxford University Press, 2003); Ahmet Yükleyen, "Sufism and Islamic Groups in Contemporary Turkey," in *The Cambridge History of Turkey*, ed. Kasaba, 381–87.

18. Jenny B. White, *Islamist Mobilization in Turkey: A Study in Vernacular Politics* (Seattle: University of Washington Press, 2002); Cihan Tuğal, *Passive revolution: absorbing the Islamic challenge to capitalism* (Stanford, Calif.: Stanford University Press 2009).

19. Soydan, *Türkiye'nin refah gerçeği*.

20. Ali Çarkoğlu and Ersin Kalaycioğlu, *Turkish Democracy Today: Elections Protest and Stability in an Islamic Society* (London: Tauris, 2007).

21. Hale and Özbudun, *Islamism, Democracy and Liberalism in Turkey*, 13.

22. Sinan Ciddi, *Kemalism in Turkish Politics: The Republican People's Party, Secularism and Nationalism* (London: Routledge, 2009); Hale and Özbudun, *Islamism, Democracy and Liberalism in Turkey*.

23. Cihan Tuğal, *Passive Revolution: Absorbing the Islamic Challenge to Capitalism* (Stanford, Calif.: Stanford University Press, 2009), 44.

24. Ayşe Buğra, "Political Islam in Turkey in Historical Context: Strengths and Weaknesses," in *The Politics of Permanent Crisis: Class, Ideology and State in Turkey*,

ed. Neşecan Balkan and Sungur Savran (New York: Nova Science, 2002), 107–44; Nilüfer Göle, "Secularism and Islamism in Turkey: The Making of Elites and Counter-Elites," *Middle East Journal* 51, 1 (1997): 46–58; Metin Heper, "Islam and Democracy in Turkey: Toward a Reconciliation?" *Middle East Journal* 51, 1 (1997): 32–46; Ziya Öniş, "The Political Economy of Islamic Resurgence in Turkey: The Rise of the Welfare Party in Perspective," *Third World Quarterly* 18, 4 (1997): 743–66.

25. Hale and Özbudun, *Islamism, Democracy and Liberalism in Turkey*.

26. Ibid., 7

27. Buğra, "Political Islam in Turkey in Historical Context."

28. R. Quinn Mecham, "From the Ashes of Virtue, A Promise of Light: the Transformation of Political Islam in Turkey," *Third World Quarterly* 25, 2 (2004): 339–58; Murat Somer, "Does It Take Democrats to Democratize? Lessons from Islamic and Secular Elite Values in Turkey," *Comparative Political Studies* 44, 5 (2011): 511–45.

29. Soydan, *Türkiye'nin refah gerçeği*.

30. Somer, "Media Values and Democratization"; Somer, "Does It Take Democrats to Democratize?"

31. Somer, "Media Values and Democratization."

32. The analysis included three Islamic conservative papers (*Yeni Şafak, Zaman,* and *Milli Gazete*) and two pro-secular papers (*Milliyet* and *Cumhuriyet*) and covered more than 40,000 articles published between 1996 and 2004. The five papers captured roughly 22 percent of total newspaper circulation in 1996. See Somer, "Media Values and Democratization"; "Does It Take Democrats to Democratize?" for a detailed discussion of the methodology.

33. Somer, "Does It Take Democrats to Democratize?"

34. Ergun Özbudun, "Democratization Reforms in Turkey, 1993–2004." *Turkish Studies* 8, 2 (June 2007): 179–96.

35. Hale and Özbudun, *Islamism, Democracy and Liberalism in Turkey*, 55.

36. Meltem Müftüler Baç, "Turkey's Political Reforms and the Impact of the European Union," *South European Society and Politics* 10, 1 (2005): 17–31; Hale and Özbudun, *Islamism, Democracy and Liberalism in Turkey*, 55–62.

37. Ziya Öniş, "Conservative Globalism at the Crossroads: The Justice and Development Party and the Thorny Path to Democratic Consolidation in Turkey," *Mediterranean Politics* 14, 1 (2009): 21–40; Murat Somer, "Moderate Islam and Secularist Opposition in Turkey: Implications for the World, Muslims and Democracy," *Third World Quarterly* 28, 7 (October 2007): 1271–89; Ciddi, *Kemalism in Turkish Politics*.

38. Ciddi, *Kemalism in Turkish Politics*.

39. Somer, "Moderate Islam and Secularist Opposition in Turkey"; Osman Ulagay, *AKP gerçeği ve laik darbe fyaskosu* (Truth of AKP and Fiasco of Secular Coup) (Istanbul: Doğan Kitap, 2008).

40. Somer, "Moderate Islam and Secularist Opposition in Turkey"; Hakan M. Yavuz, *Secularism and Muslim Democracy in Turkey* (New York: Cambridge University Press, 2009).

41. Tezcür, "Judicial Activism Activism in Perilous Times," 310.

42. Emma Sinclair-Webb, "The Turkish Trial That Fell Far Short," *New York Times*, August 6, 2013.

43. Murat Somer and Evangelos G. Liaras, "Turkey's New Kurdish Opening: Religious Versus Secular Values," *Middle East Policy* 17, 2 (Summer 2010): 152–65; Tezcür, "Judicial Activism Activism in Perilous Times; Somer, "Does It Take Democrats to Democratize?"

44. Calculated based on information in Bayram Erzurumluoğlu and Turgut Göksu, "Türkiye'deki suç eğilimleri ve polis performansinin faktörel etkisi" (The Impact of Police Performance on Crime Development in Turkey), *Polis Bilimleri Dergisi* (2013): 43; Türkiye I[uf53]statistik Kurumu (Turkish Statistical Institute), http://www.turkstat.gov.tr/, accessed May 27, 2013.

45. Biriz Berksoy, *Türkiye'de ordu, polis ve istihbarat teşkilatlari: Yakin dönem gelişmeler ve reform ihtiyaçlari* (The Military, Police and Intelligence Agencies in Turkey: Recent Developments and Reform Needs] (Istanbul: Tesev Yayinlari, 2013).

46. *Gezi Park Protests: Brutal Denial of the Right to Peaceful Assembly in Turkey*, Amnesty International Report, EUR 44/022/2013, 2013. Also see http://www.amnesty.org/en/news/turkey-accused-gross-human-rights-violations-gezi-park-protests-2013-10-02.

47. Reporters Without Borders, *World Press Freedom Index 2013*, Paris, http://en.rsf.org/press-freedom-index-2013,1054.html.

48. Radikal Online, "Sadece cumhuriyet'e dokunulmasin" (Let Us Not Touch Only the Republic), May 10, 2010.

49. Somer, "Is Turkish Secularism Anti-Religious, Reformist, Separationist, Integrationist, or Simply Undemocratic?"

50. www.diyanet.gov.tr, accessed May 27, 2013.

51. Michaelle L. Browers, *Political Ideology in the Arab World: Accommodation and Transformation* (Cambridge: Cambridge University Press, 2009).

52. Nancy Bermeo, "*Myths of Moderation: Confrontation and Conflict During Democratic Transitions,*" *Comparative Politics* 29, 3 (1997): 305–22; R. Quinn Mecham, "From the Ashes of Virtue, A Promise of Light: the Transformation of Political Islam in Turkey," *Third World Quarterly* (2004); Somer, "Does It Take Democrats to Democratize?"

53. Ihsan D. Daği, "Transformation of Islamic Political Identity in Turkey: Rethinking the West and Westernization," *Turkish Studies* 6, 1 (2005): 21–37; Ümit Cizre, "Introduction," in *Secular and Islamic Politics in Turkey: The Making of the Justice and Development Party*, ed. Ümit Cizre (New York: Routledge, 2008), 1–14.

54. Somer, "Moderation of Religious and Secular Politics," 2012.

Chapter 3. Patterns of Normalization: Islamist Parties in Indonesia

1. The only other Muslim nation delimited as "free" in 2010 was Mali. All others were classified as "partly free" or "not free." Scores are based on a scale from 1 to 7,

with 1 the "most free." For the full list of Freedom House combined scores in 2010 see Freedom in the World 2010, http://www.freedomhouse.org.

2. July 2010 statistic from CIA World Factbook, https://www.cia.gov.

3. Robin Bush, *Nahdlatul Ulama and the Struggle for Power Within Islam and Politics in Indonesia* (Singapore: ISEAS, 2009), 2.

4. Carrie Rosefsky Wickham, "The Path to Moderation: Strategy and Learning in the Form of Egypt's Wasat Party," *Comparative Politics* 36, 2 (2004): 206.

5. There are currently three major nationalist parties: PDI-P, Golkar, and Democrat; the Democrat Party did not exist in 1999.

6. The Indonesian national ideology of Pancasila consists of five principles: belief in one god, unity in diversity, humanitarianism, social justice, and democracy through deliberation and consensus.

7. Greg Fealy and Anthony Bubalo, *Joining the Caravan: The Middle East, Islamism and Indonesia*, Lowy Institute Paper 5 (Sidney: Lowy Institute for International Policy; Longueville Press, 2005), 67.

8. Ibid.

9. Marrin Van Bruinessen, "Post-Suharto Muslim Engagements with Civil Society and Democratization," presented at Third International Conference and Workshop, "Indonesia in Transition," August 24–28, 2003, University of Indonesia, Depok.

10. By election registration requirements, I am referring specifically to what Indonesians commonly but confusingly have called the "electoral threshold," a constraint on participation in future elections for failure to obtain a certain percentage of the vote in the current election. In 1999 and 2004, the constraint was minor. The party was permitted to reform under a [often slightly altered] new name and new banner. For example, the Justice Party would become the Prosperous Justice Party. In the 2009 elections, Indonesia adopted a new 2.5 percent electoral threshold, in which entry barriers applied to legislative seats rather than to the next election. Thus, in referring to the 2009 elections, the more common meaning "electoral threshold" has come into use.

11. Kikue Hamayotsu, "Beyond Faith and Identity: Mobilizing Islamic Youth in a Democratic Indonesia," *Pacific Review* 24, 2 (2011): 225–47.

12. Ibid.

13. *Memperjuangkan Masyarakat Madani: Partai Keadilan Sejahtera Falsafa Dasar Perjuangan dan Platform Kebijakan Pembagunan PK Sejahtera* [Building an Islamic Civil Society: PKS Basic Philosophy of Struggle and Policy Platform], Jakarta: Majelis Pertimbangan Pusat PKS 2008, 37

14. Yon Machmudi, "Islamising Indonesia: The Rise of Jemaah Tarbiyah and the Prosperous Justice Party," Ph.D. dissertation, Australian National University, 2006, 198–99.

15. Interview, Mutammimul Ula, former member of parliament from PKS, July 2008, Jakarta.

16. Julie Chernov Hwang and Quinn Mecham, "Institutional Incentives and Electoral Success of Islamist Parties: Explaining the Divergent Trajectories of the PKS in

Indonesia and the AKP in Turkey," presented at Association for Asian Studies Annual Meeting, Philadelphia, March 27–30, 2010.

17. Historically, two significant divisions among Indonesian Muslims were between the traditionalists, often characterized as poorer, rural Javanese members of Nahdlatul Ulama and modernists who tended to be wealthier, middle-class, educated urbanites who were members of Muhammadiyah. While traditionalism blended classical Sunni jurisprudence interpreted with Sufi, Hindu, and local cultural influences, modernists reject the four Sunni schools of Islamic jurisprudence in favor of direct interpretation of the Quran and Hadith. William Liddle, "Indonesia in 1999: Democracy Restored," *Asian Survey* 49 (January/February 2000): 37.

18. Bernhard Platzdasch, *Islamism in Indonesia* (Singapore: ISEAS, 2009), 202.

19. Ibid., 180.

20. Ibid.

21. Ibid., 178.

22. *Keterapan Muktamar VI-Partai Persatuan Pembangunan Tentang Khittah dan Program Perjuangan Partai Persatuan Pembangunan*, www.ppp.or.id (2007), 12–13.

23. Fieldwork notes, March 2009, Jakarta. I walked into an anti-Ahmadiyah demonstration in Jakarta. The leading organizations were Hizbut Tahrir and the Islamic Defenders Front. However, there were a handful of men with two PPP banners.

24. *Anggaran Dasar, Partai Persatuan Pembangunan*, 5.

25. The original Marriage Law as proposed would have unified all regulations on marriage and divorce, severely restricted polygamy, increased women's rights in divorce beyond what is allowed by Islam, and largely removed marriage and divorce from the religious courts. The Kepercayaan Law would have permitted religious mysticism to be recognized as a legitimate belief system by the state. This caused no small amount of consternation by many Muslims who saw this as a way to equalize belief and religion. Both bills sparked massive protests.

26. Platzdasch, Bernard, *Islamism in Indonesia*, 179.

27. Hamayotsu, Kikue, "The Rise of the Prosperous Justice Party in Post-Authoritarian Indonesia," *Asian Survey* 51, 5 (September/October 2011): 971–92, 975; Noorhaidi Hasan, "Islamist Party, Electoral Politics, and *Da'wa* Mobilization Among Youth: The Prosperous Justice Party," RSIS Working Paper 184, October 22, 2009, 25.

28. Interview, Mardani Ali Sera, deputy secretary general of PKS, PKS Headquarters, January 2010, Jakarta.

29. Greg Fealy, "Democracy Mengerem Kekerasan Islam," *Madina*, April 4, 2008, 34.

30. Hamayotsu, "Rise of the Prosperous Justice Party," 976.

31. Ananta, Aris, Arifin, Evi Nurvidya, and Suryadinata, Leo, *Emerging Democracy in Indonesia* (Singapore: ISEAS, 2005), 59.

32. PKS internal party data, sent by email by Mardani Ali Sera, deputy secretary general, January 20, 2010.

33. Interview with Mardani Ali Sera, deputy secretary general, January 2010, Jakarta.

Riset Perilaku Pemilih PKS, PowerPoint presentation on PKS internal survey conducted August 30–September 6, 2009, slide 18, given by Mardani Ali Sera at interview, January 2010, Jakarta.

34. Hwang and Mecham, "Institutional Incentives and Electoral Success of Islamist Parties," 42.

35. Ibid.

36. Interview, Irghan Mahfidz, secretary general of PPP, January 2010, Jakarta.

37. Ananta, Arafin, and Suryadinata, *Emerging* Democracy, 51.

38. Ibid.

39. Interview, Irghan Mahfidz.

40. Interview, Husnan Bey, editor of PPP party magazine, *Majalah Pakar*, May 2006, Jakarta.

41. Fieldwork notes, January 2010, Jakarta; Platzdasch, *Islamism in Indonesia*, 49.

42. Hamayotsu, "Beyond Faith and Identity: Mobilizing Islamic Youth in a Democratic Indonesia," *Pacific* Review (March 21, 2009): 19.

43. Platzdasch, *Islamism in Indonesia*, 49

44. Interview, Burhanuddin Muhtadi, researcher at Indonesian Survey Institute, January 2010, Jakarta.

45. Ibid.

46. Bubalo, Fealy, and Mason, *Zealous Democrats*, 64.

47. Ibid.

48. Hwang and Mecham, "Institutional Incentives and Electoral Success of Islamist Parties," 33.

49. Interview, senior cadre of PKS, January 2010, Jakarta.

50. Ibid.

51. Fieldwork notes. In all interviews conducted with PKS elites, only one has said non-Muslims could ever become members of the Majlis Syuro.

52. Interview, Anis Matta, secretary general, PKS, March 2009, Jakarta.

53. Interview, Nursanita Nasution, former member of the DPR from PKS, January 2010, Jakarta.

54. Interview, LSI researcher and scholar on PKS, January 2010, Jakarta.

55. PKS internal party data, sent by email by Mardani Ali Sera, January 20, 2010.

56. Ibid.

57. Interview, LSI researcher and scholar on PKS, January 2010, Jakarta.

58. Bernhard Platzdasch, "In Different Shades of Grey," *ISEAS Viewpoints*, October 4, 2008.

59. Platzdasch, *Islamism in Indonesia*, 248.

60. The Jakarta Charter was a seven-word addendum to the "belief in one God" principle of Pancasila that would have obliged Muslims to obey shari'a. After protests

from non-Muslims in Eastern Indonesia as well as secular Muslims, the clause was removed.

61. Nadirsyah Hosen, "Religion and the Indonesian Constitution: A Recent Debate," *Journal of Southeast Asian Studies* 36, 3 (2006): 432.

62. Interview, Irghan Mahfidz, secretary general of PPP, July 2008, Jakarta.

63. *Kekuatan Elektoral Partai-Partai Islam Menjelang Pemilu 2009*; Lembaga Survei Indonesia, PowerPoint presentation, Jakarta, September 2008.

64. Ibid.

65. *Kekuatan Elektoral Partai-Partai Islam Menjelang Pemilu 2009*; Saiful Mujani, "Macrocondition, Policy, and Electoral Attitudes on the Eve of the 2009 Election: Public Opinion Trends," Jakarta, March 2009.

66. Ibid.

67. Fealy, Greg, "Indonesia's Islamic Parties in Decline," *Inside Story*, May 11, 2009

68. Muhtadi, Burhanuddin, "Thinking Globally, Acting Locally: Analyzing the Islamist Activism of Indonesia's Prosperous Justice Party (PKS) from a Social Movement Theory Perspective," sub-thesis, Master of Arts in Asian Studies. Australian National University, July 2008, 72.

69. Hasan, "Islamist Party, Electoral Politics," 25.

70. *Kekuatan Elektoral Partai-Partai Islam Menjelang Pemilu 2009*.

71. Interview, Mohammed Razikun, head of the Election Winning Body of PKS, March 2009, Jakarta.

72. Interview, Zulkieflimansyah, senior member of parliament from PKS, March 2009, Jakarta.

73. Riset Perilaku Pemilih PKS, PowerPoint presentation.

74. Fieldwork notes from campaign trail with Anis Matta in Selayar, Sarah Handayani in villages outside Bogor, Yoyoh Yusroh in Tanggerang, and Zulkieflimansyah in Banten in the two weeks prior to the 2009 elections.

75. Interview, Saiful Mujani, professor at UIN Syarif Hidayatullah, March 2009, Jakarta.

Chapter 4. Between a Rock and a Hard Place: Reform, Reticence,
and Realignments of the Pan-Malaysian Islamic Party

1. Malays are the ethnic majority in Malaysia, approximately 50 percent of the population; they are also constitutionally defined as Muslims. The combination of Malay-Muslims with coreligionists from the minority Chinese, Indian, and Hadrami communities account for the approximately 60 percent of the Malaysian population who are Muslim. For general information about politics and society in Malaysia (albeit slightly outdated), see Harold A. Crouch, *Government and Society in Malaysia* (Ithaca, N.Y.: Cornell University Press, 1996).

2. For a detailed study of the history of PAS, see Farish Noor, *Islam Embedded: The Historical Development of the Pan-Malaysian Islamic Party PAS, 1951–2003*, 2 vols. (Kuala Lumpur: Malaysian Sociological Research Institute, 2004).

3. For a detailed discussion of how the coup materialized, see Joseph Chinyong Liow, "Creating Cadres: Mobilization, Activism, and the Youth Wing of the Pan-Malaysian Islamic Party, PAS," *Pacific Affairs* 84 (December 2011).

4. The classic study of this phenomenon is Judith Nagata, *The Reflowering of Malaysian Islam: Modern Religious Radicals and Their Roots* (Vancouver: University of British Columbia Press, 1984).

5. The Islamization "race" is treated in Joseph Chinyong Liow, *Piety and Politics: Islamism in Contemporary Malaysia* (New York: Oxford University Press, 2009).

6. This, despite the fact that until recently, Malaysian tertiary students were banned from partaking in political activities under the 1971 Universities and University Colleges Act. "Malaysia Rules Against Ban on Student Politics," *Jakarta Globe*, October 31, 2011.

7. See Maznah Mohamed, "Malaysia—Democracy and the End of Ethnic Politics?" *Australian Journal of International Affairs* 62, 4 (December 2008); Thomas B. Pepinsky, "The 2008 Malaysian Elections: An End to Ethnic Politics?" *Journal of East Asian Studies* 9, 1 (January–April 2009); Joseph Chinyong Liow and Afif Pasuni, "Debating the Conduct and Nature of Malaysian Politics: Communalism and New Media Post-March 2008," *Journal of Current Southeast Asian Affairs* 4 (2010).

8. Basiron Abdul Wahab, "Pilihan Raya Umum: Negara Kebajikan, Tabung Biasiswa Antara Tawaran PAS" ("General elections: PAS offers a welfare state and bursary fund"), *Harakah Daily*, August 28, 2007.

9. Citing examples from the *hadith* (sayings of the Prophet Muhammad) al-Bukhari, an ulama with the "professional" camp, intimated that since "Islamic law came only when religion and faith were established, likewise the implementation of Islamic law today cannot come about before the proper education of Muslims in the understanding of the religion." Author interview, Kuala Lumpur, March 23, 2011.

10. William F. Case and Liew Chin Tong, "How Committed Is PAS to Democracy and How Do We Know It?" *Contemporary Southeast Asia* 28, 3 (December 2006): 89.

11. In comparison, PAS won 27 seats in the same election. In 1995, DAP won 9 seats, PAS only 7.

12. See Lim Kit Siang, "Hadi should not cheapen political discourse by trivialising the numerous strong and legitimate DAP objections to the PAS Islamic State concept which PAS leaders have to date been unable to give satisfactory or acceptable explanations," *DAP Malaysia*, December 5, 2003.

13. *Kafir-mengafir* refers to highly acrimonious exchanges between fellow Muslims where each accuses the other of being apostate.

14. Liew Chin Tong, "PAS Politics: Defining an Islamic State," in *Politics in Malaysia: The Malay Dimension*, ed. Edmund Terence Gomez (New York: Routledge, 2007), 111–12.

15. Liow, *Piety and Politics*, 83.

16. Liew, "PAS Politics: Defining an Islamic State," 109.

17. Ibid., 107.

18. Ibid., 116.

19. Interview with PAS Central Committee Member, Kuala Lumpur, March 23, 2011.

20. http://blog.drdzul.com, June 7, 2011, accessed February 24, 2012.

21. See Joseph Chinyong Liow, "The Politics Behind Malaysia's 11th General Election," *Asian Survey* 45, 6 (November/December 2005).

22. For a discussion on how PAS has sought to integrate women into the party leadership, see Julie Chernov-Hwang, "When Parties Swing: Islamist Parties and Institutional Moderation in Malaysia and Indonesia," *South East Asia Research* 18, 4 (December 2010): 652–54.

23. See Chan Wenling, "When Islamists Play by the Rules Yet Change the Game," *RSIS Commentaries* 6 (June 16, 2010).

24. Deborah Loh, "Non-Muslims for PAS," *Nut Graph*, November 26, 2008.

25. Ahmad Pathoni, "Malaysian Hindu Woman Embraces Islamic Party," *Reuters*, February 29, 2008.

26. Ibid.

27. *Raja Petra Kamarudin, "PAS: Trapped Between a Rock and a Hard Place," Malaysia Today, January 3, 2009.*

28. *Reme Ahmad, "Islam Permits Working With Non-Muslims," Straits Times, June 14, 2010.*

29. Yow Hong Chieh, "Hudud Will Empty Out PAS"'s Non-Muslim Wing, Says Chief," *Malaysian Insider*, October 9, 2011.

30. *The Malaysian government had blocked previous PAS attempts to implement hudud on the grounds that it was unconstitutional.*

31. "Top Leaders to Openly Discuss and Resolve Matter Tomorrow," *The Star*, September 27, 2011.

32. Nik Imran Abdullah, "Serve People First, PAS Fan Club Tells Party," *New Straits Times*, October 5, 2011.

33. "Non-Muslim Supporters May Give Up on PAS," *The Star*, October 10, 2011.

34. Abdullah, "Serve People First, PAS Fan Club Tells Party."

35. Syed Azhar, "Hu Defies Party Gag Order," *The Star*, October 13, 2011.

36. Zedeck Siew, "PAS's Slim Victory in Manik Urai," *Nut Graph*, July 15, 2009.

37. Interestingly, during the Manek Urai by-elections, banners had appeared on the campaign trail raising doubts about PAS's commitment to Islam since it was prepared to work so closely with DAP. More likely than not, these banners were erected by the UMNO campaign machinery to sow doubts in the minds of potential PAS supporters.

38. Interview with Dzulkefly Ahmad, Kuala Lumpur, March 23, 2010.

39. Even in the case of the exception, APU (an alliance between PAS and Semangat '46, a breakaway UMNO party), PAS was in an indirect alliance with DAP by virtue of Semangat's formal alliance with the latter in the form of Gagasan Rakyat.

40. See H. Wilke, J. Pruyn, and G. de Vries, "Coalition Formation: Political Attitudes and Power," *European Journal of Social Psychology* 8, 2 (1978). As we saw earlier, DAP certainly suffered for its association with PAS in 1999.

41. Interview with Hassan Shukri, Petaling Jaya, August 16, 2006.

42. In fact, a group of PAS stalwarts eventually left and formed Berjasa as a breakaway party.

43. The CCC functioned as an executive board formed by PAS to spread the message of Islam to the ethnic Chinese community and other non-Muslim communities. See Ibnu Hasyim, *PAS Kuasai Malaysia?* (Kuala Lumpur: GG Edar, 1993), 345.

44. The other parties were Parti Nasionalis Malaysia (Nasma; Malaysian Nationalist Party), Parti Sosialis Rakyat Malaysia (PSRM; Malaysian People''s Socialist Party), and Sepakat Democratic Party (SDP).

45. Hasyim, *PAS Kuasai Malaysia*, 350.

46. Liow, *Piety and Politics*, 38.

47. Ibid., 363–66.

48. After PAS dissolved its relationship with the CCC, some CCC leaders including Leow Kim Hock and Ong Hua set up the Communities Consultative Council (CCC) in 1987 to achieve the original CCC objective. The revamped CCC later registered as a political party—the Community Coalition Congress—November 20, 1988, and continued support of the PAS objective of an Islamic state.

49. Crouch, *Government and Society in Malaysia*, 122–23.

50. PAS's relations with Semangat also began to experience friction. By winning the lion's share of both parliamentary and state seats in Kelantan during the 1990 elections, PAS enjoyed primacy in the state administration. This translated to PAS control over major administrative and political appointments in the state government, which went to party cadre. The gulf between PAS and Semangat widened over time, to the extent that several Semangat representatives were expelled from the PAS-controlled state legislature in late 1996. John Hilley, *Malaysia: Mahathirism, Hegemony and the New Opposition* (London: Zed, 2001), 189–90.

51. Interview with Anwar Ibrahim, Singapore, August 22, 2008.

52. Azmin Amin, "Hindraf: PAS Kesal Hak Asasi Rakyat Dicabuli," *Harakah Daily*, November 25, 2007. PAS was careful to warn, however, that it did not agree with all Hindraf's demands either. See Dato' Seri Tuan Guru Abdul Hadi Awang, "Hak Berhimpun Diakui, Tetapi Sebahagian Tuntutan Hindraf Melampau," *Harakah Daily*, December 2, 2007.

53. This point was made to the author by various members of PAS during conversations at the sidelines of the party assembly in Selangor, June 5–7, 2009. Needless to say, the history of PAS-DAP relations will be replete with anecdotes and examples of mutual hostilities.

54. Because of the federal nature of the Malaysian government and the need to contest local or state elections, most political parties have state chapters that combine to constitute the national party. For PAS, the two traditionally strongest state chapters are those in Kelantan and Terengganu (Kelantan PAS and Terengganu PAS).

55. Ian McIntyre and The Eng Hock, "PAS Chief Wants Unity Government," *The Star*, June 5, 2009.

56. Joseph Chinyong Liow, "No God But God: Malaysia's Allah Controversy," *Foreign Affairs* (February 2010).

57. Given his credentials and reputation for being a conservative hardliner, his about-face was nothing short of remarkable. After all, it was not too long ago that Abdul Hadi publicly declared through the Amanat Haji Hadi that UMNO and its supporters were kafir for defending a British-inspired constitution (1985—the same constitution that he now claims guarantees the rights of non-Muslims to use the term "Allah"), that apostasy should be punishable by death (1999), and that Malaysia should be an Islamic state with hudud as its criminal code (2003).

58. Ariffuddin Ishak, "Kufur Jika Sokong Guna Kalimah Allah—Haron Din," *MyStar Online*, January 4, 2010.

59. For a fuller treatment of the different positions among PAS leaders on this issue and the reasons behind their respective positions, see Joseph Chinyong Liow, "Islamist Ambitions, Political Change, and the Price of Power: Recent Successes and Challenges for the Pan-Malaysian Islamic Party, PAS," *Journal of Islamic Studies* 22, 3 (September 2011).

60. Interview with UMNO insider, Kuala Lumpur, March 22, 2011.

61. Interview with DAP parliamentarian, Selangor, March 22, 2011.

62. Interview with PAS Central Committee member, Kuala Lumpur, March 23, 2011.

63. Zubaidah Abu Bakar, "Pas in a Quandary over Malay Vote Loss," *New Straits Times*, March 11, 2011. Nik Aziz had commented that though Islam was not race-based, "For PAS, Malays need to be prioritised in our agenda because they are the dominant Islamic race in Malaysia," adding that "UMNO has not been upholding Islam or the Malays"; see Shazwan Mustafa Kamal, "BN to Regain Two-Thirds with 5pc Malay Swing," *Malaysian Insider*, February 19, 2011.

64. Kamal, "BN to Regain Two-Thirds with 5pc Malay Swing."

65. Interview with PAS Central Committee Member, Kuala Lumpur, March 23, 2011.

Chapter 5. Searching for Political Normalization: The Party of Justice and Development in Morocco

1. The literal meaning of *makhzan* is "storage." It was used historically to refer to the sultan's court and retinue, the regional and provincial administration, the army, and all persons linking these institutions to the general population. The makhzan's

task was collection of taxes, and when certain groups resisted, it turned to coercive measures. The notion of "makhzan" and its meaning have changed over time. It has also variously been used to refer to the state apparatus; the services that the state provides to its citizens, such as education, health care, and other forms of economic and social development; and all persons in the service of the central power (the monarchy) with official and unofficial (religious, military, economic, or political) authority.

2. See Rachida Chérifie, *Le Makhzen politique au Maroc: Hier et aujourd'hui* (Casablanca: Afrique Orient, 1988).

3. On these different perspectives see Clement M. Henry, *The Mediterranean Debt Crescent: Money and Power in Algeria, Egypt, Morocco, Tunisia, and Turkey* (Gainesville: University Press of Florida, 1996); André Bank, "Rents, Cooptation and Economized Discourse: Three Dimensions of Political Rule in Jordan, Morocco and Syria," *Journal of Mediterranean Studies* 14, 1/2 (2004): 155–79; Abdallah Hammoudi, *Master and Disciple: The Cultural Foundations of Moroccan Authoritarianism* (Chicago: University of Chicago Press, 1997); Rahma Bourquia and Susan Gilson Miller, eds., *In the Shadow of the Sultan: Culture, Power, and Politics in Morocco* (Cambridge, Mass.: Harvard University Press, 1999); Henry Munson, *Religion and Power in Morocco* (New Haven, Conn.: Yale University Press, 1993).

4. On the lack of ideology and the shared value of economic interest, see Mark A. Tessler, "Morocco: Institutional Pluralism and Monarchical Dominance," in William Zartman, ed., Political Elites in Arab North Africa: Morocco, Algeria, Tunisia, Libya, Egypt (New York, Longman, 1982), 72.

5. See "Morocco: The Constitution," *Arab Law Quarterly* 17, 3 (2002): 304–20. The 2011 constitution has not changed this reality.

6. Clifford Geertz, *Islam Observed: Religious Development in Morocco and Indonesia* (1968; Chicago: University of Chicago Press, 1988), 88.

7. See Mohamed Tozy, *Monarchie et Islam politique* (Paris: Presses de la Fondation de Sciences Politiques, 1999).

8. See Driss Maghraoui, "Constitutional Reforms in Morocco: Between Consensus and Subaltern Politics," *Journal of North African Studies*, Special Issue: *North Africa's Arab Spring* 16, 4 (2011).

9. While the person of the king is no longer "sacred," article 46 states that "the integrity of the person of the king shall not be violated." In article 47, he has the power to appoint the head of government and government ministers after a proposition from the head of government. After "consulting" the head of government, the king can dismiss government ministers. The king presides over cabinet meetings (article 48) and can still dissolve the parliament (article 51). He retains the title Amir al-Mouminin (Commander of the Faithful), the most powerful religious authority of the country (article 41). While the king has delegated some powers to the head of government, he remains supreme commander and chief of staff of the Royal Armed Forces and chair of the newly created Supreme Security Council. In addition, the king keeps the power to declare a state of exception under extraordinary circumstances.

10. The full text of the revised 2011 Moroccan Constitution is available in the *Bulletin Officiel* 5964, July 30, 2011, http://www.sgg.gov.ma.

11. Abdeslam Maghraoui, "Depoliticization in Morocco," *Journal of Democracy* 13, 4 (2002): 24–32.

12. Mohamed Tozy, "Morocco's Elections Islamists, technocrats, and the Palace," *Journal of Democracy* 19, 1 (January 2008).

13. In 1983, the regime arrested hundreds of Islamic activists. They were all charged with plotting against the monarchical institution, thus threatening the stability of the state.

14. In 1980 Hassan II established by decree the regional councils of Ulama and a new high council. Both institutions were under the presidency of the king. For the more recent religious reforms under Mohamed VI see Driss Maghraoui, "The Strengths and Limits of Religious Reforms in Morocco," *Mediterranean Politics* 14, 2 (July 2009): 195–211.

15. University campuses served as venues for Islamic groups to mobilize the youth to counter and compete with the Marxist groups, which led to violent confrontations between the two groups, especially in Fes and Rabat.

16. Authors' interview with a member of the bureau of the PJD, February 2, 2011, Rabat.

17. Khadija Mohsen-Finan and Malika Zeghal, "Opposition islamique et pouvoir monarchique au Maroc: Le cas du Parti de la justice et du développement," *Revue Française de Science Politique* 56, 1 (February 2006): 79–119.

18. Quoted in the daily newspaper *Al Asr*, October 3, 1997, 4, author's name not mentioned.

19. Idrissi Moqrie Abou Zaid, for the Arabic newspaper *Annabae*, December 3, 1997.

20. Rassouni Ahmed in *Al Asr*, November 3, 1997, 2.

21. On February 8, 1997, there was the signature of a memorandum between the Ministry of Interior and the main political parties that the elections will be conducted under transparent elections. They decided to create a national committee in charge of following the electoral operation and thus according to a royal decree. The committee was composed of the minister of interior, at that time Driss Basri, the secretary general of the government, and the leaders of political parties represented in parliament, presided by the president of the supreme court. The committee created regional committee to serve the same purpose.

22. New electoral lists were established in August 1996 and reviewed between December 1996 and March 1997, and some reforms were introduced through the computer under the control of a technical committee composed of the technicians of the administration and those who represent the political parties. A new electoral code was adopted in the chamber of representatives in March 1997. This code offers new guarantees for different stages of the electoral operation, from enrollment on the electoral lists to declaration of the results.

23. The House of Representatives formed a fact-finding committee to investigate a public financial institution known as the Crédit Immobilier et Hotelier (CIH).

24. Myriam Catusse and Lamia Zaki, "Gestion communale et clientélisme moral au Maroc: Les politiques du Parti de la justice et du développement," *Critique Internationale* 42 (2009/1): 73–91.

25. Mohammed succeeded his father in July 1999 in a stable and consensual political context.

26. From 9 seats in the 1997 legislative elections, it won 43 seats in the 2002 elections.

27. For a discussion of the process and problems of the application of the moudawana, see Katja Zvan Elliott, "Reforming the Moroccan Personal Status Code: A Revolution for Whom?" *Mediterranean Politics* 14 (2009).

28. The new family code responded to many of the requests formulated by the women's NGOs since the beginning of the 1990s. It gave women equal rights over custody and welfare of their children and restricted the practice of polygamy. The legal age of marriage was raised from fifteen to eighteen and the family was legally under the responsibility of both husband and wife. Wives could seek divorce in the same way as husbands and this could be obtained only by mutual consent as opposed to the practice of repudiation, which did not require involvement of the court. The practice of *wilaya* (tutelage) in marriage was abolished. In the new legal text *wilaya* is a right women have, to exercise according to their will and with their consent.

29. Quoted in an interview in the daily newspaper *Al-Ayyam*, October 5, 2003, 4.

30. In a speech before the parliament, October 10, 2003, the king said: "As Amir al-Mouminin, I cannot allow what God prohibited nor forbid what God has permitted."

31. The law enclosed dispositions, among which the security forces have the right to hold suspects up to eight days without access to a lawyer and to intercept telephone and postal communications without warrants. In the same vein, it defines as a terrorist act any disturbance of public order.

32. This survey was conducted by the International Republican Institute in 2006; results at http://www.iri.org

3. See Farid Bousaid, "The Rise of the PAM in Morocco: Trampling the Political Scene or Stumbling into it? *Mediterranean Politics* 14, 3 (November 2009): 413–19.

34. See El Oddi, Bahia, Ferrali Romain, en collaboration avec Youssef Benkirane, "Veni, Vidi, Vici: La victoire du parti authenticité et modernité aux élections communales marocaines de 2009," *Revue Averroès* 2, Thème 1: Les élections dans le monde arabe en 2009, 12.

35. Interview by M. Sehimi and N. Jouhari with Abdelilah Benkirane, *Maroc Hebdo*, July 4, 2010.

36. See Saloua Zerhouni, "The Moroccan Parliament," in *Political Participation in the Middle East*, ed. Ellen Lust-Okar and Saloua Zerhouni (Boulder, Colo.: Lynne Rienner, 2008).

37. See Driss Maghraoui, "The Dynamics of Civil Society in Morocco," in *Political Participation in the Middle East*, ed. Lust-Okar and Zerhouni.

38. See the official Arabic *communiqué* of the movement: *al-bayan arrasmi li harkat 20 fibrayar.*

39. Ramid today occupies the post of minister of justice.

40. Interview with the authors in November 2011, Rabat.

41. Ibid.

42. Quoted in an interview in the Arabic newspaper *Akhbar al yawm*, November 27, 2011, 2.

43. Quoted in an interview in *La Vie Économique*, November 26, 2011.

Chapter 6. Mapping the Terrain of Reform
in Yemen: *Islah* over Two Decades

The research for this chapter draws on fieldwork conducted in Yemen between 2004 and 2009. It was funded through the generous support of Hobart and William Smith Colleges, the American Institute of Yemeni Studies, the Harvard Academy for International and Area Studies, and the Graduate School of Arts and Sciences at the University of Pennsylvania. The author thanks the editors, as well as Janine Clark, Jillian Schwedler, Ali Saif Hassan, Sami Ghaleb, Nabil al-Sofee, Sayeed Thabit Sayeed, Amina Steinfels, Kavita Datla, and Vikash Yadav for their help in considering (and reconsidering) parts of this chapter.

1. Sayeed Thabit Sayeed, interview with author, Sana'a, February 26, 2005.

2. The overwhelming majority of Yemeni Jews left the country after the establishment of the State of Israel in 1948. See Yael Katzir, "Preservation of Jewish Ethnic Identity in Yemen: Segregation and Integration as Boundary Maintenance Mechanisms," *Comparative Studies in Society and History* 24, 2 (1982): 264–79. The small community that remains has largely disengaged from formal political institutions and debates.

3. Paul Dresch, *A History of Modern Yemen* (Cambridge: Cambridge University Press, 2000), 173.

4. Shelagh Weir, *A Tribal Order: Politics and Law in the Mountains of Yemen* (Austin: University of Texas Press, 2007); Shelagh Weir, "A Clash of Fundamentalisms: Wahhabism in Yemen," *Middle East Report* 204 (1997): 22–26; Gabriele vom Bruck, *Islam, Memory, and Morality in Yemen: Ruling Families in Transition* (New York: Palgrave Macmillan, 2005).

5. 'Abd al-Bari Taha, "The Islamic Movement in Yemen and Democracy," in *Islamists in Yemen*, vol. 2. Proceedings of the Aden University conference on Religious Fundamentalists and the Dialogue of Civilizations, June 12–16, 2002 (Aden: General Center for Studies, Research, and Publications, 2002), 106 (In Arabic)

6. J. Leigh Douglas, *The Free Yemeni Movement, 1935–1962* (Beirut: American University in Beirut Press, 1987), 124. For an elaboration on the notion of Islamo-nationalism in relation to the Muslim Brotherhood and the movements it has inspired,

see Olivier Roy, *The Politics of Chaos in the Middle East* (New York: Columbia University Press, 2008), 92–98.

7. Sheila Carapico, *Civil Society in Yemen: The Political Economy of Activism in Southern Arabia* (Cambridge: Cambridge University Press, 1998), 98. These two organizations dedicated to the "promotion of virtue and prevention of vice" might be colloquially glossed as vigilante or semi-official "morality police."

8. Lisa Wedeen, *Peripheral Visions: Publics, Power, and Performance in Yemen* (Chicago: University of Chicago Press, 2008); Weir, *A Tribal Order.*

9. Weir, *A Tribal Order*; vom Bruck, *Islam, Memory, and Morality in Yemen.*

10. Franck Mermier, "L'Islam politique au Yémen ou la 'Tradition' contre les traditions?" *Monde Arab Maghreb Machrek* (1997): 12–13.

11. Robert Burrowes, *The Yemen Arab Republic: The Politics of Development, 1962–1986* (Boulder, Colo.: Westview Press, 1987), 131; Laurent Bonnefoy, *Salafism in Yemen: Transnationalism and Religious Identity* (New York: Columbia University Press, 2012).

12. Constitution of the GYA, in Douglas, *The Free Yemeni Movement*, 87.

13. Carapico, *Civil Society in Yemen*, 98–99.

14. Dresch, *A History of Modern Yemen*, 142.

15. Susanne Dahlgren, *Contesting Realities: The Public Sphere and Morality in Southern Yemen* (Syracuse, N.Y.: Syracuse University Press, 2010).

16. Muhammed Qassem No'man, interview with author, Aden, September 17, 2005.

17. 'Abdallah Hashim Al-Siyani, *The Muslim Brothers and the Salafis in Yemen* (Sana'a, Yemen: Raed Center for Research and Studies, 2002), in Arabic.

18. Dresch, *A History of Modern Yemen*, 190.

19. Michaelle Browers, *Political Ideology in the Arab World: Accommodation and Transformation* (Cambridge: Cambridge University Press, 2009); Stacey Philbrick Yadav, *Islamists and the State: Legitimacy and Institutions in Yemen and Lebanon* (London: Tauris, 2013).

20. Bonnefoy, *Salafism in Yemen.*

21. Western scholarship on Islah in the 1990s has often characterized the party as composed of three distinct "trends" and identified these as the Muslim Brothers, the tribes, and a coalition of socially conservative businessmen or entrepreneurs (Carapico, *Civil Society in Yemen*; Dresch, *A History of Modern Yemen*; Jillian Schwedler, "Yemen's Aborted Opening," *Journal of Democracy* 13, 4 (2002): 48–55). By the early 2000s decade, Islahi leaders themselves, as well as some Yemeni academics writing on the origins of Islah, retrospectively characterized the triumvirate differently, essentially replacing the social conservatives with the party's salafi wing, under the leadership of Shaykh 'Abd al-Majid al-Zindani (Taha, "The Islamic Movement in Yemen and Democracy"). Whether this retelling of Islah's history is more or less accurate than the earlier scholarly accounts, or simply reflects change, is difficult to know. What *is* clear is that the latter characterization reflects well the prominence of one of Islah's

major players and the anxieties felt by people inside and outside Islah about his ability to shape the party in recent years.

22. 'Abd al-Wahhab Al-'Anisi, interview with author, Sana'a, September 27, 2005.

23. Moreover, this Northern base was distinctly tribal in foundation, led by Shaykh 'Abdallah bin Hussein al-Ahmar (speaker of parliament from 1993 to his death in 2007), Muhammed al-Yadoumi, and 'Abd al-Wahhab al-'Ainsi. None of the three had received what might be considered an "Islamist" education, but all had deep ties to the Northern tribal system, unlike the leaders of the Muslim Brotherhood contingent, who tended to be from the Ta'iz area, with weaker tribal ties and more formal education. The Brothers would come to dominate the policy-making apparatus in the party, while the tribal contingent would serve as the party's public face. According to several party leaders, the Salafi contingent under Zindani's influence was largely seen as a voter base, with little formal decision-making power within the party.

24. Carapico, *Civil Society in Yemen*, 137.

25. Ibid.

26. Jillian Schwedler, "The Islah Party in Yemen: Political Opportunities and Coalition Building in a Transitional Polity," in *Islamic Activism: A Social Movement Theory Approach*, ed. Quintan Wiktorowicz (Bloomington: Indiana University Press, 2004), 205–28, 209.

27. *Agence France Presse*, April 19, 1990.

28. Yemeni Congregation for Reform, *Political Program* (Sana'a: Yemeni Congregation for Reform, 1994), 5.

29. Schwedler, "The Islah Party in Yemen," 210.

30. These are the figures for members of the respective parliaments of the YAR and PDRY who were installed as members of the provisional parliament. An additional thirty-one members were appointed to achieve parity (Carapico, *Civil Society in Yemen*, 137). This brought the total number of MPs to 301, the number elected in each subsequent parliamentary election.

31. Marsha Pripstein Posusney, "Multiparty Elections in the Arab World: Election Rules and Opposition Responses," in *Authoritarianism in the Middle East: Regimes and Resistance*, ed. Marsha Pripstein Posusney and Michele Penner Angrist (Boulder, Colo.: Lynne Reinner, 2006), 101.

32. Renauld Detalle, "The Yemeni Elections Up Close," *Middle East Report* 185 (1993): 8–10.

33. Abdo Baaklini, Guilain Denoeux, and Robert Springborg, *Legislative Politics in the Arab World: The Resurgence of Democratic Institutions* (Boulder, Colo.: Lynne Reinner, 1999), 209.

34. Schwedler, "Yemen's Aborted Opening," 49.

35. Muhammed Qahtan, interview with author, Sana'a, September 27, 2005.

36. Wahabiyya Sabra, interview with author, Sana'a, January 10, 2009.

37. Dresch, *A History of Modern Yemen*, 197.

38. Sabra interview, 2009.

39. Schwedler, "The Islah Party in Yemen," 217–20.

40. Baaklini, Denoeux, and Springborg, *Legislative Politics in the Arab World* , 211.

41. Ibid., 213.

42. Ibid.

43. Carlo Binda, interview with author, Sana'a, August 29, 2005

44. Mermier, "L'Islam politique au Yémen ou la 'Tradition' contre les traditions?," 12.The term "scientific institutes" a translation from the Arabic, denoting Yemeni usage to refer to a veritable cottage industry of institutions teaching the "Islamic Sciences." Mermier offers an excellent discussion of the growth of these institutes (10–11).

45. No'man interview, 2005.

46. 'Abd al-Rahman Al-Khalq, interview with author, Aden, September 16, 2005.

47. Stacey Philbrick Yadav, "Segmented Publics and Islamist Women in Yemen: Rethinking Space and Activism," *Journal of Middle Eastern Women's Studies* 6, 2 (2010): 1–30.

48. Mermier, "L'Islam politique au Yémen ou la 'Tradition' contre les traditions?," 12.

49. Ibid., 13.

50. Schwedler, "The Islah Party in Yemen, 219.

51. Ibid., 217.

52. Steven Levitsky and Lucan Way, *Competitive Authoritarianism: Hybrid Regimes After the Cold War* (Cambridge: Cambridge University Press, 2010); Thomas Carothers, "The End of the Transitions Paradigm," *Journal of Democracy* 13, 1 (2002): 5–21.

53. In this chapter, as elsewhere, I contend that Islah's principal goal is to pursue specific policy objectives related to Islamization of the public, through reform of state institutions and shaping of public discourse (Yadav, *Islamists and the State*). I see no evidence that Islah seeks to win an absolute majority and assume power. This impression was shaped mainly through conversations with Islahis about Islamist electoral experiences in Algeria and the Palestinian Authority, wherein Islahis tended to praise the "Moroccan strategy" of electoral influence.

54. Stacey Philbrick Yadav and Janine A. Clark, "Disappointments and New Directions: Women, Partisanship and the Regime in Yemen," *HAWWA* 8, 1 (2010): 55–95, 74–77.

55. Yadav, *Islamists and the State. Takfir* may be loosely understood as a form of excommunication, a statement by a Muslim labeling another Muslim an apostate. Though there is juristic disagreement over the specific requirements for punishment, apostasy is generally considered a capital crime. In the absence of a state willing to enforce Islamic legal sanctions against apostasy, allegations can encourage vigilante violence. Though the state does not enforce the statute, Article 4 of the Yemeni penal code lists apostasy as a capital offence, thus creating a shared knowledge of the (potential, if unrealized) consequences of the allegation.

56. Michaelle Browers, "The Origins and Architects of Yemen's Joint Meeting Parties," *International Journal of Middle East Studies* 39, 4 (2007): 565–86; Browers, *Political Ideology in the Arab World*.

57. *Qat* chews are ubiquitous events in which Yemenis gather to chew *qat* leaves, a mild stimulant, while discussing politics, doing business, or socializing. These can, in some instances, be understood as "focus groups," but also function as minipublics, in which concepts are debated and refined and through which political actors formulate joint strategies for action. See Wedeen, *Peripheral Visions*, 2008.

58. Yadav and Clark, "Disappointments and New Directions"; Sarah Phillips, "Politics in a Vacuum: The Yemeni Opposition's Dilemma," *MEI Viewpoints* 11 (2009): 11–13; Stacey Philbrick Yadav, "Antecedents of the Revolution: Intersectoral Networks and Postpartisanship in Yemen's Revolutionary Movement," *Studies in Ethnicity and Nationalism*, 11, 3 (2012): 550–63.

59. Yadav, "Segmented Publics and Islamist Women in Yemen."

60. Browers, *Political Ideology in the Arab World*.

61. Yadav and Clark, "Disappointments and New Directions."

62. These include the al-Huthi uprising in the North from 2004, a secessionist movement in the South beginning in 2007, and growing relevance of Al Qaeda in the Arabian Peninsula since 2009.

63. Phillips, "Politics in a Vacuum"; April Longley-Alley and Abd al-Ghani al-Iryani, "Southern Aspirations and Salih's Exasperation: The Looming Threat of Secession in Southern Yemen," *MEI Viewpoints* 11 (2009): 2–5.

64. Yadav, "Antecedents of the Revolution."

65. As one prominent member of the ruling party put it, while al-Zindani is "'*eeb* [a source of shame] for the government," if he were ever to be forced out of Islah by the reformist wing, the GPC would "snap him up" and his grassroots popularity along with him.

Chapter 7. Islamist Parties, Elections, and Democracy in Bangladesh

1. Quinn Mecham, this volume.

2. Ibid.

3. Guilain Denoeux, "The Forgotten Swamp: Navigating Political Islam," *Journal of Middle East Policy* 9, 2 (2002): 56–81.

4. These elections include parliamentary elections in 1973, 1979, 1986, and 1988 and presidential elections in 1978 and 1986. Three elections—1979, 1986, and 1988—produced parliaments with very limited power as they were elected under a presidential system of government and because effective power remained in the hands of the military establishment. During this period (1975–1990) the country also witnessed a number of successful and abortive coups, including an uprising of the soldiers. One of the presidents and a military ruler, Ziaur Rahman, was assassinated in a failed

putsch in May 1981. For details of the events, see Ali Riaz, *Unfolding State: The Transformation of Bangladesh* (Toronto: de Sitters, 2006).

5. Shakhawat Liton, "Islamic Parties' Boom After 1976 Ban Lifting," *Daily Star*, August 29, 2006, 1.

6. Before the ninth general elections in December 2008, the EC obtained 117 applications for party registration, but temporarily registered only 39 parties following submission of their draft constitutions. Later, the EC confirmed registration of 38 parties on submission of their revised constitutions, and later canceled registration of one party.

7. *Pirs*, literally translated "saints," are a very common feature of politicoreligious life in Bangladesh. The tradition grew out of a specific mode of preaching Islam in the subcontinent. Some of these early preachers drew the attention of the local people irrespective of their religious beliefs through their spiritual power, morality, and principles of tolerance. These pirs originally represented mystic Islam and one or more mystic orders. Following their deaths their graves are turned into *mazars* (shrines) and are visited by their *muridan* (disciples). But over the years the practice has degenerated and has created cult-like organizations headed by pirs who exert influence over their disciples and whose residential-cum-worship compounds have become headquarters of complex social networks and places where patronage is exchanged between high-ranking people.

8. Islamic educational institutions called *madrasas* are broadly divided into two categories in Bangladesh: Aliya and Qwami. Institutions belonging to the former strand are part of the state-approved education system and supervised by a government-appointed education board. Their degrees are recognized by the government and are equivalent to general education. Institutions belonging to the later strand are privately operated and do not receive any government funding. The curricula of these two strands are markedly different. Qwami madrasas usually follow the tradition started in 1876 in Darul Uloom in Deoband, commonly known as the Deobandi tradition. There are allegations that Qwami madrasa infrastructure has been used by the militants. There are no reliable figures of the total number of Qwami madrasas in Bangladesh. In an application to the prime minister seeking official recognition of these madrasas, supporters estimated the number of Qwami madrasas at 15,250 with 1.85 million students and 132,150 teachers.

9. In 2001 Bangladesh was divided into six administrative divisions—Rajshahi, Khulna, Barisal, Dhaka, Sylhet, and Chittagong. Each division comprises a number of districts. The number of seats in each division varies by population.

10. Ali Riaz and Kh Ali Ar-Raji, "Who Are the Islamists?" in *Political Islam and Governance in Bangladesh*, ed. Ali Riaz and C. Christine Fair (London: Routledge, 2010), 60–63.

11. Ibid.

12. For details see *Daily Star*, November 21, 2008.

13. Pippa Norris, *Muslim Support for Secular Democracy* (Sydney/Boston: University of Sidney and Harvard Kennedy School, 2011).

14. Mecham, this volume.

15. For internal schisms in the IOJ see Ali Riaz, *Islamist Militancy in Bangladesh: A Complex Web* (London: Routledge, 2008), 42–43. Details of the split between the JI and IOJ are documented in a U.S. Embassy Confidential Cable sent from Dhaka May 24, 2005 (Ref05DHAKA2409), leaked by Wikileaks and available at http://leaks.hohesc.us.

16. The demand for a caretaker government (CTG)grew out of the experience of the transitional arrangement devised in late 1990 as a constitutional way out for the military regime of General Ershad. In December 1990, the opposition alliances agreed to a formula that Ershad would hand over power to an interim government headed by the chief justice of the Supreme Court.

17. The Thirteenth Amendment stipulated that on dissolution of the parliament at the end of its five-year term, an eleven-member nonparty CTG headed by the chief advisor would function as an interim government for ninety days. The amendment provided that the immediate past chief justice would be head of it. The constitution stipulates four other options for appointing the chief advisor if the immediate past chief justice is unavailable or unwilling to take up the job. If all other options prove unworkable, the president will head the caretaker government in addition to his presidential duties.

18. JMB, an Islamist militant organization founded in the late 1990s, became very active beginning in 2001. In 2005 it was proscribed by the BNP-led collation government after intense pressures from the international community. The organization responded with synchronized bomb attacks throughout the country on August 17, 2005, when about 450 homemade devices were exploded. It was followed by a series of suicide attacks on judges and local courts. For details see Riaz, *Islamist Militancy in Bangladesh*; International Crisis Group, "The Threat from Jamaat-ul Mujahideen Bangladesh," *Asia Report* 187 (March 1, 2010).

19. "Khelafat Majilisher Shathe Panchdofa Chukti, Awami Leagu Khomotai gele Alemder Fatwar Odhikar Debe" (Five Point Agreement with Khelafat Majlish: If Elected to Power, Awami League Will Allow Alims to Issue Fatwa, in Bengali), *Prothom Alo*, December 24, 2006, 1.

20. Hasan Jahid Tushar, "2 'Militants' Get AL Tickets," *Daily Star*, December 27, 2006, 1.

21. "AL Says Its Islamist Allies to Work for 'Secularism,'" *Daily Star*, December 28, 2006, 1. The AL finally scrapped the deal on February 17, 2007, more than a month after the election was canceled.

22. "Chardoleyo Jote ke vote na diley Islam rakshya hobe na" (Islam Won't be Saved Without the Four-Party Alliance Voted to Power, in Bengali), *Shamokal*, December 26, 2006, 1.

23. "Islami Shaktir Shohayota Chara Keu Khomotai Jete Parbe na: Aminee" (No One Can Attain Power Without the Support of the Islamic Forces: Aminee, in Bengali), *Ittefaq*, December 26, 2006, 1.

24. Golam Azam, *Bangladesher Rajniti* ("The Politics of Bangladesh," in Bengali) (Dhaka: Al Azad, 1987), 5.

25. The Ahmadiyya, also called Qadiani, is a small Muslim sect. They are the followers of reformist Mirza Ghulam Ahmad (1835–1908) who hails from Qadian, in Punjab. Ahmadiyyas claim to practice the Islam taught and practiced by the Prophet Muhammad and his companions. Some Muslim groups—from both Sunni and Shi'a sects—insist that the Ahmadiyyas are non-Muslims. The acceptance of the finality of Muhammad as the last prophet has been cited as the main source of contention between the mainstream Muslim sects and the Ahmadiyyas. In 1973 the Pakistani government declared Ahmadiyyas non-Muslims.

26. "Khulna Bigots Threaten to Attack Ahmadiyyas," *Daily Star*, April 20, 2005, 1.

27. "Declare Them Non-Muslims to Get Electoral Support," *Daily Star*, March 12, 2005, 1.

28. To claim oneself the sole or true interpreter of Islam is essentially against the teachings of Islam. Yet, the JI in Bangladesh has begun openly insisting on this. In early 2005, JI chief and cabinet minister Matiur Rahman Nizami warned that "speaking against Jamaat is tantamount to speaking against Islam" ("Speaking Against Jamaat Is Tantamount to Speaking Against Islam," *Daily Star*, April 1, 2005, 1).

29. "Women Will Have Equal Rights in Properties," *Prothom Alo*, March 9, 2008, 1.

30. In August 2007 the government came down hard on student demonstrations and arrested students and faculty. The day the police allowed the Islamists to demonstrate, a small gathering of left political parties against price hikes was dispersed by force.

31. Bangladesh Jamaat-i_Islami, Statement of Matiur Rahman Nizami, April 16, 2008, www.http://jamaat-e-islami.org/index.php?option = com_statement&task = de tail&info_id = 18.

Conclusion: The New Dynamism of Islamist Parties

1. Electoral results are scored for average percentage of votes earned over the last three elections in a given country, which have all occurred in the last two decades. The most recent legislative elections have been held in Bangladesh (2008), Indonesia (2009), Malaysia (2008), Morocco (2011), Turkey (2011), and Yemen (2003).

2. The current AKP leadership previously held positions in the party's forerunners, the Welfare and Virtue parties. Welfare received 17 percent of the vote in the 1995 elections, and Virtue 15 percent of the vote in 1999, the two elections prior to the AKP's inaugural election of 2002.

3. Khalil Al-Anani, "Will the Salafis Change Tack?" *Al-Ahram Weekly* 1083 (February 2–8, 2012).

4. John Thorne, "Tunisian Police and Conservatives Clash over 'Blasphemous' Film," *National*, Abu Dhabi, October 16, 2011.

5. Sarah Lynch, "Egypt Has Second Thoughts on the Muslim Brotherhood," *USA Today*, April 5, 2012.

Contributors

Wenling Chan is an Associate Research Fellow at the S. Rajaratnam School of International Studies, Nanyang Technological University, Singapore.

Julie Chernov Hwang teaches in the Department of Political Science and International Relations at Goucher College. She is author of *Peaceful Islamist Mobilization in the Muslim World: What Went Right*, which examines state-Islamist group relations in Indonesia, Malaysia, and Turkey. In 2011, she was Luce Southeast Asia Fellow at the East West Center in Washington, D.C. Her articles have been published in *Asian Survey*, *Nationalism and Ethnic Politics*, *Southeast Asia Research*, and *Asia-Pacific Issues*. She is also the author of book chapters on disengagement of Indonesian jihadists, Islamic education in Malaysia and Indonesia, and mainstreaming of political Islam in Indonesia. Her current research examines the processes of radicalization and disengagement of Indonesian jihadis from Jemaah Islamiyah, KOMPAK, and other militant groups.

Joseph Chinyong Liow is Associate Dean and Associate Professor at the S. Rajaratnam School of International Studies, Nanyang Technical University, Singapore. His research interests lie in Muslim politics in Malaysia and Thailand. His most recent publications include *Piety and Politics: Islamism in Contemporary Malaysia* and *Islam, Education, and Reform in Southern Thailand*. His articles have been published in *Asian Survey*, *Third World Quarterly*, *Commonwealth and Comparative Politics*, *Contemporary Southeast Asia*, *Southeast Asia Research*, *Studies in Conflict and Terrorism*, *Journal of Islamic Studies*, *Harvard Asia-Pacific Review*, and *NBR Analysis*.

Driss Maghraoui is Associate Professor of History and International Relations at the School of Humanities and Social Sciences at Al Akhawayn University, Ifrane, Morocco. His publications have appeared in international academic journals and edited volumes in Morocco, Germany, Italy, the United Kingdom, and the United States. He is co-editor of *Reforms in* *the Arab World: The Experience of Morocco, Mediterranean Politics*, and editor of *Revisiting the Colonial Past in Morocco*. He is currently working on a book project on *The Predicament of Democracy in Morocco*.

Quinn Mecham teaches political science at Brigham Young University and is a research associate at Middlebury College. His research interests include political Islam, identity politics, civil conflict, electoral behavior, and democratic development. His publications include articles on Islamist parties in Turkey, the development of the Muslim Brotherhood in Egypt, and comparative Islamist movements. His forthcoming book examines the comparative processes of political mobilization by religious actors in the Muslim world from 1970 to 2010. He has done ethnographic work on Islamist movements and parties across the Muslim world, including Morocco, Bahrain, and Senegal. He served as Franklin Fellow on the policy planning staff of the U.S. Department of State in 2009–10, and has been a visiting scholar at George Washington University and an Academy Scholar at Harvard University. He received MA and PhD degrees in Political Science from Stanford University.

Ali Riaz is Professor and Chair of the Department of Politics and Government at Illinois State University. He has previously taught at universities in South Carolina, England, and Bangladesh. His recent publications are *Faithful Education: Madrassahs in South Asia, Islamist Militancy in Bangladesh: A Complex Web*, and edited volumes *Religion and Politics in South Asia, Political Islam and Governance in Bangladesh*. He earned the ISU College of Arts and Sciences first Dean's Award for Outstanding Scholarly Achievement in 2004 and Outstanding College Researcher Award in 2005. He also received the Pi Sigma Alpha Excellence in Teaching Award in 2006. In 2012 he was designated University Professor based on his international reputation.

Murat Somer is Associate Professor of International Relations at Koç University, Istanbul. His research addresses questions of democratization, ethnic conflict, religious politics and secularism, elite beliefs and values, public and private polarization, the Kurdish question, and political Islam. His writings have appeared in book volumes and journals including *Annals of the American Academy of Political and Social Science, Comparative Political Studies, Middle East Journal*, and *Third World Quarterly*.

Stacey Philbrick Yadav teaches political science at Hobart and William Smith Colleges, where she also directs the Middle East Studies program. She is author of the forthcoming *Islamists and the State: Legitimacy and*

Institutions in Yemen and Lebanon and several journal articles focusing on cross-ideological opposition alliances in both countries, based on field research in 2003–2009. She has published collaborative work on the role of women as both objects and subjects of Islamist politics in Yemen and is a regular contributor to *Middle East Report* and *Foreign Policy*.

Saloua Zerhouni is Associate Professor at in the School of Juridical, Economic, and Social Sciences at Mohammed V University in Rabat, Morocco. In 2000, she was a visiting researcher at Georgetown University. In 2001–2003, she was a research associate at the German Institute for International and Security Affairs (SWP), Berlin. She has done extensive research on elites as agents of change and theories of political transformation, Islamist movements, political parties, the parliament, elections, youth and politics, and protest movements in Morocco. She has served as a consultant of national and international organizations such as the European Commission, USAID, and the Royal Institute for Strategic Studies. Her publications include an edited book with Ellen Lust, *Political Participation in the Middle East*.

Index

Acknowledgments

This volume has been several years in the making. The initial idea arose in the aftermath of an International Studies Association panel on Islamist parties in 2008 in San Francisco. We wanted to produce an edited volume on Islamist parties that was both theoretically grounded and comparatively useful for students of political Islam. We sought to emphasize the more open and democratic cases in the Muslim world where religiously oriented parties were engaging in politics in innovative ways and helping shape their political systems as a result. In this endeavor, we received support from many sources.

We want first to acknowledge the hard work of our contributors: Murat Somer, Joseph Chinyong Liow and Wenling Chen, Driss Maghraoui and Saloua Zerhouni, Stacey Philbrick Yadav, and Ali Riaz. It is their thoughtful analysis and country expertise that collectively make this volume stand out. We are also grateful to the Project on Middle East Studies (POMEPS) at George Washington University for generously funding the 2010 conference where we first discussed our drafts and tested our original theoretical arguments. Additionally, there have been many colleagues who gave us input to improve the chapters and opened doors to contacts. They include Marc Lynch, William Liddle, Greg Fealy, Kikue Hamayotsu, Burhanuddin Muhtadi, Saiful Mujani, Suzaina Kadir, A'an Suryana, Nathan Brown, and many others.

The staff at the University of Pennsylvania Press has been helpful throughout. Bill Finan has been a supportive editor from the very beginning, and the copy editing team has helped us to refine the final product. Alison Anderson as Managing Editor and Sara Davis as Marketing Manager have guided our book through the revision process and beyond. The anonymous reviewers invested substantial effort in assessing the project, and the suggestions they made aided us in strengthening the volume.

The summer research funding and faculty development grants provided by our colleges were instrumental in the success of this project for enabling the fieldwork and data collection. Our research assistants, Rudy Stoler, Jack Swallow, Samuel Wyer, Abraham Katz, Tik Root, and Micah MacFarlane, among others, deserve special mention. Jack and Rudy's efforts in reviewing the full chapters from a student point of view was an important asset to the project.

We also wish to thank the officials from the political parties who agreed to be interviewed as well as those scholars who have built up a substantial literature on the subjects of the volume over many years.

Finally, our deepest gratitude goes to our families: Dae, Sophie, Maren, Sonja, Laurel, Torin, and Peter for their love and support, for understanding the travel and long hours that go into a volume such as this, and for making free time something to be treasured.